Sacred Departures

The Sociology of Death and Dying

Sacred Departures

The Sociology of Death and Dying

Veenat, PhD

THE BROWSER

Title: Sacred Departures: The Sociology of Death and Dying
Author: Veenat

ISBN: 978-93-49042-27-8

Published by:
JGS Enterprises Pvt Ltd
Imprint: The Browser

Publisher's Address:
SCO 14-15, FF, Sector 8-C, Chandigarh 160 009

Website: thebrowser.org
Email: service@thebrowser.org

Printed in India

© Layout and Cover Design by 99 beagles
99beagles.com

THE BROWSER
Publishers & Booksellers

Contents

Preface

Death is the one truth we all share, yet each culture finds its own way of meeting it. Some light candles, others chant prayers, some gather in silence, while others celebrate a life well-lived. This book is about those different ways of facing death—how our beliefs, traditions, and modern choices shape what happens when life ends.

For centuries, religion gave us the main answers: What happens after death? How should we honour the dead? Why must we die at all? But today, things are changing. Medicine, science, and modern lifestyles have introduced new questions: Should I pledge my organs? Should cremation be electric instead of traditional? Is euthanasia a dignified choice? These are not just abstract debates—they are real dilemmas that families in India and around the world are facing. This book grew out of my research in Chandigarh, a city that is both modern and deeply rooted in tradition. There, I spoke with families from Hindu, Sikh, Muslim, Christian, and Buddhist backgrounds who had recently lost loved ones. I also spent time with sacred specialists who guide communities through mourning rituals. Through these conversations, I discovered how people balance faith and modernity, tradition and practicality, while dealing with death.

After completing my research in Chandigarh, I was awarded the Residential Research Library (RRL) Fellowship by Durham University, UK. During my one month stay as a visiting fellow at the Centre for Death and Life Studies, I gained access to extensive literature on death and dying, including the rare collection on cremation and burial archives of the Cremation Society of Great Britain. I even had the chance to explore emerging cremation trends in the UK, which revealed how rapidly death practices are evolving globally. This experience broadened my horizon. It allowed me to view the Indian deathscape through a wider lens. These insights reflect in the chapters of this book.

The book is structured into six chapters. The first chapter, **The Journey of Death**, establishes a foundational understanding of the book. Explaining the concept of death and how it has transformed over time, the chapter explores how death, far from being a purely biological or medical event, is deeply embedded in socio-cultural contexts. It highlights the journey of death: how death's perception has transitioned from the primitive societies to the present times. Different theoretical perspectives that have contributed to the understanding of death are presented. Finally, the chapter sets the stage for the rest of the book by underscoring the importance of a sociological lens in understanding death and its various aspects.

The second chapter, **Death and the Divine**, takes on the happily married relationship of death and religion. Death and religion are so deeply connected that death is considered the prime source of organised religious beliefs, and it is believed that without death, there would be no need for religion. Based on the readings of the sacred texts from five religions—Hinduism, Sikhism, Buddhism, Christianity, and Islam—this chapter illustrates a cross-religional understanding of death and its related themes like Reincarnation/ Transmigration and Resurrection, Determinants of the Fate of the Deceased, Afterlife Journey and Salvation, etc. In integrating theological perspectives with sociological analysis, the chapter underscores religion's dual role: reinforcing social cohesion through shared death rites and providing personal solace through metaphysical narratives. This exploration establishes a foundation for understanding how every religion, having its own mortality thesis, shapes the understanding of death and dying of its adherents.

Based on the death philosophy presented in the preceding chapter, the third chapter, **Prescribed Death Practices**, explores religiously prescribed death rituals and mourning practices in Hinduism, Sikhism, Buddhism, Christianity, and Islam. The chapter highlights prescribed death-related practices, ranging from the anticipation of death to dealing with death, the afterlife journey of the deceased, and the final closure of the mourning. It examines the socially constructed nature of death rituals.

The fourth chapter, **Perceptions of Death and Its Related Aspects**, presents an empirical exploration into the perceptions of people on death and its related themes. Based on the intensive fieldwork conducted in Chandigarh, this chapter seeks to highlight the extent to which the perception of death of people following different faiths is in line with their religion and how much it has changed. Chandigarh is a religiously plural city and has facilities for electric cremation, organ donation, and corpse donation. Respondents, selected through purposive sampling, were the people who had experienced the death of their loved ones belonging to Hinduism, Sikhism, Buddhism, Christianity, and Islam. Their narratives articulated a wide spectrum of emotions and meanings associated with death. The influence of the religious doctrines in shaping their perceptions of death, rebirth, salvation, and other themes has been significant, and it has been the highlight of the chapter. However, the spark of change and inclination towards modern practices, like organ donation, euthanasia, and the use of electric crematoriums, etc., also stood out.

The fifth chapter, **Death Practices and the Paradoxical Situation**, is an account of the death practices followed by individuals from diverse religious backgrounds. The chapter elucidates how people navigated the death of their loved ones and the extent to which their actions aligned with traditional, prescribed rituals. Key themes include the commercialisation of death practices and the interplay between personal grief and communal obligation. The chapter also interrogates the role of gender, caste, and socio-economic status in shaping access to and performance of prescribed rituals. The chapter also highlights variations in mourning periods, prayer ceremonies, and body disposal methods across religious groups, noting both continuity and change. The paradoxical situation of perception of death and dealing with it, is the takeaway from this chapter. While religious frameworks continue to guide most of the death-related practices across religions, there is a noticeable shift as well. Overall, this chapter illustrates how prescribed death practices are negotiated in the urban milieu of Chandigarh.

Chapter six, **The 'Three Cs': Conformity, Conviction, and Change**, is the last chapter that synthesises the findings from ethnographic fieldwork and the changing paradigms with which death is understood and dealt with. To articulate the complex, evolving relationship between religion and death, the chapter introduces the conceptual framework of the 'Three Cs': Conformity, Conviction, and Change. Conformity refers to the societal and ritualistic adherence to traditional death practices. The chapter highlights how religious rites often remain anchored in society not merely because of conviction, but also due to family expectations, community norms, and a collective need for structure during bereavement. Conviction explores the deep personal beliefs of individuals in their religious faiths regarding life after death, *karmic* justice, and divine will. These beliefs provide existential meaning and emotional anchorage, especially in times of grief. However, despite conviction, there is a possibility of non-conformity. Change captures the dynamic shifts in death practices resulting from medicalisation of dying, and individual agency. The chapter emphasises how deathscapes are being reshaped—rituals are abbreviated due to pragmatic reasons, and mourning practices are becoming more secularised or customised. By triangulating narratives from different faiths and weaving doctrinal prescriptions with lived realities, the chapter argues that while religion continues to structure death practices, individual autonomy and social transformation are leading to changes in deathways. It concludes by elaborating the changing paradigm of death and dying from the pre-modern to the modern and post-modern eras.

The stories in this book show how people navigate the end of life: some hold firmly to rituals handed down for generations, while others quietly adapt or even challenge them and choose to go by what their loved ones wanted. Some find comfort in the promise of an afterlife, while others place their hope in science, organ donation, or simply in leaving a legacy of love. What I found is that death is never just about the end of life—it is also about love, memory, faith, and identity. This book is not just about rituals—it is about grief and hope, fear and courage, old traditions and new choices. My hope is that these reflections will not only help you understand how societies deal with death but also make you pause and think about what death means in your own life. I am glad that you have chosen to spend time with death. Most people wait for a lifetime to do that :)

I extend my heartfelt gratitude to my mentor Prof. Sherry Sabbarwal, former Professor, Department of Sociology, Panjab University, Chandigarh, for her invaluable guidance and support.

Veenat

❦

CHAPTER 1

The Journey of Death

As Homo sapiens are the only species that can reflect upon their own mortality, different attempts have been made for ages to unfold this mystery and define it. Anthropologists have discovered that in many tribal societies, death was perceived as the separation of some essence of the person from the flesh. In a few tribes, it was believed that the loss of blood could lead to death, and that the paleness in the body of the dead implied that he/she had lost the physical essence of life. Traditionally, it was also believed that death does not happen all at once, and it was declared by clearly observing physical signs of cessation, like lack of respiration and responsiveness, as well as paleness and stiffening of the body. Death was not considered complete until the spirit had liberated itself from the body. Some ideas and methods of making the spirit leave the body and travel in other realms were developed by aborigines before the organised system of religion evolved. And, they had developed a variety of ways to deal with it.

An anthropologist in his very famous book, *Primitive Culture*, has stated that the concept of the soul arose when primitive people reflected on death, visions, and dreams. He logically deduced this statement based on two experiences of primitives. First, the primitives' awareness of the sudden transformation of the vibrant human body into a corpse at the moment of death led to the realisation that the animating source of life cannot be found in the physical body. Second, people conversed with the dead in dreams and visions and thought that dead persons seemed to exist in some form even after their bodily demise. This led to the logical deduction that an animating spirit exists that was invisible, immaterial, and detachable from the physical body. This concept of spirit was later extended to animals, plants, and objects, and it developed into the 'belief in spiritual beings', which he called animism, the closest definition and starting point of the concept of religion.[1]

Another explanation says that the primitive people would envision the dead people of their clan in dreams, and that made them believe in the existence of the dead even after their physical disappearance. This was the beginning of ancestor worship. Moreover, the most important and powerful members of society were believed to retain their positions and power even after death. Over time, these ancestors evolved into revered deities. Thus, making sense of this natural mystery of death was always an agenda for the primitive people, which gradually gave way to the evolution of rigorous belief systems called religion.

Death and Religion

When societies transitioned from nomadic ways to agricultural settlements, the organised system of religion evolved, and death gained more definite meanings.

Religion is the cultural institution built up around the idea of the relationship between some supreme being and human beings. Religion is conceptualised around three aspects. First, the idea

1. Tylor, E.B. (1871). *Primitive Culture: Researches into the Development of Mythology, Philosophy, Religion, Art, and Custom.* USA: Franklin Classic Trade Press.

of the presence of some divine power; second, a set of doctrines generating connections between this divine power and humanity; and third, the assumption that individual behaviour has to be in line with the divine order. Therefore, religion is the institution that has set the behaviour pattern in line with the divine order. The idea of religion has always been out of the purview of science, as the presence of some divine beings has no logical or scientific explanation.

Death and religion are so deeply connected that death is considered the prime source for the origin of organised religious beliefs, and it is believed that without death, there would be no need for religion. Anthropologists have written that religion was born out of real tragedies of human life and out of the conflict between human plans and realities. The fact of death is the most upsetting of all human events and perhaps the main source of religious belief. Malinowski, a renowned anthropologist, said:

> *'forebodings around death and immortality forms the nucleus of religious belief and practice'*[2]

Death is also called a 'marginal situation' (such situations that push social actors to the margins of meaningful stability), leading to the innate instability in life and imposing an anomic threat to society. Religion was invented to make sense of such marginal situations and to address the problem of how to bear the end of life.

Examining different religious traditions of the world, namely Hindu, Buddhist, Greek, Chinese, Mesopotamian, Egyptian, Christian, Herbaic, and Islamic, it has been established that religious belief systems interlace physical, psychological, and spiritual aspects of death.

---

2. Strenski, I. (2015). *Understanding Theories of Religion: An Introduction*. UK: Willey Blackwell.

Religion created a belief system about 'the dead', their probable fate after death; methods to look after the corpse; providing a new status to the dead; ways to fulfil their vacated roles; reaffirming group solidarity and re-establishing and comforting the bereaved. It brought about the concepts of salvation, reincarnation, heaven, hell, and rituals to tackle death and became the only institution that speculated on death and produced all knowledge about understanding and dealing with it. Not just about dealing with death, but religiosity also had an impact on people's orientation towards contemporary death issues like euthanasia, suicide, capital punishment, etc.

Some psychologists have conducted experiments on religious and non-religious people, and they have concluded that people with deep religious conviction showed less anxiety towards death as compared to non-religious people. Further, in terms of feelings related to visiting cremation grounds and attending funerals, non-religious subjects were less likely to recognise or report feelings connected with death and burial; however, religious groups reported calmness after attending a funeral.

Therefore, religions developed as coalitions of beliefs and practices, addressing various human phenomena, with death being of utmost importance. Death is one of the central themes in Hinduism, Sikhism, Buddhism, Christianity, and Islam. The death philosophy prescribed in these religions revolves around the meaning of death, the fate of the deceased after death, the possibilities in the afterlife journey, and liberation.

The Coming of Science

As societies advanced, attributes like rationality and reasoning became more important than religious orientation. After the historic industrial revolution, different aspects of human phenomena were understood and explained scientifically. In this phase, death and dying also came under the purview of science, and their indicators were medically defined in a rational manner.

One of the indicators of identifying death was the heart and lung criterion. It means the absence of cardiac activity, respiration, and responsiveness. For instance, life had passed into death if the heart did not beat, if air did not flow in and out of the lungs, and responsiveness was checked by simple indicators like no movement in the body, finding no response on pinching or pricking the skin, etc.

Gradually, medical technology advanced, and things became less clear. Machines could keep hearts pumping and lungs breathing artificially. With the development of Cardiopulmonary Resuscitation (CPR) technique and the invention of life support systems, the heart and lung criterion failed. Advancements in medical technology led to the survival of individuals even after losing cardiac and respiratory functions and resulted in a new state of living called 'Persistent Vegetative State' (PVS). Now the challenge was whether the person whose heart is beating on artificial systems should be considered alive or dead. Also, for medical procedures like organ donations, it was clearly required to demarcate life and death. So the new criteria of brain death were developed by the Harvard Medical School Committee. The following three definitions fall under brain death criteria:

- **Neocortical brain death:** This refers to the irreversible cessation of the function of the cerebral cortex. It means the end of cognitive functions of the brain, like mental processes of perception, memory, reasoning, and judgement, and a body living in an irreversible vegetative state.

- **Brainstem death:** The brainstem controls and regulates functions such as circulation, breathing, temperature, blood pressure, and the arousal of consciousness. According to this criterion, death can be declared if the brainstem stops functioning. This criterion is considered advantageous for carrying out organ donation procedures by medical practitioners.

- **Whole brain death:** This refers to the irreversible cessation of all brain activity. A person is considered dead when he or she has suffered irreversible loss in all capacities of the brain and is no longer capable of performing any physical and mental functions. This has become the most acceptable criterion for determining death in recent times. It is also popular because it facilitates organ donation. When the brain suffers irreversible damage, the heart is made to pump blood artificially. This is also confusing because the person declared dead could still breathe. The declaration of brain death is not based on any subjective measures. There is a clinical way to identify it. The electroencephalogram (EEG) is the test conducted; if it doesn't show any electrical activity, the person is declared dead. An injection of mild radioactive isotopes into the brain reveals the absolute absence of blood flow. The sense organs of brain-dead people also do not respond. Their pupils do not respond to light, and they do not blink. They do not respond to pain, and in the absence of signals from the brain, their lungs stop working, and only a ventilator keeps them functioning.

So, the advancement in medical sciences made death a more précised event happening in the hospitals, surrounded by medical experts who would do their best to prolong life and keep death at bay. However, while medical science brought about clear indicators of determining death, religious faiths still sustained as they provided knowledge on ways to deal with it, journey beyond death, the possibilities of coming back, and so on.

Socio-Cultural Understanding of Death

As the civilisations evolved, death got socio-cultural meanings as well. The biological sameness in medical terms is not sufficient to define the larger-than-life concept of death completely.

'Sociologically, death is viewed as the nucleus of the particular culture complex involving a group of interrelated cultural traits which function together in a more or less consistent and meaningful way. The study of the specific areas which make up this complex, such as culturally defined meaning of death, the roles of the functionaries, bereavement, death rites and practices, and the effect of attitudes toward death upon the general life organization of the individual, could be made more meaningful by viewing these areas as aspects of a larger configuration surrounding death.'[3] Thus, various terms and phrases are used to explain death socio-culturally.

- **Death System:** Death system refers to the interpersonal, socio-cultural, and symbolic network that exists around death in every society.[4] Death has a role in the maintenance and change of the social order. The death system contains the following components:
    - *People* are the first component in the death system, as no person in the world can avoid death, and no one can stay isolated and unaffected—if not by one's own death, then by the death of others. In addition, there are people who play various kinds of roles in the death system, such as funeral directors, health care workers, priests, etc.
    - *Places* like hospitals, funeral homes, cemeteries, etc., which deal with the dead and dying, are the second component of the death system. Memorials, hospices, and battlefields are some other places that are linked to death.

3. Faunce, W.A, & Fulton, R.L (1958). The Sociology of Death: A Neglected Area of Research? *Social Forces, 35,* 205–209.

4. Kastenbaum, R. (2001). *Death, Society, and Human Experience* (7th edition ed.). Boston: Allyn & Bacon.

- *Time* is the third component of the death system. It refers to a specific day or phase which is associated with the dead. All Saints' Day, Good Friday, and memorial days in Christian traditions, and in India, death anniversaries of influential people and days of *shradh*, called *pitru paksha,* etc., are examples of this component of the death system. Different cultures may hold different times to remember their dead.

- *Objects and Symbols* are the remaining components of the death system. Death-related objects include coffins, mourning clothes, wood, oil, etc. Symbols refer to the culturally diverse funerary rituals and mourning practices.

The death system survives because it fulfils certain manifest and latent functions that help in maintaining the social order. The death system is not static. It constantly evolves to deal with changing circumstances and situations. For example, the terrorist attacks of 11 September 2001, in the U.S., have led to the development of whole new systems for airline security that include new personnel, regulations, and places such as screening and identification. As causes of death have changed, new institutions such as hospice and nursing homes have developed. A change in one part of the system is likely to generate a change in other parts of the system.

Functions of Death

Though marking the end of life, death is seen as socially contributing by playing some important functions.

1. **Death as a Means of Control:** Death acts as a means of control. For instance, in war, death or the threat of death is involved. Wars are won by increasing the death count of the enemy. Also, capital punishment is an effective means of social control. The

very idea of capital punishment is an outcome of the belief that the fear of death can influence the behaviour of people and make them conform to the social norms.

2. **Death as an Indicator of Social Status:** The procedure and the gathering at the mortuary or funeral ceremony is an indicator of one's social status. In western societies, for instance, factors such as the number of floral offerings, the quality of the casket, and the size and type of marker used at the grave indicate the social status of the deceased and the family. In India, the elaborate and extravagant funeral ceremony of socially and politically affluent people is a pointer to their influential status.

3. **Death as an Entertainment:** Death is also seen as a form of entertainment. It is significant in the bullfights of Mexico and Spain, which have been very popular in the West. People are fascinated and entertained by watching the art performances and sports activities where the risk of life is involved. Without the death elements, the act would apparently be less entertaining. Instances of people enjoying adventure sports, car racing, thrill driving, etc., reinforce the notion that death is entertaining.

4. **Death as Means of Escape:** Death is also seen as a means of avoiding life and many problems associated with living. Death is also a tool used by people in an effort to escape from potential responsibilities and obligations. Instances like killing deformed children and female infants reflect that death helps in escaping from certain responsibilities. Further, the assumption behind committing suicide is also escaping from some disturbing realities of life. Thus, in some contexts, for individuals, the fear of life overshadows the fear of death.

Therefore, medically, death has been understood in terms of cessation of bodily functions, primarily the brain. Socially, it became a much broader concept. It is seen as a system that has functions to perform for society. It has been interpreted as a means of social control, a means of escape, entertainment, and an indicator of social status.

Social Death

Social death is a phenomenon implying that a person is declared socially dead by society, regardless of his/her actual state of life. There are circumstances which lead to social death before biological death. For instance, a person suffering from a chronic illness may not be able to continue with their societal roles. This is referred to as a state where the social existence of the dying patients is reduced and almost eliminated by physical, emotional, and communicative withdrawal. Social death occurs when a person becomes a 'non-person'.[5] 'Non-person' means that the individual is no longer an active agent in the ongoing social world, and other people no longer seek to communicate with that person and no longer take the deceased into consideration for their actions. Social death is also perceived as a situation when a person is ostracised or boycotted by the members of society. Thus, social death implies cessation of an individual as an active agent in others' lives.

Death in the Modern Period

The period from the late eighteenth century to the twentieth century is marked as the modernisation phase. During this time, societies transitioned from simple to complex forms, from homogeneity to heterogeneity. In this phase, societies witnessed significant social changes like scientific and technological advancement, globalisation, individualism, changing family

5. Mulkay, M. (1993). Social Death in Britain. In D. Clark (Ed.), *The Sociology of Death: Theory, Culture, and Practice* (pp. 31–49). Oxford: Blackwell.

structure and gender roles, etc. The situation emerged whereby religion shifted its position from the central pillar of society and was replaced by attributes like scientific thinking, rationality, and logic. Human phenomena like polity, economy, education, individual decision making, etc., were now understood on the basis of these attributes and not religion. In this phase, the phenomena of death and dying also underwent change, and many new dimensions were added to it.

Death Became a Problem to Be Solved

In the modern era, with the advancement in medical science, there has been a significant change in Attitude towards Death. While religion focused on accepting death, medicalisation and technology in modern times focused on conquering death. The traditional medicine system prescribed by various religions attempted to restore the 'vigour', the 'suppleness', and the 'fluidity' of the body. In the nineteenth century, medical attention shifted from illness of the body to disease, resulting in the pathologising of mortality.[6] Death is considered a failure of the doctor, and people have become non-receptive towards it. Therefore, the modern attitude towards death is one of non-acceptance. Death is perceived as a problem to be solved with the help of medicine.

Commercialisation of Death

In the times of capitalism, death and dying have also been commercialised with the extensive growth of the funeral industry, where funeral services are sold, demonstrating the class and status of the deceased. Because of advanced medicalisation, the deceased

---

6. Lupton, D. (2009). Foucault and Medicalisation Critique. In S. Earle, C. Kamaromy, & C. Batholomew (Eds.), *Death and Dying: A Reader* (pp. 20–24). London: Sage.

first becomes the property of medical institutions and, after death, the corpse becomes the property of funeral directors. A huge amount of money is spent on dealing with death. The ritualistic services that evolved as part of sacraments in different religious faiths are now sold by the service providers with the intention of making a huge profit. Extravagant death ceremonies also indicate the commercialisation of death. While in the West, the funeral industry is centred on the profit-making of funeral directors, in India, places like Banaras, Haridwar, Bodh Gaya, etc., are the centres where the 'sacred specialists' (priests) who facilitate the bereaved organise their business around death.

Secularisation of Death

Secularisation is one of the by-products of modernisation. It refers to the process whereby religion loses its significance in different spheres of human life. Secularisation of death means understanding death and dealing with it in a non-religious manner.

> *'The reference point in death, as in life, is no longer God but man and death is seen as the end of the person's life rather than the beginning of a life in heaven, and after death we are exhorted to attend to the mourner's grief rather than to the deceased's soul.'*[7]

Since death is no longer perceived in a religious manner, non-religious ways to deal with it have started emerging. Inviting a rock band for a post-funeral ceremony, playing the favourite music of the deceased instead of reading scriptures in the funeral mass in a church, embalming and plastination of the dead bodies, organ donation, pledging the cadaver, etc., are some of the examples of secular ways of dealing with death.

7. Walter, T. (2015). Secularisation. In C.M. Parkes, P. Laungani, & B. Young (Eds.), *Death and Bereavement Across Cultures* (p. 133). London: Brunner-Routledge.

Sequestration of Death

Sequestration of death means sidelining and bracketing the subject of death from everyday life. This sequestration is done by concealing and ignoring the fact of death to the greatest possible extent. Removal of death and dying from domestic spaces to hospitals, hospices, and funeral parlours is an example of sequestrating death. Death is not just sidelined as a phenomenon but also as a subject of study. Instead of focusing on the actual reality of death, most of the modern thinkers pick up subjects like bereavement, the funeral industry, hospice, etc. Thus, the sequestration of death in everyday life involves practices like not talking about it; a large number of deaths happening in isolation at hospitals rather than at home, hiding corpses and death-related practices from children, and considering death practices as morbid and sad, etc.

'Irrationality' and Fear of Death

Rationality is the quality of being reasonable, which is founded on fact, reason, and logic. To be rational in the context of death would mean the use of logic and a lack of emotion while understanding and dealing with it. Acceptance of death as a natural order of things signifies the rationality of death. It is irrational to fear death. While in traditional times death was accepted as a normal event in life, it has become a fearsome reality in modern times. Thus, another notable feature of death in modern times is that it is perceived irrationally with an emotion of fear.

Planning for Death

Planning of death has become a popular practice in modern times. It involves practices like making a will, pledging organs, making death insurance, etc. Will-writing is an appropriate way to plan one's death. It is the legal testimony of a person, where the testator legally assigns persons to manage his/her movable and immovable assets after death. It also involves assigning heirs and inheritors of one's property after death. A Will may include pledging of organs, wishes (if any) pertaining to what is to be done with one's body, unclear debts (if any), rituals, in particular, to be followed, etc.

Use of Electric Crematorium

An electric crematorium disposes of the dead body using electricity. It is a furnace built with brick walls; the combustion is carried out at a high temperature generated by electricity. In the modernisation phase, in the light of preserving wood, preventing pollution, and the lack of space for burial, the use of crematoria became very popular in Western countries, even where the majority of the population followed religious faiths that prescribed burial as the appropriate way of body disposal. Also, in some countries, crematoria became the ideal model as they attempted to convert the heat generated by cremation into electricity. In India, it came into practice in January 1989 as part of the Ganga Action Plan. The intention was to initiate environment-friendly cremation, as the conventional process of cremation required huge quantities of firewood, which was expensive and hazardous for the environment. An electric crematorium is less expensive and saves resources. Electric crematoria are set up in different parts of the country, especially in the metropolis. Their usage is promoted by the government, NGOs, and environmentalists.

Liberal Views on Euthanasia

Euthanasia, also called mercy-killing, refers to the intentional ending of the patient's life at a stage from which the person is so ill that he/she cannot recover. Religious faiths, by and large, are against the practice of euthanasia, and largely, it is equated to sin as severe as murder. However, legally, it has been allowed in some countries. Some aspect of it is legal in India as well. The Supreme Court of India, in 2011, laid out the guidelines for euthanasia and distinguished between active and passive euthanasia. Passive is allowed, which refers to the situation whereby the person suffering from persistent vegetative state is left without an artificial life support system, which the court stated is not a 'positive act of killing'. Studies have shown that in recent years, people's attitudes towards issues of euthanasia and suicide have liberalised.

Hence, in modern times, new dimensions of death and dying started emerging. With the help of medical technology, more précised ways to determine death have developed. From absolute control of religion, death shifted into the lap of science, consequently leading to its secularisation, commercialisation, and changing people's attitude towards it. Therefore, in contemporary times, we have entered a situation whereby there are two choices to comprehend death and deal with it: 1) believing and following whatever is prescribed in one's religion; or 2) comprehending death logically and opting for non-religious ways like organ donation, whole body donation, and not mourning the death in the religiously prescribed ways.

Theoretical Approaches to Death and Dying

The first genre of anthropologists is called evolutionary theorists, who explored the non-biological side of death and dying.

The idea of regenerating life is central to human societies, as it ensures continuity and strengthens human existence in the world. In the subconscious minds of human beings, there is an existence of powerful forces of survival that indicate the regeneration of life. These forces are visible in phenomena like sexual drive to reproduce, hunting to obtain food and shelter, and expressing joy or profound bereavement through art, music, song, dance, etc. Anthropologists highlighted certain death-related practices amongst primitives that indicate the vigour of the regeneration of life after death.

Anthropologist Johann Jakob Bachofen studied symbolism in funerals and revealed that the symbols of fertility and sexuality are reflected in the funerals of aborigines. He found the symbols of fertility (eggs and women) on tombs of ancient Greeks and Romans and interpreted them as indicators of the belief that life comes out of death.[8] In some communities, there was a practice of naming a newborn child after a recently dead person.[9] Bloch & Parry (1982), in their anthology, *Death and Regeneration of Life*, have developed an equation between mortuary rituals and the symbols of birth and fertility of various communities from China, India, New Guinea, Latin America, and Africa. The studies highlight that the complex funeral rites of some tribes, like dancing in tight circles on heavy rhythm and the slaughter of cattle, are also practised while planting rice. This expresses the power of vitality, indicating death as the regeneration of life.[10]

Thus, evolutionary theorists believe that forces of survival are inherent in human beings. So, when they make sense of death (annihilation of the physical body), they do not see it as the end, but rather consider it as a regeneration of life.

Functionalist School

While the first genre of evolutionary theorists discussed above reflected upon the symbolic and ritualistic aspects of death,

---

8. Bachofen, J.J. (1967). An essay on ancient mortuary symbolism. In *Myth, Religion, and Mother Right* (R. Manheim, Trans.). London: Routledge & Kegan Paul.

9. Ebersole, L.G. (2005). Death. In L. Jones, *Encyclopedia of Religion, Second Edition* (pp. 2235–2245). USA: Mcmillan.

10. Bloch, M., & Parry, J. (1982). *Death and Regeneration of Life*. Cambridge: Cambridge University Press.

in later years, functionalists, Emile Durkheim, Robert Hertz, Malinowski, and Radcliffe-Brown focused upon the social aspects of death. In *Elementary Forms of the Religious Life*, Durkheim (1912) argues that the most important function of death rites is to regulate societal bonds. He explained that death is not to be seen as an instant annihilation of an individual's life, but rather as a social process, whereby the dead person becomes an ancestor. The most important function of death is to promote the reorganisation of the social order and the restoration of faith in the permanent existence of the society, which has been temporarily challenged by the death of the individual. Social and emotional reactions following death are culturally determined, and these reactions depend upon different variables of the dead person, like his/her age, gender, and social status.

Functionalists also studied death in terms of mortality rites and stated that the function of these rites, like other ceremonies, is to resolve the disruptive tendencies which operate at times of social crisis. The ceremonies of death are the most powerful means of reintegration of the group's shaken solidarity and re-establishment of its morale. Also, death is a phenomenon that leads to issues of inheritance, redistribution of rights and statuses, and reintegration of mourners into day-to-day life. They believe that death leads to a partial destruction of social cohesion until a new equilibrium is established. Weeping at the time of death affirms the social bond between people, especially the bereaved.

The Death Anxiety Approach

In a very famous work of Sigmund Freud on psychoanalysis, there is a psychological explanation of death. He explained that sometimes people express fears of death, called 'Thanatophobia'. People do not fear their own death because it is quite unimaginable, and nobody believes in his/her own death, but they fear the death of others. This fear is a manifestation of emotional ambivalence at the unconscious level, which is projected in dreams. It is this fear of facing others' death that is the cause of death anxiety. People also fear the return of the dead and the demonisation of the dead.

Modern Approaches to Death

Modern sociological thinkers understand death by relating it to the peculiar features of modernity, like individualism, advanced medical technology, and secularisation. They propound that in modern society, death is a denied phenomenon both as a reality and as a subject of study. It is considered a negative phenomenon. Advanced medicalisation, dying lonely in hospitals, surrounded by professionals and not by family, and dealing with death with the help of professionals, instigates a sense of denial of death amongst modern people. In modern societies, due to extensive individualism, the vital function of death-related rituals to re-bond the social relationships across the community is also not happening.

Another famous book, *The Denial of Death* by Ernest Becker, explains that death anxiety is real and is people's deepest source of concern. This anxiety is so intense that it generates many fears and phobias that people experience in everyday life. For him, the denial of death is important because if the reality of our end keeps alarming us all the time, it will be difficult for humans to function. So the denial of death in everyday lives keeps our basic anxiety under control. In his analysis of society, he points out that funeral homes with their flowers, hospices, and the advanced medical system are among societal elements that contribute to maintaining the denial of death.

Many also argue that since it is not possible to fully deny death, it is sequestrated. Just like modern societies brush the significant problems of society under the carpet, they attempt to sequestrate (hide) death. Sequestration of death also means that as the event of death breaches the sense of security that keeps people leading a peaceful life, it has become a private and personal event. It is no longer a social or communal event and, therefore, less visible in society.

Post-Modern Approach: Revival of Death

The 'revival of death' perspective, however, contradicts the above-mentioned modern approaches and emphasises that in contemporary times, the noise being created about death being death denied and sequestrated, in fact, makes it more popular. A book, *The Revival of Death*, points out, first in agreement with sequestration approach theorists, that death in a Western modern society is an individualised and private affair, but disagrees with the idea that death is less visible in society. It emphasises that death is more visible, particularly in the realm of advanced mass media.

Highlighting individualism in death and dying-related issues, in contemporary times, individuals are exercising their agency on matters pertaining to their death. Individuals' discretion is involved in decisions like whether they want to be in hospice or in a hospital, and whether they want medication or want to stop it, etc. This is not the hiding of death but its revival. Death is in the forefront, as in the process of dying, the agency of the deceased is given more importance as compared to earlier times, where religion or the doctors would impose their choices.[11] This approach states that in earlier times, it was religion that dictated all do's and don'ts for one's death, and in the modern phase, the medical staff and the doctors took the position of deciding not just about the moment of death but also the last phase of the dying—the medicines to be given or withdrawn, and the ward to be kept in, etc. However, in the post-modern times, it is the

11. Seale, C. (1998). *Constructing Death: The Sociology of Dying and Bereavement.* Cambridge: Cambridge University Press.

deceased (actor) who is involved in making sense of his/her last phase of life, relatively free from the compulsions of institutions like religion and medicine. Post-modern theorists also point out that mass media have helped in making death more visible and exuberant than hidden or sequestered.[12]

Therefore, the early genre of theorists focused on death as its functionality for society and how the rites meant to manage death contribute to the restoration of the societal order and strengthen the social bonds. The modern thinkers focus on the aspect that as societies transformed from traditional moorings to modern ways, their ways to comprehend and deal with death also underwent change. The denial of death thesis explains that in present times, death as a reality is denied by modern people. It is understood as failure and rejection. Another approach to the sequestration of death contests the earlier extreme position taken by the scholars that death is a denied phenomenon in modernity. This approach emphasises that death is not denied but hidden and bracketed in modern times, as it breaches the sense of security that keeps people leading a peaceful life.

The 'revival of death' school opines that, instead of hiding or bracketing, death has become more visible in different mediums. Individualism, the by-product of modernity, has not just confined death to personal and private space, but it also means the role of individual agency in deciding how one prefers to die and how one decides to grieve.

---

12. Jacobsen, M.H. (2016). 'Spectacular Death'—Proposing a New Fifth Phase to Philippe Ariès's Admirable History of Death. Humanities, 5 (19), 1–20.

CHAPTER 2

Death and the Divine

Death is one of the central themes in Hinduism, Sikhism, Buddhism, Christianity, and Islam. The death philosophy prescribed in these religions revolves around the meaning of death, the fate of the deceased after death, the possibilities in the afterlife journey and liberation. Major themes pertaining to death and dying are prescribed in the sacred texts of these religious faiths. However, before discussing the death philosophy of these religions, let's have an overview of these religions.

An Overview of the Major Religions and Their Sacred Texts

Hinduism

In the history of world religions, Hinduism is a unique phenomenon; it does not have the concept of only one God as being central to it. Hinduism does not revere any particular person as its sole prophet or founder. It also does not recognise any particular book as its absolutely authoritative scripture. There are numerous gods and goddesses who are revered; rivers, places, and mountains that are considered sacred; there is a variety of mystics, saints, sects, and cults; diverse schools of thought; and a vast canopy of literature from which its philosophy has emerged. Interestingly, despite so many variations, it has persisted through centuries as a distinct religious entity and is followed by millions of people in India. The beginning of the Hindu tradition is traced back to the coming of the Aryans into India from the northwest, and it was the transitional time from nomadic life to agricultural settlements.[1] The sacred literature in Hinduism has accumulated since then and been collected over centuries, composed over so many years. There is a huge variety of literature dedicated to different gods, composed by different people (saints/*rishis*) of different sects and cults. Broadly, the entire literature is categorised into two parts: *Sruti* (heard/revealed) and *Smriti* (remembered). An interesting feature of *Sruti* literature is that, for centuries, it survived orally (heard literature), received and transmitted from *guru* (teacher) to *shishya* (disciple) verbally. Thus, in *Sruti* literature, the revelation is acknowledged as the *sabda* (eternal word), the word which is not composed by humans or even different gods, but 'heard' by ancient *rishis* (sages). The ancient seers were endowed with such powers that when they would get deeper into their inner selves, the truths of the universe would come automatically into their consciousness. *Sruti* literature, in totality, is a collection of four Vedic *Samhitas*: Rig, Sama, Yajur, and Atharva. Each of these *Samhitas* has its own collection of the Brahmanas, the Aranyakas, and the Upanishads.

Smriti literature comprises the whole body of sacred wisdom remembered by *rishis* (sages) and their interpretation of *Sruti* texts. However, *Sruti* literature is considered superior, and it is

1. Friess, H.L., & Schneider, H.W. (1960). *Religion in Various Cultures.* New York: H. Holt and Co.

believed that in case of conflict between *Sruti* and *Smriti*, the former should prevail.[2] Largely, literature in the *Smriti* canon consists of *Vedangas* (texts on subjects of astronomy, astrology, grammar, etc.), *Shastras* (law books like *Manusmriti*), eighteen *Maha-puranas* and eighteen *Upa-puranas* (mythological stories for conveying the religious code to laity), and epics such as Ramayana, Mahabharata, and Bhagavad Gita (sacred song of God). Other than these, the teachings of different *rishis*, books on yoga, *tantras, mantras, yantras, mandalas*, and cosmograms, etc., are also part of the *Smriti* canon. *Smriti* literature has contributed to the formulation of a righteous code of conduct for a Hindu.

Therefore, such a huge spectrum of sacred literature that was accumulated over centuries has led to the development of assorted beliefs and practices that prevail in Hinduism in contemporary times. Death-related philosophy, too, has not emerged in one shot but has been built up in different phases of Hinduism. Some aspects of *Sruti* literature still persist, many have become obsolete, and many practices emerged in the later phases. As a result, in Hinduism, there exists a potpourri of ideas that explain the meaning of death and offer guidelines to deal with it.

Sikhism

Sikhism is amongst the youngest religions of the world. The religion evolved and progressed in the Punjab region of the Indian subcontinent over the years 1469–1709, propagated by the ten successive Sikh Gurus and later designating the scripture (anthology of teachings of all Gurus and of other saints of those times), Guru Granth Sahib, as the eleventh Guru. To date, adherents of Sikhism revere Guru Granth Sahib as their living divine Guru. Guru Nanak was the first Guru, and Sikhism's origin is rooted in Guru Nanak's teachings that date back to the

2. Leaman, O. (2001). *Encyclopedia of Ancient Philosophy.* London: Routledge.

fifteenth century. Nanak was born in a Hindu family in 1469 in a predominantly Hindu area. In those times, different cults within Hinduism (Vaishnavites and Shaivaites) were popular, and at the same time, Islam was also prevalent as the Mughals were ruling some parts of the country. At that time, in both religious doctrines, too much importance was given to performing rituals to please God. So Guru Nanak took a different position and developed and preached a non-ritualistic method to revere the divine power. It is believed that Guru Nanak's understanding of God was derived from his experience. The story goes that he was taken to God's court, and he became aware of God as one and only, pervading the entire universe. He was given a cup of nectar of God's name to drink and was commanded to go into the world to preach the divine name. '*From then onwards, he not only found God within himself, but he perceived God as pervading in all forms, all castes and all hearts*' (AG, 223).

Thus, in the beginning, Sikhism emerged as an offshoot of Hinduism and gradually developed into a full-fledged religion.

Sikhism is a monotheistic religion that believes in one God,[3] addressed as *Waheguru*. *Waheguru* is defined as *nirankar* (shapeless), *akal* (beyond time), and *alakh* (sightless). God is stated as *ik omkar* (one constant), who is omnipresent and infinite. Sikhism rejects the view that God descends into the world and takes any kind of bodily form. Sikhism preaches that God is *Ajuni* (one who does not take birth). But not taking birth does not mean that God is not active. Sikhism propounds that God is the creator from whom the entire universe has manifested. Existence of the universe and its sustenance depend upon God's *hukam* (will), which is supreme. Sikhism preaches that God doesn't come to earth in the form of any incarnation but communicates the eternal word through legendary humans like Moses, Mohammad, Gurus, saints, etc. These legendary humans are the torchbearers in the pursuit of

3. '*Sabẖnā kā parabẖ ek hai ḏūjā avar na koe*', GGS, p. 757, line 4.

enlightenment for the masses. It is preached that humans are the highest product of the evolutionary process, and it has happened because of God's intention.

The core philosophy of Sikhism is based upon the teachings of Gurus compiled in the Guru Granth Sahib, which contains compositions by six Gurus: namely, Guru Nanak, Guru Angad, Guru Amar Das, Guru Ram Das, Guru Arjan Dev, and Guru Teg Bahadur. While the philosophy of Sikhism, including death-related beliefs, is based upon Guru Granth Sahib, the righteous code of conduct for Sikhs is prescribed in the manuals called *Rehatnamas.* In 1699, the last Guru, Gobind Singh, declared that the scripture was his successor and designated the authority to carry forward the legacy of Gurus to not any one individual but to the community as a whole. Hence, it was felt that since there is no authorised person who could answer the queries of the community, manuals called *Rehatnamas* were written to describe the Sikh code of conduct. The tradition of *Rehatnamas* can be traced back to the eighteenth century, and these have been rewritten on different occasions. These texts give instructions pertaining to rites of passage in the light of *Gurbani.*[4] The latest version was written by the Shromani Gurdwara Parbandhak Committee (SGPC), called *Rehat Maryada: Sikh Code of Conduct and Conventions.* It is called a modern standard *Rehatnama.* This document has been accepted as the official account which provides guidelines to deal with various aspects of life for Sikhs around the world.

Buddhism

Buddhism is a very diverse religious tradition with its origins in India around the sixth and fifth centuries B.C. The religion was founded by Buddha Shakyamuni, who was a royal prince of the Shakya family in Nepal. According to the traditional stories of Buddhism,

---

4. *Gurbani* refers to the text in holy scripture, Sri Guru Granth Sahib.

the prince decided to seek enlightenment after witnessing four sights: a sick person, an old person, a corpse, and someone who has renounced the world. These sights troubled him so much that he realised that all humankind was subject to *dukkha* (the sufferings). Such thoughts made him renounce his luxurious life, and he left to seek solutions for these sufferings. He lived a life of an ascetic and practised austerities and meditation for many years. Finally, on the verge of starvation while meditating, he achieved enlightenment. Thereafter, he started preaching his sermons.

As Buddhism evolved and spread across different parts of the world, various schools of thought emerged within it, making Buddhism a very diverse religious tradition. Scholars have captured its diverseness in different ways. Historians have classified it into philosophical epochs (era-wise). Some theologians have offered a regional typology, like Tibetan, Sri Lankan, Chinese, and Japanese Buddhism. Other Buddhist scholars have formulated a schema based on diverseness in the doctrines within Buddhism. According to this typology, Buddhism is divided into three categories: namely, *Theravada* (Way of Elders), *Mahayana* (the great vehicle), and *Vajrayana* (Diamond Vehicle) Buddhism.

The *Theravada* school is the oldest and reveres Buddha as the single, supremely gifted, yet mortal teacher and claims to abide by the original teachings of the Buddha. *Theravadins* trace their descent from the monastic community called the original *sangha* (community of ordained Buddhist monks), that first followed Buddha. The *Theravada* school is widespread in South-East Asia, particularly in countries like Thailand, Myanmar, Vietnam, Cambodia, and Sri Lanka. The central theme of *Theravada* doctrine is that salvation (freedom from the cycle of birth and death) is possible only for *arhats* (monks); they can attain salvation through ascetic life and tough meditative practices, and the laypersons can only seek to be reborn as a monk after many rebirths.

This core philosophy of *Theravada* Buddhism became the point of its criticism. It was accused of being too orthodox and self-obsessed. So, after some years, the Buddhists came up with a new doctrine, which preached that using virtues like compassion, *arhats* can help the laity on the path of enlightenment and liberate them from the birth/death cycle. They called their philosophy *Mahayana* (the great vehicle) and named the earlier one, *Theravada*, *Hinayana* (the lesser vehicle). *Mahayana* Buddhism is popular in China, Korea, Japan, and some parts of India.

Around 747–749 A.D., *Vajrayana* Buddhism emerged in Tibet. This was founded by Indian Master Padmasambhava, also popularly known as Guru Rimpoche, who travelled from Afghanistan to preach Buddhism in Tibet and Bhutan.[5] During those times, the Chinese religious philosophy called Bön was popular in Tibet. Hallucinations and paranormal experiences were integral to Bön philosophy. They believed that humans consist of twin spirits that depart on death, and after death, the departed part might come back and haunt, if not handled properly. So, to ward off the evils created by the spirits that might have existed because of being mishandled at the time of death, the practice of human and animal sacrifice was also prevalent. These pre-existing beliefs had an impact on the Buddhist teachings preached by Guru Rimpoche, leading to the emergence of another school: *Vajrayana* Buddhism. It is also known as Tibetan Buddhism and *Tantric* or Esoteric Buddhism. The literal meaning of the term '*tantra*' is 'thread', which refers to a chain of teachers who pass their teachings from generation to generation. *Vajrayana* Buddhism is predominant in Himalayan nations like Tibet, Bhutan, Nepal, Mongolia, and India (the Himalayan region). The very popular Dalai Lama cult also belongs to the *Vajaryana* school of thought. Like Hinduism, Buddhism also has a variety of sacred texts. *Triptikas* (Pali canon) are the traditional texts and are believed to be the writings based on the original teachings of Buddha, and are written in the Pali

5. Becker, C.B. (1993). *Breaking the Circle: Death and the Afterlife in Buddhism.* Carbondale, Illinois: Southern Illinois University Press.

language. These texts are revered by the *Theravada* school. In addition, the *Mahayana Sutras* and *The Tibetan Book of the Dead* are popular texts of *Mahayana* and *Vajrayana* Buddhism.

Christianity

Historically, it is believed that there are three monotheistic Abrahamic[6] religions: namely, Judaism, Christianity, and Islam. Judaism is the oldest religious belief, while Christianity and Islam are its offshoots. Christianity, which is believed to be the world's largest religion, originated almost two thousand years ago and is popular worldwide, with numerous denominations and sects. Though there are notable differences in various schools of thought in terms of apostolic succession, degree of acceptance of the scripture, sacraments, authority of the Pope, etc., the core of Christianity (involving all variations) is the belief in the existence of one God and Jesus Christ. It is believed that Jesus Christ came to earth in a human form as the only son of God and sacrificed his life for the entire human race. The sacred literature of Christianity belongs to the Biblical canon, and its most popular and revered texts are the Old Testament and the New Testament. The former comprises 46 books of the Bible, written before Christ, including the first five that the Jews call the Torah. The latter is the anthology on the life, death, and resurrection of Christ, written by the early disciples of Jesus, consisting of 27 books. As explained in the New Testament, the core tenets of Christianity revolve around the following aspects of the life of Lord Jesus:

1. ***He is the Son of God:*** The Gospels[7] call Jesus the Son of God. They explain that he was the manly manifestation of God's

6. Faiths that trace their common origin to Abraham and recognise him as their first prophet are called Abrahamic faiths.

7. Gospels are any one of the first four books of the Christian Bible that tell of the life of Jesus Christ.

dunamis (Greek term for dynamics). He was born as a human who was subject to the penalty of death (like other human beings), but he acted as a superhuman figure, like angels or the Messiah. He also believed that he would be vindicated by God. Though he was human, his actions were miraculous like God. He spoke and acted against the existing major political and religious issues of that time. He claimed that he got the right to question the prevailing systems directly from God, whom he addressed as *Abba* (father). This attitude of Jesus provoked the ruling and the superior class of that time. Therefore, he was put on trial.

2. ***Trial in Jerusalem:*** As he was found deviating from God's command according to the boundaries of the covenant and the Torah prevailing in those times, he had to face the trial in Jerusalem (the religious/political centre of Israel in those days).

3. ***The Last Supper and Crucifixion of Jesus:*** The night before the trial is considered to be the most significant event in the life of Jesus. The Bible notes that Jesus, on the night before his trial, offered a piece of bread and wine to his followers, referring to it as his body and blood. Sharing the food is considered symbolic of believers participating in the death of Jesus. The Gospels note that Jesus' trial seemed to have been the kind of investigation envisaged in Deuteronomy (the book of law for Jews) to establish whether he was deviant or not. The accusation against him had nothing to do initially with blasphemy or any other offensive act in the light of Deuteronomy, but it was his silence that put him in the Deuteronomic category of an obstinate and aberrant teacher. Bearing these charges, he was punished with crucifixion. The event is described as being very dreadful and torturous. As Jesus claimed that he was the Son of God, it was expected that God would come and save him. Two rebels were also crucified with him. It is quoted that until 3 p.m., the

darkness spread all over, and he cried in a loud voice, '*Eli, Eli, lema sabachthani?*' (My God, my God, why have you forsaken me?) And he gave up his life. He said, '*It is finished,*' *and he bowed his head and gave up His spirit* (John 19:30).

4. ***Rising of Jesus:*** The most significant event in history, according to Christianity, is the 'Rising of Christ' (later termed as resurrection) and being seen alive after death. So, Christianity evolved from the very idea that God, in the form of Jesus Christ, came to the earth, died for mankind, and rose again to establish reconciliation with the entire human race. Apostle John's Gospel notes, '*For God so loved the world that he gave his only son, that everyone who believes in Him shall not perish and have an eternal life*' (John 3:16).

So, events in Jesus' life: his coming on earth as a Messiah, crucifixion, sacrificing his life, shedding his blood for cleansing the entire human race, and his ascension (rising again) form the central themes in Christianity. It is preached that God, in the form of a human being, came down to earth to establish a covenant of love with mankind. He gave assurance to the entire human race that God will take everyone into his embrace in eternal bliss.

Islam

The word 'Islam' has an Arabic root, with the literal meaning 'surrender' or 'submission'. It is the youngest of the three Abrahamic faiths. Islam is not viewed as an altogether different religion but as an offshoot of Judaism. The historical origins of Islam go back to the seventh century. It is believed that about 600 years after the origin of Christianity, a new religious doctrine called Islam started emerging. Prophet Muhammad, an Arab, experienced a revelation in his fortieth year, and thereafter he started preaching Islam. It is a monotheistic religion which strongly preaches believing and worshipping one God *(Allah)* as the creator of life and its final judge. Proponents define Islam as a way of life and not just a religion. The righteous way to lead a life is disseminated to Muslims through the sacred texts of Islam, namely, the Quran and the Hadith. The Quran is referred to as the primary text revealed to the Prophet Muhammad by God himself, and the Hadith, second to the Quran in terms of authority, comprises sayings of Muhammad and later Islamic sages. Verses from these texts are translated into righteous actions called *Sharia,* the Islamic law. It is stated that every aspect of a Muslim's life is governed by *Sharia.* Though Islam too has different sects, the most popular ones are *Sunni and Shi'a,* with further divisions and sub-sects, but interestingly, these sects have differences only in terms of successors after the death of the Prophet, but the basic tenets and the main themes are largely the same. The core tenets of Islam across various sects and sub-sects are *Iman* (the six articles of Islamic faith) and the Five Pillars of Islam.

Iman (The Six Articles of Islamic Faith)

1. ***Belief in Allah*** **(God):** It is strongly prescribed in Islamic texts that *Allah* is the only God, who has created the universe and is the sustainer of life on earth. Islam rejects all other claimants of divinity and supreme authority.

2. ***Belief in Farishte*** **(Angels):** Islam prescribes that angels are one of the sapient creatures of God, like humans and *jinns* (demons). But, unlike the other two, angels do not enjoy free will and act only upon God's will. Angels are made up of light, and Muslims are supposed to believe in the existence of these unseen beings. There is a mention of ten angels in the Quran, namely, *Jibril, Mikail, Israfil, Izrail, Munkar, Nakir, Raqib, Atib, Malik,* and *Ridhuan.* It is believed that these angels, at the will of God, intervene in different aspects of human life.

For instance, *Izrail* takes the souls of living beings, *Munkar* and *Nakir* question men/women in the graves, *Malik* is the guardian of hell, etc.

3. ***Belief in the Messengers of Allah:*** Islam teaches that a Muslim is supposed to have faith in the messengers and Prophets sent by *Allah* to this world at different stages to guide mankind. Many names of messengers like Moses, Aaron, Muhammad, etc., are noted in the Quran.

4. ***Belief in Allah's Book:*** For Muslims, it is mandatory to believe in the Quran, the Holy Book revealed by God.

5. ***Belief in Qiyamah* (The Day of Judgment):** Islam prophecies that there will be a last day when all life on earth will come to an end; everything will be destroyed. It is prescribed that this event is already mentioned in the Quran, and Muslims are supposed to believe in this. It has been maintained in the texts that the deeds of all mankind will be judged by God on an appointed day, and all human beings will be rewarded or punished.

6. ***Allah Has the Power to Determine Destiny*:** It is pertinent for Muslims to believe that all good and bad manifest from *Allah.* So, keeping in view that Muslims have to revere God for all deeds (good and bad both), it is prescribed that the followers of Islam have to be grateful and thankful to *Allah* for the goods in life and face failures acknowledging them as *Allah's* will.

The Five Pillars of Islam

According to Islamic teachings, every action done with the intention that it fulfils the will of God is considered an act of worship. However, there are five specific acts that provide the framework for Muslim spiritual and social life.

1. ***Shahadah*** **(Testimony of Faith)**: This is the initial act of faith that testifies one's commitment to follow the path of God's guidance for living one's life. It is fulfilled by declaring the foundational creed of Islam. It is prescribed that one has to recite the following to commit oneself to Islam:

   'Ashhadu an la ilaha illa 'llah; ashhadu anna Muhammadan rasulu 'llah'[8]

2. ***Salat*** **(Prayer)**: Prayer is the second pillar of Islam and is a mandatory act for all Muslims. It is preached that although Muslims can offer any number of prayers at any place, an adult Muslim is obliged to pray five times a day. The timings are fixed according to the movements of the sun. It is preached that offering these prayers is the most important act, so important that when *Allah* decides the eternal fate of the soul on the Final Day of Judgment, this will be one of the major factors. *Salat* is a Muslim's ascension to heaven! It is a symbolic reminder to people of their temporary existence on earth. '*The dawn prayer reflects one's coming into the world; mid-day is perceived as the end of youth; the afternoon prayer is considered as old age; the sunset prayer as death and the evening prayer portrays the darkness of the grave, and the next dawn prayer is seen as the awakening and resurrection of the dead.*[9] Therefore, the praying pattern prescribed in Islam is also the way to contemplate one's death on an everyday basis.

3. ***Zakah*** **(Purification of Wealth)**: It refers to the obligation of giving alms once in every lunar year. The act requires giving a

---

8. I bear witness that there is no God but Allah; I bear witness that Muhammad is His servant and His Prophet.

9. Hanson, H.Y., (n.d). *Encyclopedia of Death and Dying*. Retrieved 1 June 2020, from www.deathreference.com: http://www.deathreference.com/Ho-Ka/Islam.html#ixzz3AftMnR6X

fixed percentage of one's personal assets for the benefit of the poor and the deprived. It serves as a reminder to Muslims that all beings manifest from the will of God.

4. ***Sawm* (Fasting)**: The fourth pillar of Islam is fasting, which implies abstaining from food, drinks, and sexual relations from dawn to dusk for the entire month of *Ramadan* (holy month). It is preached that fasting inculcates the feelings of patience, social conscience (as the community does it collectively), and willpower to bear hardships in life.

5. ***Hajj* (Pilgrimage to Mecca)**: Mecca is believed to be the first place of worship, restored by the Prophet Muhammad. It has been preached that Muslims have to perform the act of worship in Mecca at least once in a lifetime. The *Hajj* gathers the believers from different places, irrespective of class, for a common act of worship. This ritual is a symbolic reminder of the 'Grand Assembly' on the Day of Judgment, when people will stand in front of God, waiting for the final decision of God on their deeds and destiny.

Thus, the core philosophy of Islam is built around six articles of faith and five pillars. It is prescribed that Muslims subscribing to various sects and sub-sects believe in these six articles of faith and adhere to the five pillars.

Death

Reflecting upon the manifestation of the entire creation, these religious faiths explain death as not an ultimate end of the being but a transitional phase that leads to something new.

In Hinduism, the subject of death has been addressed since its very origin in Vedic texts, but the core meaning of death evolved in the Upanishads and the Bhagavad Gita. It is explained that the whole creation is manifested from one common source, *Brahmand* (universe). This *Brahmand* is infinite with numerous realms, the earth being one of them. All life forms that are manifested from this *Brahmand* are dual in character; they carry a physical body and an underlying-self, *atman* (soul). Death is a temporary moment that separates the body and the soul. The body, which is the cover, gets destroyed, and the *atman* moves on. This *atman* wanders for a little while and is born again in a new body. This new life again has a limited span and is bound by death.

So, the soul lives endless life-death cycles till it attains immortality by merging with its source of origin, i.e., *Brahmand* (pursuit to attain the same is prescribed). So, death in Hinduism is a moment that either gives a new life to the soul or frees it from the birth/death cycle.

For Sikhism, however, the entire creation (including the universe) is believed to have manifested at the will of God. *Gurbani* calls this phenomenon of creation a self-pleasing sport of God; '*when he desires he extends part of himself (soul) into various names and forms, and when he so wishes, he dissolves and contracts this whole cosmos in Himself* (GGS, 292).[10] This game of creation of cosmos by God happens time and again at His sweet will, and the whole universe might merge into its primaeval source, *Akalpurkh* (God), at His will (GGS, 276).[11] Like Hinduism, Sikhism also prescribes the dual aspect of composition, the body and the underlying soul. As all creation in the universe manifests at the will of God, so death, too, is explained as the creation of God. Before the beginning of time, only the *hukam* (command or order) of God existed. There was no birth or death, nor coming and going in a reincarnation. Death came to the living because of the will of God, and it is explained that death is the inevitable destiny of everyone. Even the divine humans and the prophets have no exemption from it.

---

10. *Apan khelu api kari dekhai, khel sankochai tau nanak ekai.*

11. *Sagal samagrī apnai sūṯ ḏẖārai.* (He has strung the entire creation upon His thread); *Kẖin mėh thāp uthāpanhārā* (In an instant, He creates and destroys).

Sikhism explains death as *kal* (time). The term '*kal*' has a dual meaning. It means death as well as time. Death is just a happening; it is inevitable, and its time is predestined. Opposed to *kal* is the *akal* (eternal), which signifies both an attribute of God and the state beyond time and mortality. It is prescribed that the ultimate goal of human life is to reach this state. Further, in Sikh philosophy, dying is called '*chadai kar jaana*', which means to climb up. This is explained as a stage of evolution; as an opportunity to unite the part (soul) which manifested from God with him (*akalpurkh*). It is preached that the universal fact of mortality can lead to *amarapad* (immortality)—union with the eternal—which is also called the ultimate objective of life. So, death is an opportunity for evolution towards the further stage of meeting the Lord. However, if this opportunity is missed, the soul will come back to life in a new body. Thus, like Hinduism, Sikhism also explains death as a moment whereby the underlying-self gets an opportunity to get back to its source of origin or come back to life in a new form.

In Buddhism, too, death has been the central theme, as it was the encounter with death that provoked Prince Gautama (later called Buddha) to leave his princely life and worldly pleasures to seek enlightenment. Further, as Buddhism evolved and spread across different parts of the world, it became so engrossed in death-related ceremonies and rituals that, in Buddhist countries like China and Japan, Buddhism is given the name of a 'religion of the dead'. Like Hinduism and Sikhism, Buddhism also believes in the existence of an infinite universe with many material and immaterial realms.

In the early schools of Buddhism, it is explained that a human being is the sum total of five *khandas* (ever-changing aggregates): *rupas* (matter or form), *vednas* (feelings, both physical and psychological), *sannas* (perceptions), *samkharas* (mental states, activities, and volitions) and *vinnanas* (conscious awareness). Basically, the material form is called *rupa*, and the remaining four are the mental faculties called *nama*. The entire existence, ranging from a minute microbe to a genius human being, is based upon three facts: (a) *Annicam* (impermanence); (b) *Dukkha* (sufferings); and (c) *Anattaa* (No-self). Unlike Hinduism and Sikhism, early Buddhist thought refuted the idea of the existence of any permanent self underlying the physical cover. At the same time, these schools also propagated continuity of some aspect of *nama* (mental faculties) after death. However, the later schools, including the Tibetan school of thought, accepted the doctrine of an underlying-self (consciousness) that is released from the body after death.

According to the Tibetan school of thought, death is not an instant event. It is seen as a process taking several hours or sometimes even several days. It is through the process that the element of consciousness departs from the physical body and experiences out-of-body travel. In the book, Breaking the Circle: Death and the Afterlife in Buddhism by Carl B. Becker, death is explained as a process comprising the following eight events:

- seeing the cloud or illusion: it happens due to the shrinking of the limbs and gives a feeling of sinking;
- appearance of blue smoke: it happens at the cessation of hearing and drying of the mouth;
- appearance of light like fireflies due to the cessation of smell and cooling of the body;
- a vision of sputtering butter lamps happens on the cessation of taste and the end of breath and movement;
- a vision of blank whiteness like moonlight happens as all conceptions cease;
- further, energy moves from the sexual organs to the heart, and there is a vision of the rising of a red-orange appearance;

- energy from the heart is lost, the dualism ceases, and there is a vision of radiant black vacuum like autumn light; and
- the last event in this process is the leaving of consciousness and the appearance of clear light.

This chronological order explains the condition of the dying person and the process of death that leads to the departure of consciousness from the body. However, the texts explain this sequence only for natural deaths; there is no reference found for death occurring due to accidents, seizures, sudden strokes, or explosions. In Tibetan Buddhism, the departure of consciousness on death is correlated with the out-of-body travel experience, possible for accomplished *yogis* through meditation. Thus, meditative yoga and death experience are considered alike, with the only difference that in the yogic act, this consciousness will come back to the same body, but in the case of death, it cannot happen. Death is the moment of opportunity for this consciousness to merge into Clear Light and annihilate forever; else it will get back to life in a new form.

As discussed earlier, Christianity is an offshoot of Judaism, so some of its beliefs are inherited from Judaism. It is explained that the entire creation is the manifestation of God himself. The very famous story of Genesis in the Bible reveals that when God created the earth, the first set of human beings (Adam and Eve) was crafted in his own image, powerful and stronger over all other creatures. *Yahweh* (God) fashioned Adam of dust from soil and then breathed into his nostrils the breath of life, and thus man became a living being (Genesis 2:7). But, they disobeyed God, and this act of disobedience led to the entering of sin in the world, and the punishment of sin is death. Since the entire human race is linked to the first set of humans, all human beings are indirectly sinful. God, still being kind, wants to repair and restore his relationship with his creation, so he sent Jesus, his only son, to earth. Jesus lived on earth and sacrificed himself to pay for the sins of Adam, forever. He established a new covenant of love with the human race and assured them of eternal bliss. Hence, death in Christianity is an outcome of sin; thus, it is inevitable. It marks the separation of the physical body and the breath (spirit). While the physical body turns out to be the dust, the spirit begins its eternal journey. Christianity also prescribes that the present life is the only life that has been bestowed by God, and it has to be lived as the covenant of love established by God.

Like Christianity, Islam also explains death as not the ultimate end but only the cessation of physical life on earth, and a beginning of eternal life in God's realm. Significantly, present life is the only chance for better prospects after death. Islam elaborates that when *Allah* created Hazrat Adam, the first man and his progeny, the angels got concerned about the possibility of the world getting overpopulated. So Allah said, '*I will create death*'.[12] Angels were alarmed, and they mentioned that this could instil fear amongst humans and may remove all pleasure from life. So Allah replied, '*I shall create for them hope and ambition*'.[13] It is also mentioned that when Adam was sent to the earth, he was told, '*O Adam! Construct buildings destined for destruction and ruination, and beget for death*'.[14]

> *'Every person (nafs) will taste death....'*
> *'... no one knows (where) in what land (or place) he will die.'*
> *'Allah does not give any breather (or let up) to anyone for death when its fixed time comes.'*
> *(Surah 3:185, 31:34, 63:11)*

12. Petrowski, R. (2011). *Death: The Long Journey Home.* Indiana, USA: Xlibris, Corporation.

13. Quoted by Hasrat Hasan Basari and reproduced by Imam Ahmedin Kitab Ul Zuhad in Robert Petrowski (2011), *Death: The Long Journey Home*, USA: Xlibris Corporation, p.15.

14. 'Death – A Gift for a Believer', www.inter-islam.org/faith/dthgft.htm

These verses imply that death is a reality that can be either sweet or bitter in taste. Therefore, one should not fear death but take it as crossing the bridge from this temporary life to the permanent, everlasting life. Islam prescribes that every person is given a fixed period of life at birth; when this fixed period is over, the angel of death, *Azrael,* takes the *ruh* (soul) from the body.

Therefore, all five religions explain death as an inevitable reality but not an absolute end of a person. Death is the moment of separation of the physical body and the subtle essence (soul/spirit/consciousness/*ruh*). Hinduism, Sikhism, and Buddhism prescribe that only the physical body dies, and the underlying essence either gets back to its origin—*Brahmand* or *Akalpurkh*—in Hinduism and Sikhism and Clear Light in Tibetan Buddhism or gets a new life in human or some other physical form in this infinite universe. Christianity and Islam, however, propound that the earthly life will end with death and there will be no coming back to earth or any other realm in human form or any other form, but death will lead the spirit towards its permanent, eternal settlement in God's realm.

Continuity After Death: Reincarnation/Transmigration and Resurrection

Another death-related theme addressed in various religions is the fate of the deceased after death. As discussed above, Hinduism, Sikhism, and Tibetan Buddhism prescribe that if the underlying-self doesn't get absorbed into its source of origin, it will come back to the earth or to another realm in a new body (human/non-human). This process of coming back to life is called reincarnation or transmigration. However, the doctrine of resurrection refers to the ecstatic revival of the dead person, with the same body. It also refers to the continuity after death, however, not on earth or any other material realm, but on some eternal plane with God's will. Christianity and Islam preach resurrection as a form of continuity after death.

For Hinduism, the origin of all existence is from one source, *Brahmand*, and therefore the final goal for all is explained as union with that *Brahmand*. However, in between lie different rounds of births, implying the continuity of the soul after death. It is argued that when the physical body dies, the underlying soul takes a new birth. This rebirth of the soul is called reincarnation or transmigration. The word reincarnation has different elements: *re*: again, *in*: into, *carn*: flesh, *ate*: cause or become, *ion*: process. So, reincarnation is the process of coming into flesh again. This doctrine of the *atman* coming back to life in human or in another form evolved in the Upanishads. The Vedic *Samhitas* explained that on death, when the underlying-self (*atman*) leaves the body, it becomes a *preta* (disembodied self), ascends to *pitrlok* (realm of ancestors), and on reaching there, it becomes a *pitr* (ancestor). Special rituals are prescribed in Vedic texts for making a *preta* become a *pitr*. Further, from *pitrlok,* there is another possibility for the disembodied self to reach *devlok* (the realm of gods). To ensure one's prolonged presence in the *pitrlok* and ascend to *devlok*, some prescribed *yajnas* (sacrifices) are to be performed while alive. The benefit attained from performing these *yajnas* is called *sukñta* (immortal food) that ensures one's lifespan in the *pitrlok* and eventually in *devlok*. And, this realm of gods is described as *amrta-bandhu* (not bound by death). The immortal food, earned through hard *yajnas*, keeps the disembodied self well nourished and helps in retaining the immortal state, but its depletion leads to *punarmrityu* (the repeated death). This implies that death occurs at *pitrlok* and even at *devlok*. In the *Yajur Vedic* hymns, there are hints of *pitrs* falling back to earth like shooting stars.[15] However, there is a lack of description on this process of re-death and what happens upon this re-death, but the concrete doctrine on rebirth that was formulated

15. Lopez, C. (1997). Retrieved 23 March 2020, from www.academia.edu: https://www.academia.edu/3647011/Food_and_Immortality_in_the_Veda_A_Gastronomic_Theology

in the Upanishads has its roots in this Vedic idea of *punarmrityu.*[16] The *Katha* Upanishad is believed to be the text where this theme of reincarnation got concretised and has been reinforced by later texts, primarily the Bhagavad Gita and the *Puranas.*

> *'Even as a man casts off worn-out clothes and puts on others which are new, so the embodied casts off worn-out bodies and enters into others which are new.'*
> *(Bhagavad Gita, 2.22)*

Many references are found in Hindu texts regarding reincarnation. It is stated that divine incarnations remember their past lives, and pure-minded saints who achieve mastery in *samadhi* can also recall their past lives. Even laypersons sometimes remember traces from their previous births, though they may not be provable. However, Hinduism proposes that reincarnation is certain as it is the only theory that explains adequately certain phenomena that are otherwise not explainable. For instance, the extraordinary intelligence of a child that cannot be explained by genes and heredity theories is justifiable by the doctrine of reincarnation. One explanation of the cause of reincarnation is the unfulfilled desires of human beings. When a person dies with a strong desire in the mind that can be fulfilled only on earth, he/she comes back. Secondly, it is believed that reincarnation gives a person an opportunity to grow spiritually. The various valuable experiences that a soul gathers in numerous reincarnations make it nearer to God's realisation.

Reincarnation is often interchangeably used with transmigration, which means *trans*: across, *migr*: to go or move, and *ation*: the process of causing and becoming. It is a process of moving across, from one to the other. While reincarnation refers to the rebirth of the soul in a human body, transmigration means

16. Shushan, G. (2011). Afterlife Conceptions in Vedas. *Religion Compass,* 5 (6).

the rebirth of the soul into any other living form after death. Hindu texts preach both. It is stated that the soul may not always get migrated into a human body; it can transmigrate into different species, like plants, insects, fish, birds, mammals, etc. *Smriti* literature elaborates on many permutations and combinations for rebirths in different forms. For instance, *Manusmriti* notes, '*Action which springs from mind, from speech, and from body, produces either good or evil results; by action are caused the various conditions of man: the highest, the middle, and the lowest. A man obtains the result of a good or evil mental act in his mind, that of a verbal act in his speech, and that of a bodily act in his body. In consequence of many sinful acts committed with his body, a man becomes in the next birth an inanimate thing; in consequence of sins committed by speech, a bird or a beast; in consequence of mental sins, he is reborn in a low caste*' (*Ganth*, *Manusmriti*).[17]

Hinduism propagates the existence of the infinite *Brahmand* (universe), and this infinity is not just limited to one earth; there are many more *lokas* (planes). Though there is mention of innumerable planes, mainly fourteen *lokas* (categorised as higher and lower planes) have been repeatedly talked about in different texts. *Satyalok*, *tapoloka*, *maharloka*, *janaloka*, *svarloka*, and *bhuvloka* are referred to as higher *lokas*, whereas *bhurloka*, *atalaloka*, *vitalaloka*, *sutalaloka*, *rasatalaloka*, *talatalaloka*, *mahatalatalaloka*, and *patalaloka* are considered as lower planes. *Bhurloka* (earth) serves as the reference point for explaining the conditions on other planes. Better than earth are the higher planes, and worse than earth are the lower planes. Each *loka* is explained as a world of different sets of vibrations.[18] Apart from visible living beings, many souls and spirits exist as demonic beings that may not be felt

---

17. www.academia.edu. Retrieved 2 December 2019, from www.academia.edu:https://www.academia.edu/31478379/Manu_Smriti_Sanskrit_Text_With_English_Translation

18. Bhaskarananda, S. (1994). *The Essentials of Hinduism: A Comprehensive Overview of the World's Oldest Religion.* Chennai: Shri Ramakrishna Math Printing Press.

through the sensory organs, like *daityas*, *danavas*, *raksasas*, *asuras*, *pisachas*, *bhutas*, etc. In Hindu mythological stories, these terms are mentioned in various contexts, like wandering spirits, the ones who have not been treated in the prescribed manner after death, beings disturbing seers, enlightened ones, etc. The transmigration theory states that the transmigration of the soul is possible into these realms as well. However, like on earth, the lifespan on all these planes is short-lived and bound to death and transmigration.

Sikhism also preaches reincarnation and transmigration of the *atman*. So, if the soul doesn't merge with the supreme, it is transmigrated to earth. Transmigration of the soul is an accepted theory in Sikhism, to such an extent that it is believed that ten successive gurus are also one soul in different bodies. It is mentioned in Guru Granth Sahib that when Guru Nanak selected Bhai Lehna as his successor, as Guru Angad, he was blessed with the spirit of Nanak. Referring to this episode in Sikh history, Guru Granth Sahib quotes:

> *'Lehne di pheraiye, nanaka dohi khatiyai*
> *Jot uha jugat sai, she kaya pher paltiae'*
> *(GGS, 966)*[19]

The fundamental principle of the Sikh religion is that the same spirit of Guru Nanak animated all the succeeding nine Gurus, and it is believed that it is for this reason that the word 'Nanak' occurs in the word of all Sikh Gurus. And, all succeeding Gurus are often ordained as Nanak II, Nanak III, Nanak IV, etc. (*The Sikhs and Their Way of Life*).[20] It is also prescribed that the soul goes through many rounds of rebirth and death on this earth. Soul

---

19. It has been announced that Lehna is now in place of Nanak on the throne of the kingdom of the Guru. The Divine Light was the same, the Way and Mode were the same, the Master had merely changed the body.

20. http://www.gurmat.info/sms/smspublications/thesikhsandtheirwayoflife/chapter3/

is born in various forms, though the sequence of births or forms is not specified. It is emphasised that the human form is superior to all, and it takes the course of birth in *chavraasi lakh joon* (eighty-four lakh species) to be born as a human being. Therefore, human life is in the topmost position in this ladder of evolution.

> *'Kai janam gaj min karunga,*
> *Kai janam pankhisarap hoeo,*
> *Kai janam haivar, barikh joeo,*
> *Mil jagdis milan ki baria,*
> *Chirankal eh deh sanjaria,*
> *Kai janam sail gir karia,*
> *Kai janam sakh kar upaia,*
> *Lakh chaorasih jon bharmaia, Sadhsangh bhaio janam prapat'*[21]
> *(GGS, 176)*

In all schools of Buddhism, it is prescribed that there is continuity of life after death through rebirths. However, the early schools like *Theravada* Buddhism do not subscribe to the idea of one permanent underlying-self taking a new physical body after death. It is explained that at the time of death, the five *khandas* of the form are broken down, and nothing is left, but this event of breaking down is a cause that has an effect on the outer cosmos and leads to continuity in some way.

According to the early Buddhist teachings, when the five *khandas* are dissolved at death, the four non-material *khandas* continue like a causal current or stream of *bhava-sota* (energy), and this energy influences a foetus in a receptive womb, creating

---

21. O man thou hast seen many births as worms and moths; thou has passed through many lives, as elephant, fish, and deer; thou hast been bird and snake in many births; for many lives, thou hast been horse and ox, with a yoke; Secure the union with the master of the world; this is the time for it; after long time, thou hast obtained this human body; for many lives, hast thou been trees and plants; thus hast thou been revolving in the cycles of births and deaths.

another form. This phenomenon of continuity is explained by offering different allegories in Buddhist texts. In *Milindapanha*,[22] Nagasena Monk illustrates the case of the man who steals mangoes and later pleads that the mangoes he stole were different from the ones the owner planted. It is explained that mangoes are not identical with the ones planted—there is continuity of some kind—neither the same nor totally different. This is the outcome of a causal sequence. Rebirth is explained as another case of this same sort of process. Early Buddhism preaches that there are various realms of existence, and this rebirth can take place in any of these realms.

Later schools, however, preach that there is an underlying, subtle essence that is reborn after death. Tibetan Buddhism also subscribes to this idea of the soul getting a new form and being born again. This reincarnation can happen in different realms, too. After the consciousness departs from the physical body, it becomes a *bardo* body that gets various opportunities to choose its new birth. Initially, it gets the opportunity to submerge in Clear Light and annihilate forever. If that doesn't happen, the departed consciousness can enter into spiritual realms or sub-human forms. If that also doesn't happen, it wanders for a few more days and ultimately chooses a human womb for itself. The process takes place in forty-nine days.

Christianity does not subscribe to this doctrine of the soul coming back to earth or being reborn in any form. However, it is prescribed that on one unknown day, God will descend on earth and will raise all the dead souls and will announce their permanent fate. This eternal fate could be either in God's realm or away from him. This raising of souls from graves is called resurrection. Christianity claims its very origins in the testimonies that Jesus was resurrected and was seen alive after death. Theologians believe

---

22. *Milindapanha* (questions of Milinda) is a famous text on Buddhist doctrine. It comprises the dialogue between Milinda, a Greek ruler, and a monk, Nagasena.

that had there been no resurrection of Jesus, then all the faith would be in vain and all the preaching in Christianity would have no meaning. The resurrection of Christ is explained in the Gospels as a fact and not as an opinion or a mythological fable. Christianity prophesies that Christ will come again to earth to end the whole creation, and resurrection will happen on that very day. Apostle Mark writes that at death, the soul becomes naked until rejoined to its resurrected body, which will occur when the Son of Man comes in clouds with great power and glory; he will send his angels and gather his elect from the ends of the earth to the ends of the heavens (Mark 13:26–27). Apostle Paul, in his Gospel, quotes that when Christ returns in glory, at the sound of God's trumpet, the dead will rise first, and then '*we who are alive, who are left, shall be caught up together with them in the clouds to meet the Lord in the air*' (Thessalonians 4:17).

Unlike Hinduism and Sikhism, in Christianity, the physical body is also given due importance. According to the theory of Genesis, it is believed that God himself created the first human being (Genesis 2:7). By taking dust from the earth, Adam's body was created and animated by the breath of life directly by God. Thus, both the material and immaterial parts of humanity originated directly from God. Later, God created Eve by Adam's side, and since then, all human bodies and souls have originated by natural procreation, and every human being bears the image of God; God's original creation! It is prescribed that body and soul are not opposed to each other, even though they are distinct entities. In the integral person, they are interdependent. Therefore, the body is viewed as a gift from God, so it has to be honoured equally as the soul and is not perceived as a prison or cage for the soul. Thus, the body will also be raised. Soul and body will be united again and will forever live in God's embrace. Therefore, resurrection in Christianity is explained as the transformation of *psychikos* (earthly body) to the *pneumatikos* (spiritual body). This resurrected body is the consummation of one's entire personal reality and earthly history.[23] After resurrection, the body that was once merely physical becomes very glorious and eschatological, too mysterious to comprehend. Thus, in Christianity, with the strong conviction on resurrection, it is explained that the final fate after death on earth is the continuity of life by rising again with God's bliss and living eternally on a higher plane.

Like Christianity, in Islam, it is prescribed that resurrection will take place on the Day of *Qiyamah* (Day of Judgment). Believing in *Qiyamah* is one of the six articles of Islamic faith. Islam also prescribes that the *ruh* (spirit) that lies under the physical body will begin its journey towards God's abode at the moment of death. This journey will end with the final judgment of all souls by *Allah* on the Day of Judgment (that will take place on an unknown day), and depending upon the result it gets, the soul will be accorded a permanent realm by *Allah* to live ever after. The Quran describes that on this day of resurrection, all life on earth will come to an end. In the Quran, this day is depicted as a frightening event. It is stated that on this day, mankind will see massive destruction and terror. However, the specific hour has been appointed by *Allah,* and only He knows about it. God's angel, *Israfil*, will make the trumpet sound to declare that the day has come; apparently, that is the only job of this angel. The Day of Judgment will come only once, and there is no mention of it being a cyclic concept.

'When the sun shall be folded up;
And when the stars shall fall;
And when the mountain shall be set in motion;
And when the pregnant she-camels are abandoned;
And when the wild beast shall be gathered together;
And when the seas shall boil;
And when the souls shall be paired with the bodies;

---

23. Kramer, K.P. (1989). *The Sacred Art of Dying: How World Religions Understand Death.* New York: Paulist Press.

And when the girl child that was buried alive shall be asked,
For what crime was she put to death;
And when the leaves of the books shall be unrolled;
And when the heaven shall be stripped away;
And when hell shall be made to blaze;
And when paradise shall be brought near;
Every soul shall know what it hath produced.'
(Surah 81:1–14)

Thus, according to Hinduism, Sikhism, and Buddhism, the continuity after death is explained by the possibility of the soul coming back to the physical world in a new body (human or non-human). Christianity and Islam, however, prescribe that the present life is the only one and there is no scope for coming back to earth, but death is not the ultimate end. After cessation of life on earth, the spirit will continue to live eternally in God's realm. However, the eternal fate of all the spirits will be decided on one unknown Day of Judgment when God (Jesus or *Allah*) will descend on earth and resurrect everyone.

Who Becomes What? Determinants of the Fate of the Deceased

As religious faiths prescribe continuity after death, so the sacred texts of Hinduism, Sikhism, and Buddhism have also listed various determinants that decide the fate of the deceased. Christianity and Islam have also laid out the criteria to receive eternal bliss or damnation after death.

Hinduism and the Law of *Karma* (Action)

The law of cause and effect in materialism is called the law of *karma* in Hinduism. It implies that human beings are the architects of their own fate. Every act performed in life leaves an impression on the soul, just as the saffron leaves an impression on the cup after it is emptied. When the soul leaves the physical body, it takes these impressions attached to the astral body in the journey ahead, and these materialise into rewards or punishments. The sum total of everything that one sees, hears, does, and thinks creates an internal impression on the soul. These *karmic* impressions on the soul are the cause of good or bad situations in life. On death, one can leave behind weaknesses, excellences, merits, demerits, but cannot nullify the *karmic* impressions of the soul.

In Hinduism, the prevailing heterogeneity is explained in the light of *karma*. Some people are born rich, others are born poor; some are born sick, disabled with some congenital disorders, and others are born healthy; some are born geniuses, and some are born with low intelligence. This differentiation in Hinduism is explained in the light of the law of *karma*. The proponents of the doctrine of *karma* argue that accumulated *karmic* impressions create certain conditions for human beings. Despite the fixed conditions, the scope of free will also persists. An analogy of a cow explains this phenomenon. Man's freedom is like that of the cow tied to the post. Although the cow cannot go beyond the length of the rope, it can gaze, lie down, stand up or sit down, and do many other things within its reach. Similarly, *karmic* impressions create conditions for humans, but it's the consciousness and element of free will that enable human beings to deal with the situations and create new impressions on the soul. The *Bhagavad Gita* also emphasises the importance of deeds and their relation to death and rebirth. Lord Krishna convinced Arjuna to fight for the sake of performing his *karma*:

> *'Perform the prescribed duties: for action is superior to inaction;*
> *Moreover, if you are inactive, even the maintenance of your body will be impossible.*
> *This world is bound by action other than that for sacrifice;*
> *Therefore, perform actions for the sake of that, O son of Kunti*

(Arjuna), free from attachment.'
(Bhagavad Gita, 3.8)

In the context of the extent to which the effect of *karma* can be mitigated, the following typology of *karma* is explained:

a. ***Sanchita Karma:*** It is the sum total of past *karma* that is yet to be resolved. It is stated that some actions, because of their inherent nature, yield results very slowly. They mature so late that a lifetime period is very short, so they are carried forward to the next life. The way term deposits get accumulated and fructify after a specific period, likewise, *sanchita karma* yields fruits after a specific time span.

b. ***Prarabdha Karma:*** This refers to that portion of *sanchita karma* which is being experienced in the present life. When *sanchita karma* gets activated from the potential state and starts affecting, it becomes *prarabdha karma.* This *prarabdha karma* causes a person's birth and determines one's lifespan. This *karmic* force is responsible for the pleasures and pains that one experiences during the course of life. When this force is exhausted, the body dies. This *karmic* force is believed to be so powerful that even the spiritually enlightened souls have to bear its fruits till it is fully exhausted. An analogy of a bow and arrow is offered to explain this. *Sanchita karma* is like a hunter's quiver (container) full of arrows. It is in the potential state. *Prarabdha karma* is the portion of *sanchita karma* in the kinetic state, like a shot arrow; once it is out, it cannot be reverted. It is no longer in the control of the hunter, either.

c. ***Kriyamana or Agamin Karma:*** The actions being done in this life are called *kriyamana* or *agamin karma*. These are the actions that have immediate *karamphala* (results). By and large, the fruits of *kriyamana* are borne in the same life itself.

> Nevertheless, the portions of *kriyamana karma* that do not fructify in the same life get accumulated as *sanchita karma*, the storehouse of *karmic* forces.

Hindu sacred texts explain that the impact of *sanchita* and *kriyamana karmas* can be nullified to some extent, as they are in the potential state, but *prarabdha* cannot be stopped. It resolves only after its fructification. Thus, *karma* theory is retributive and considers the individual himself/herself accountable for the ongoing conditions (sufferings and pleasures) in life and in the future.

Sikhism and the Doctrine of *Karma* (Action)

Like Hinduism, Sikh texts also prescribe that transmigration depends upon the retribution of *karmas* (actions) performed in the preceding life. *Karmas* of previous life are held responsible for the favourable or unfavourable conditions in the present life. It is the doctrine of *karma* and transmigration that offers the solution for the extensive diversity prevailing in every existing form of life. Various quotes are found in Guru Granth Sahib on the retributive justice of *karma*:

> *'Karmi-karmi hoye vichar'*
> *(GGS, 7)*[24]
>
> *'Lekha ikho avu jaho'*
> *(GGS, 25)*[25]
>
> *'Karmi avai kapra nadri mokh duar'*
> *(GGS, 2)*[26]

---

24. By their deeds and their actions, they shall be judged.

25. According to the account of our actions, we come and go in reincarnation.

26. By the *karma* of past actions, the robe of this physical body is attained.

However, the idea of *karma* in Sikh theology is slightly different from that of Hinduism. In Hindu philosophy, as discussed, the fruit of *karma*, particularly the fruits of *prarbdha karma*, are borne even if it takes multiple lives. According to Hindu philosophy, in one life, only a fraction of the pile of one's *karma* cumulated in previous births is exhausted; the major portion remains in reserve to go with the soul in its journey onwards to future births. Sikhism differs on this notion. It is prescribed that there is a possibility to shed off the impact of *karma* in this very life, through reciting *naam* (bearing in mind the Lord's attributes). Also, in Sikhism, it is believed that some humans are excused from the cycle of *karma*; they are born to light the path of liberation for others, to enlighten.

Sikhism prescribes that, having been born as a human being, by virtue of contemplation on God's name, the burden of *karma* can be shed. By the divine will, the creature is forgiven for his past deeds and accepted as the child of the divine father, who further frees him/her from the cycle of births and deaths, and his soul merges into the universal soul forever. However, like Hinduism, Sikhism also prescribes that *karmas* determine only a few aspects of life. Like birth in a particular stratum of the society, life conditions like abundance and luxuries or vice versa, the *chintan* (thoughts) of a person in the present life determine his/her *sabah* (character), and that is independent of the baggage of *karma*s. Thus, according to Sikhism, one's birth in the kind of family, his/her caste, physical and mental faculties, health, wealth, etc., are the conditions determined by the cumulative *karma* of previous birth. Yet, one's thoughts are the result of an individual's free will. The power of one's thoughts and actions done in the present life is so strong that it can also curtail the hanging burden of *karma* on one's soul.

Buddhism and the Concept of *Cuticitta* (Last Conscious Thought) of the Dying and Rebirth

Buddhism, since its early schools of thought, doesn't directly consider only actions as an influencing factor for rebirth. Buddhism preaches that more than actions, it is the thoughts at the moment of dying that have the potential to ripen as future happiness or future suffering. If an individual has done good deeds in life, at the moment of death, these deeds will bring pleasant and positive thoughts that will lead to a good rebirth and vice versa. In Buddhist teachings, it is suggested that the total balance sheet of good and bad deeds performed by a person in his/her lifespan is summarised by the dying person's state of mind. And that state of mind at the moment of death influences the consciousness/spirit in its journey after death.

The Tibetan school of thought, in particular, emphasises dying with a wholesome mind (alertness). It is prescribed that dying alert would ensure the consciousness to visualise the Clear Light and get submerged into it. Thereafter, dying with alertness enables the departed consciousness to stay connected with the accomplished *lamas* (Buddhist priests) in its wandering phase for guidance for rebirth.

Christianity and the Notions of Love for Jesus and Eternal Bliss

Christianity preaches that more than deeds, a life led in submission to God's love is the gateway to eternal bliss after death (John 3:16).[27] Jesus established a new covenant of love with human beings, and according to this covenant, those who will lead a life with love for Jesus will certainly be resurrected and embraced by

27. John 3:16: For God so loved the world that He gave His one and only son, that whoever believes in him shall not perish but have eternal life.

him eternally. The faith preaches that sin prevails in the entire human race, but sins are forgiven if one submits oneself to God's love. So, the final fate of the soul doesn't merely depend upon the actions performed by an individual while alive, but rather on whether he/she has lived upto God's covenant of love.

Islam: Conformity to the Prescribed Righteous Actions Leads to Eternal Bliss

Islam also subscribes to the idea that actions performed in life are the deciding factor for the fate of the *ruh* (spirit) on the Day of Judgment. However, righteous actions in Islam are the ones that are in line with Islamic texts: the Quran, Hadiths, and *Sharia* (the Islamic law). It is believed that righteous conduct for every situation and aspect of life is mentioned in these texts. The only way to eternal bliss is leading a life in conformity with the righteous code prescribed in Islamic texts. There is a mention of the term '*hisab*', which means accountability of one's actions. It is stated that on the Day of Judgment, every human being will be asked for the *hisab* of his/her actions. The entire creation, including animals, will be given justice. Each one will fully and fairly be rewarded on the basis of how he/she conducted oneself in this life. It is prescribed that the scores of all creatures will be settled.

> *'Allah will judge between His creation, jinn, men, and animals. On that Day, Allah will let the hornless animal settle its score with the horned until, when there is nothing left to be settled, Allah will say to them, Be dust.'* [28]

While in the end animals will turn into dust, the humans' fate

28. 'Settling the scores among the animals on the Day of Resurrection', https://islamqa.info/en/answers/10673/settling-of-scores-among-the-animals-on-the-day-of-resurrection

will depend on the deeds they have performed in their lives. It is stated that all humans who are alive on that day will die, and *Allah* will make them rise again by giving them a body, and their fate will be decided. Based on the conformity to the Islamic code of conduct, people are categorised as *Mu'min* (the believers), *Kafir* (disbeliever), *Fasiq* (open sinner, corrupt), *Fajir* (sinner by action), *Munafiq* (hypocrite). Each category has a fixed fate after death.

Thus, all the above-discussed religious faiths have laid out the criteria that determine the fate of the deceased after death. Largely, they all subscribe to the doctrine that righteous actions performed while alive are the deciding factors for the fate of the deceased after death. However, righteous actions are portrayed differently by different religions. Hinduism preaches that all deeds (good or bad) and the intentions behind those deeds form impressions on the soul that are carried forward in different rounds of birth. Who will be born as what and how much is going to be the lifespan, depends upon the *karmic* impressions. It is a retributive system in which human beings are themselves responsible for their fate after death. According to Hinduism, *karmic* force is so powerful that even the spiritually accomplished saints are not free from the clutches of *karma.* However, these actions just create the conditions (good/bad and pleasures/pains) in life, and within these conditions, human consciousness is free to act and create new *karmic* imprints on the soul.

Like Hinduism, Sikhism also advocates that the *karmas* of the present life determine the conditions in the new life, but *chintan* (thoughts) and *sabah* (character) of a person are independent of this *karmic* influence. Through *chintan* and good character, one can shed off the burden of past *karma.*

Buddhism, on the other hand, propounds that more than actions, it is the thoughts of the dying person that influence their fate after death. However, the deeds of a person indirectly impact the fate of the deceased, as his/her actions might trigger the thoughts of the person in the last phase of life. Tibetan Buddhism emphasises that dying with an alert mind will lead to better prospects in the next life of the deceased.

Christianity, on the contrary, doesn't emphasise actions but prescribes that if life is lived in submission to Christ's love, then God will surely embrace the spirit eternally. Islam prescribes that to secure a position in *Allah's* realm forever, one has to lead a life in conformity with the prescribed code in its sacred texts. Interestingly, while in Hinduism, Sikhism, and Tibetan Buddhism, one has the opportunity to ascend spiritually in different rounds of birth, Islam and Christianity prescribe that the present life is the only opportunity to achieve eternal bliss. There will be no chance for the same after this life.

Adventures in the Afterlife Journey

As discussed above, all these religious faiths preach that death is not the ultimate end of the person. For Hindus, Sikhs, and Buddhists, there is the possibility of a new birth in a new body (human/non-human) on earth or in some other realm. For Christians and Muslims, it is a transitional moment, leading the deceased towards his/her eternal life in God's realm. This final fate will be declared on one unknown day. However, till the rebirth (in Hinduism, Sikhism, or Buddhism) happens or the resurrection (in Christianity or Islam) takes place, there is an intermediate phase. In this intermediate phase, the disembodied self undertakes a journey and passes through different realms.

Hinduism: *Swarg* (Heaven) and *Narak* (Hell) as Temporary Stations

Hindu sacred texts from the very beginning have reflected upon the journey of the soul after death. The Vedic seers could foresee the limitlessness as the ultimate destiny for every soul. So, in Vedic hymns, there is not much focus on the afterlife, but there is mention of terms like *pitr* (ancestor) and *pitrlok* (realm of ancestors). These terms indicate the journey of the deceased after death. On death, when the physical body ceases, an underlying essence leaves the body and joins the *pitrlok* (realm of ancestors), whose deity is Yama. In the earliest hymns of the *Rig-Veda,* Lord Yama regulates this process of death. Lord Yama is portrayed as a generous God who nurtures and protects the ancestors in *pitrlok.*

> *'In the Tree clothed with goodly leaves where Yama drinketh with the Gods,*
> *The Father, Master of the house, tendeth with love our ancient Sires.'*
> *(Rig-Veda, 10.135.1)*

> *'Go hence, depart ye, fly in all directions: this place for him the Fathers have provided.*
> *Yama bestows on him a place to rest in, adorned with days and beams of light and waters.'*
> *(Rig-Veda, 10.14.9)*

To ensure that this journey is smooth and the disembodied self doesn't deviate from the path, certain *yajnas* are prescribed in the Vedic texts. Since *agni* (fire) is an important element for *yajna* (sacrifice) performance, the body of the deceased is also placed on the pyre and lit with fire with the intention to send the disembodied self to the realm of ancestors. This is the rationale behind the cremation process, which is the popular method of body disposal amongst Hindus across the globe, even in present times.

> *'Burn him not up, nor quite consume him, Agni: let not his body or his skin be scattered.*
> *O Jātavedas, when thou hast matured him, then send him on his way unto the Fathers.'*
> *(Rig-Veda, 10.16.1)*

An elaborate account of the afterlife journey of the soul is given in the *Garuda Purana*. It comprises the dialogue between Lord Vishnu and Garuda (the king of birds). *Garuda Purana* explains that at the moment of death, the messengers of Yama reach the dying person and drag the soul out. It is an extremely painful experience for the deceased.

> *'The man of the size of a thumb, crying out "oh, oh," is dragged from the body by the servants of Yama, all the while looking at his own body.'*
> *(Garuda Purana, 1.32)*

The distance to *Yamlok* (Yama's abode) is colossal, and the entire way is full of torments. Interestingly, all painful and unpleasant experiences are quoted as per the standards of earthly life. There is mention of immense darkness, huge mountains to be climbed, lakes of blood, pus, and excrement, etc., that the soul has to cross.

> *'Yamlok, the extent of the way of Yama, measures eighty-six thousand Yojanas, without Vaitaraṇī, O Bird'*
> *(Garuda Purana, 1.56)*

> *'In one place there is pitch darkness; in another, rocks difficult to climb over; in others, lakes filled with pus and blood and with excrement.'*
> *(Garuda Purana, 2.14)*

In addition, there is mention of an extravagant river that the soul has to cross in order to reach the *Yamlok*. A very dreadful account of this river is presented in the *Garuda Purana*.

> *In the midst of the way flows the terribly horrible Vaitaraṇī River, which, when seen, inspires misery, of which even an account arouses fear. Extending a hundred yojanas, a flow of pus and blood, impassible,*

with heaps of bones on the banks, with mud of flesh and blood, unfordable, impassible for the sinful, obstructed with hairy moss, filled with huge crocodiles, and crowded with hundreds of dreadful birds. When it sees the sinful approaching, this river, overspread with flames and smoke, seethes, O Tārkshya, like butter in the frying-pan:

Covered all over with dreadful throngs of insects with piercing stings, infested with huge vultures and crows with adamantine beaks, filled with porpoises, with crocodiles, with leeches, fish, and turtles, and with other flesh-eating water-animals.

Covered with many scorpions and with black snakes—of those who have fallen into the midst of this, there is no rescuer whatever.... (Garuda Purana, 2.15–26)

On reaching *Yamlok,* the soul temporarily halts at either of the two sectors of *Yamlok,* namely, heaven (celestial) and hell (place of torments). In line with the pains and pleasures of life on earth, heaven is portrayed as a place of abundance, joy, flowers, music, fragrance, food delicacies, etc; hell, on the other hand, is a prickly, painful, suffocated, and stinky place. Depending upon the merits and demerits based on *karma,* the soul is placed in either of the two by Lord Yama. In the *Garuda Paurana,* even the portrayal of Lord Yama changes from a helping God in Vedic Hymns to a terrifying personality.

'Large teeth, wide mouth, frowning eyebrows, face twisted into a frightening shape, lord for innumerable disabilities, a long hand holding the rod (of authority) and another holding the deadly noose (to catch the erring), he directs good and bad deserts for all creatures going there.'[29]

---

29. Ghosh, S. (2002). *Hindu Concept of Life and Death.* New Delhi: MRML.

The *Garud Purana* also prescribes the rituals that have to be performed by the kin of the deceased to keep the *atman* nourished on its way to *Yamlok*. Along with the prescriptions, there is also a detailed account of the terrifying repercussions that may happen to the deceased and their kin on non-compliance with these rites.

Sikhism: No Afterlife Journey for the Soul

Sikhism does not prescribe any intermediary phase after death and rebirth. It is explained that the soul is reincarnated immediately after death. Sikh Gurus explain that even if these realms existed, they are of no use because the aim of a Sikh is union with *Akalpurkh*. Moreover, these are temporary halts; ultimately, the soul will be reincarnated. At some places, in Guru Granth Sahib, heaven and hell are portrayed as states of mind and not as distinct realms. Whenever one remains attached to God, he/she is in the state of heaven. On the other hand, when one possesses vices like lust, anger, greed, attachment, and pride, it is the state of hell.

> *'In the cave of intuitive wisdom I sit, absorbed in the silent trance of the Primal Void. I have obtained my seat in the heavens.'*
> *(GGS, 97)*

> *'Wherever you keep me is heaven. You are the Cherisher of all.'*
> *(GGS, 106)*

> *'The mortal has fallen into the deep, dark pit of household attachment; it is a horrible, dark hell.'*
> *(GGS, 1223)*

Tibetan Buddhism: The Three Bardos (Stages)

According to *Bardo Thodol* (*The Tibetan Book of the Dead*),[30] there are three stages through which the consciousness passes after death, till it is born again; these are called *bardos*. Each *bardo* gives an opportunity to the consciousness to enter the different realms of existence, namely, *dharmakaya* (Buddha mind), *sambhogakaya* (spiritual realm), and *nirmanakaya* (material realm). The following three *bardos* are mentioned in *The Tibetan Book of the Dead*:

1. ***Chikai Bardo* (Glimpse of the Clear Light):** At the moment of death, when consciousness leaves the corpse, there is a first glimpse of the Clear Light. It is the only solution for escaping from the birth cycle. It provides the consciousness with the opportunity to enter the *dharmakaya* (Buddha mind) realm. If the consciousness merges in this Clear Light of void, it is the perfect experience of Buddha Mind. It is prescribed that at the moment of death, this glimpse of light appears to everyone, but the dying person might miss it because of being trapped in other illusions. So, it is very crucial that the person dies in a wholesome mind-state, being fully aware of one's death and ready to spot the spontaneous appearance of Clear Light and get merged with it. It is believed that for the enlightened saints or highly accomplished individuals, Clear Light is visible for a longer time span, and they easily identify it and get absorbed. Lesser *yogis* (saints) and blessed people may be able to retain this vision of light, but they are eventually distracted by their thoughts. For all others, the experience of light is no more than a flash of light. On missing this chance, the consciousness gets pulled by the illusions. These illusions are the outcome of the thoughts of the dying person.

30. *Bardo Thodol* is the sacred Buddhist text that describes the stages after death and the afterlife journey.

2. ***Chonyid Bardo* (Crossing Holy and Evil Illusions):** If the consciousness gets trapped in the illusions created by its own thoughts and misses the flash of pure light, it moves downward to other levels. The next stage is called *Chonyid Bardo*. In this phase, the consciousness experiences of having an imaginary physical appearance like its previous life and wanders. It is called the *bardo* body. In the initial seven days, seven *Bodhisattvas* (Buddha-like images) appear to the consciousness. If the consciousness merges with these images, it enters the realm of *sambhogakaya* (the spiritual realm). Further, at this level also, the *bardo* body is repelled by fearful and terrifying illusions of one's own *karmic* imprints. If it misses the Buddha images and gets attracted to these illusions, it will be reborn in the realm of ghosts and demons. In the event of missing out on both, for the next seven days, it has to face some *herukas* (terrifying deities and lord of death). Buddhist texts prescribe that these images are the projections of one's own subconscious mind and are not real.

3. ***Sidpa Bardo* (Phase of Material Existence):** After two weeks of death and missing out on the opportunity to merge with *Bodhisattvas* and enter *sambhogakaya*, this wandering consciousness trickles down further to the material world. Consciousness has the power of moving across distances, visualising previous homes, mourning relatives, etc. It wanders here and there, homeless and disturbed. As the consciousness is in its pure state, it doesn't know how to overcome these realisations. It proceeds towards strange landscapes prior to the material rebirth. It is also believed that even at this phase, when the consciousness is going through illusions of misery and suffering, *Amida Buddha* (another Buddha-like image) or any other form of Buddha appears, giving one more chance to it to get submerged into it and enter the spiritual realm. However, texts note that in most cases, it becomes very difficult for the *bardo* body to hold the image of Buddha in this state of

confusion and illusions, so it enters the material realm. In this realm, it finds itself in surroundings where bodies are engaged in sexual intercourse, and the *bardo* body chooses its womb. Some interpreters believe that the consciousness might also enter an animal's womb. The lamas narrating the book of the dead to the deceased, being assured that the consciousness is still listening, advise it to choose the womb not merely because of physical attraction, but look for the parents of pious character, adequate wealth, and those who are spiritually elevated, so that in the next round of life it can have a better and elevated life.

This intermediate phase and afterlife journey lasts for 49 days, and the *bardo* body gets a womb after 49 days.

Ironically, in Tibetan Buddhism, it is believed that lamas and spiritually elevated persons are immediately merged with the Clear Light or with *Bodhisattvas* and are born in the spiritual realms. They do not envision any illusion during the 49 days. Political leaders like the Dalai Lama and other influential spiritual leaders are perceived to be the material incarnations of *Bodhisattvas*. Before their death, they indicate the region and the characteristics of the family where they will be reborn. So, after 49 days of their death, babies showing miraculous signs are identified, and efforts (specific prayers and rituals) are made to find out any physical similarities with the previous Dalai Lama, and on identification, these children are selected for intense religious education (Becker, 1993).

Christianity: Hades/Paradise, Heaven/Hell, and Purgatory

Like other religious faiths, Biblical scripture also focuses on different stages in the afterlife journey. In the early texts, there is mention of words like '*sheol*',[31] which, in Hebrew tradition, was

31. http://www.biblestudytools.com/dictionary/sheol/

called the grave. Words like 'Hades' and 'Paradise' are also found in the Hebrew scriptures. Hades denotes the doomed future of the souls, and Paradise is the state of bliss for the righteous soul. Lately, in the New Testament, heaven (the blissful state with God) and hell (the state away from God) are found instead of Paradise or Hades. Though there is a variety of interpretations of the literature and diverse understandings of the afterlife journey in various Christian denominations, the common theme is that those who have lived a life in submission to Jesus, accepting his love, will certainly have a blissful eternal life after death. The journey goes as follows:

1. **Purgatory:** The fundamental belief in Christianity is giving assurance to mankind that Jesus will resurrect those who live unto him. So the very idea of eternal punishment is not focused upon, but there is a reference to an intermediary stage, where the soul goes, before it is resurrected. This stage is called Purgatory. The term has its origins in the Latin word '*purgare*', meaning to make clean or to purify. It is a place or condition of temporary punishment. It is stated that the minor sins that leave their stains on the soul, even after death, are cleansed here and later sent to heaven. Purgatory is projected as a place of torments. Roman Catholics believe in Purgatory, and there are memorials observed to remember the dead and help them pass through the stage of Purgatory. However, this belief as a place or process is rejected by all Protestants and Eastern Orthodox churches. They assert that the idea of Purgatory is based more on church tradition than on scripture. These denominations preach that the soul lies in an unconscious state during the intermediate phase between bodily death and resurrection; it sleeps in peace.

2. **Heaven and Hell:** Heaven and Hell are the permanent destinations for the spirit after resurrection. The soul embodied in a resurrected body will attain either heaven or

hell on the Day of Judgment. As the origin of Christianity lies in the story that Jesus sacrificed himself to cleanse the sins of the entire human race and established a new covenant of love, the scripture doesn't focus much on the punishment aspect of hell. Heaven, on the other hand, is a trans-temporal, invisible domain of God's presence, which is far beyond the comprehending capacity of human beings. Heaven is the fullness of the presence of God (Psalm 16:11). For Roman Catholics, the souls with venial sins, who go to Purgatory, will be raised and enjoined with the spirits, and they will also be given a place in heaven on the Day of Judgment.

Islam: *Barzakh, Jannah,* and *Jahannum*

Islam describes the period between one's death and the Day of Judgment as *Barzakh. Jannah* (heaven) and *Jahannum* (hell) are described as the final destinations. *Barzakh* is the phase where time has no meaning, and a soul is punished or rewarded for the actions performed while alive. It is prescribed that when the believer (who lived according to the tenets of Islam) dies, the bright and glowing angels descend from heaven and take the soul to heaven. As per the will of *Allah,* angels register the soul's name in the book of '*Illiyoon*' (register in which deeds of the righteous are noted) and take him/her back to the grave, where the body was buried.

Thereafter, two angels, *Munkar* and *Nakir,* appear and quiz the soul with three standard questions:

Who is your Rubb (God)?
What is your religion?
Who is your Prophet?

The believer is expected to say, *Allah*, Islam, and Muhammad as answers. Having given these correct answers, the soul is believed to have passed the first stage of the journey of the afterlife. The angels grant the soul of the believer a comfortable stay in the grave, with soothing light and breeze coming from heaven's window.

> *'A handsome, well-dressed man will appear to him and will say, "I will bring you the good news", and when the ruh (soul) in the grave asks him who he is, the reply is "I am your good deeds". It stays in the grave as a companion and helps the soul in learning the Quran till the day of resurrection.'* [32]

However, for the disbeliever (who has not lived according to the Islamic tenets), this *Barzakh* period is explained in terms of chastisement and pain. The black-faced angels descend from hell to receive the deceased, and he/she feels intense pain and torture when the *ruh* leaves the body. Further, the gates of heaven do not open for this *ruh,* and as per *Allah's* will, this soul's name is registered in the book of '*Sijjeen*' (the register in which deeds of evil people are recorded). Thereafter, the soul is taken back to the grave, and when the three questions are asked by angels, the disbeliever never gives the appropriate answers. They have to experience darkness, pain, and torments in the grave. For the disbeliever, it is mentioned that a man with an ugly face, claiming to be his/her bad deeds, will come and stay as a companion.

> *'A dumb, deaf, and blind man will come with an iron rod and the deceased soul will be beaten up until it turns into dust till the day of resurrection.'*

Further on the Day of Judgment, when resurrection will take place, the souls will be either rewarded with *Jannah* (heaven) or

---

32. Petrowski, R. (2011). *Death: The Long Journey Home.* Indiana, USA: Xlibris, Corporation.

Jahannum (hell). Heaven in Islam is described as a place of peace and bliss, rewarded to the righteous believers. It is mentioned that '*believers will enter the gardens of paradise beneath which rivers flow. They will dwell there forever*'.[33] However, getting to heaven has nothing to do with earthly riches and delights; it all depends upon one's record of deeds. On the contrary, hell is described as an infinite space opposite to heaven, with seven gates and 19 angelic guards, led by the angel *Malik,* whose duty is to supervise the tortures for the damned. Hell is explained as a place of absolute horror; it is hot and smelly, full of blazing fire, winds, and wells of salty boiling water. It is the destination for disbelievers and evil-doers after the Day of Judgment.

> *'Those who reject Faith, and die rejecting, on them is Allah's curse, and the curse of angels, and of all mankind. They will abide therein: their penalty will not be lightened, nor will they receive respite.'*
> *(Surah 2:161–162)* [34]

> *'They are (men) whom Allah hath cursed: And those whom Allah hath cursed, thou wilt have no helper.'*
> *(Surah 4:52)* [35]

In Islam, heaven and hell are the permanent destinations assigned to the *ruh* from where there is no coming back. However, a few Islamic scholars believe that *Allah*, in his infinite mercy, will release inhabitants of hell after some time, and all will dwell in heaven.

---

33. Morgan, D. (2010). *Essential Islam: A Comprehensive Guide to Belief and Practice.* California: Greenwood Publishing Group.

34. Huda (2018), 'Hell in the Quran', *http://islam.about.com/od/heavenhell/tp/Hell-In-The-Quran.htm*

35. ibid.

Therefore, there is a belief about the afterlife journey in various religious faiths except Sikhism. Hinduism prescribes that the soul will travel through temporary realms, so there is a possibility that it might wander here and there and also come back to its old acquaintances in its disembodied state and disturb the living. So, different rituals (discussed in the next chapter) are described so that it doesn't lose its way and sails smoothly in the afterlife journey. Buddhism also propounds that consciousness experiences out-of-body travel before it gets a new form, so it is important that it is not disturbed, frightened, or confused and should make the right choice for the next birth. Accomplished lamas (monks) connect to the disembodied consciousness and guide it in this intermediary phase.

As Christianity and Islam do not subscribe to the doctrine of rebirth and the fate of the deceased is fixed (either heaven or hell), no amount of ritual or practice after death would affect the fate of the spirits. Interestingly, the explanation of hell and heaven in Islam is quite similar to the *Puranic* version of heaven and hell explained in Hinduism. The only difference is that in Hinduism, these are explained as temporary halts for the soul till its rebirth is decided, and in Islam, these are explained as permanent destinations accorded on the Day of Judgment.

Arnold Van Gennep, in his very famous work, *The Rites of Passage*, stated that in various phases in a lifetime, when an individual attains a new status, there is a transitional phase when the person is in a betwixt state (neither here nor there).[36] The afterlife journey in Hinduism, the three *bardos* of Buddhism, Purgatory in Christianity, and *Barzakh* in Islam are the betwixt conditions for the disembodied self.

Liberation from the Birth and Death Cycle

For Hinduism, Sikhism, and Buddhism, the soul/consciousness

36. Gennep, A.V. (1960). *The Rites of Passage*. London: Routledge.

is trapped in a continuous cycle of life and death. So these faiths prescribe a pursuit for the release of the soul from this cycle, called liberation – the ultimate goals for humans.

Hinduism: *Moksha* (Salvation)

In Hinduism, an individual is a small part of the huge quantum of cosmic consciousness that keeps wandering in different realms and varied forms. The ultimate goal of this portion of cosmic consciousness is to unite with the whole.[37] And, this final union is called *moksha* or salvation. So, in the sacred texts of Hinduism, the pursuit of salvation is also laid out. As Hinduism evolved in stages, from Vedic *Samhitas* to Upanishads, the pursuit for attaining *moksha* also evolved in phases. Vedic writings prescribe various kinds of oblations *(yajnas)* to achieve freedom from the cycle of birth and death; the later texts have offered more elaborate ways.

In Hinduism, based on the inner qualities, human beings are divided into four categories: 1) the emotional person; 2) the rational person; 3) the meditative person; 4) the habitually overreactive person. Considering these varied qualities of human beings, four different *yogas* (paths) are prescribed to attain freedom from the cycle of birth and death.

1. ***Bhakti Yoga* (The Path of Devotion)**: This path is prescribed for those who are emotional. This path enables an emotional person to have a direct vision of the personal God or *Ishvara.*[38] The emotion of love, which is abundant in this category of people, helps them to be used as a skill to attain God's vision. *Bhakti yoga* is a technique of transferring worldly love towards divine love. It consists of maintaining physical and mental

37. Ghosh, S. (2002). *Hindu Concept of Life and Death.* New Delhi: MRML.

38. Bhaskarananda, S. (1994). *The Essentials of Hinduism: A Comprehensive Overview of the World's Oldest Religion.* Chennai: Shri Ramakrishna Math Printing Press.

purity (*shauchta*), prayer (*prarthana*), the chanting of God's holy name (*japa*), the singing of devotional songs, and the adoration and worship of God (*puja/upasana*).

2. ***Jnana Yoga* (The Path of Rational Enquiry):** This is the path recommended for those who do not accept things/phenomena only on faith and possess the virtues of questioning, reasoning, critically analysing, and then believing. In this pursuit, the seeker assists the spiritual teacher who guides an individual.

3. ***Raja/Kriya Yoga* (The Path of Mental Concentration):** *Raja yoga* was founded by a sage called Patanjali. This is the path prescribed for a meditative person who is inclined towards exploring and mastering one's own mind. *Kriya yoga* preachers offer the analogy of a lake to explain this phenomenon. It is explained that the uncontrolled and impure mind of a person is like a lake with many waves, ripples, and impurities in it. At the bottom of the lake is the powerful light. So the aim of *Raja yoga* is to make an individual reach a state of mind that is still and free from all sorts of impurities. This advanced stage of mind is called *asamprajnata samadhi*. The attainment of this level is described as the highest form of saintliness.

1. ***Karma Yoga* (The Path of Right Action):** This path of liberation is prescribed for the laity who is always bound by *karma* (actions). As discussed, *karma* also includes the very thought of doing, undoing, or not doing something; therefore, this is a holistic path, recommending being very judicious about one's actions. According to Hinduism, work, which is inevitable for human beings, comes with psychological bondage for the doer. Every action done by humans with an attachment to its fruits puts the doer in bondage. *Karma yoga* teaches how to perform actions while being unattached to their fruits. The attachment is selfish involvement and rooted in selfish expectations. So, the work done without attachment to its fruits is a work done

unselfishly. The follower of this pursuit is taught to perform actions for the pleasure of God, not for some fruits. When action is done not for one's own sake but for God, it becomes an unselfish action. Such action is called *nishkam karma.* It doesn't mean not doing action, but doing it with all zeal, without getting attached to its fruits. It suggests that man's right is to work alone, but never to the fruits thereof.

'But the self-controlled person, moving among objects, with his senses free from attachment and malevolence and brought under his own control, attains tranquillity.'
(Bhagavad Gita 2.64)

Karma Yoga liberates the practitioner from the chain of repeated births and deaths. Every link of this birth/death cycle is because of karamphala (fruits of actions), and when a person works in such a manner that the fruits of his/her actions do not come back, then no new links are created, and the chain of births and deaths is broken, leading to salvation.

Sikhism: *Sach Khand,* the Stage of *Mukti* (Liberation)

The ultimate end of rounds of births and deaths and emancipation from the fruits of acquired *karma* is called *Mukti* in Sikhism. Liberation in Sikh texts is described as union with *Akalpurakh* (God). To attain this goal, meditation on the name of God *(naam japna)* is the prescribed method and is called the utmost important duty of a human being. Sikhism is a non-ritualistic religion, so the Hindu idea of asceticism and yogic practices in order to attain *moksha* (liberation) is rejected in the Sikh sacred literature. It is preached that contemplating on the name of God is the only way to attain ultimate bliss.

'Stubborn self-torture only wears out the body. Fasting and penance do not soften the soul. Nothing is efficacious as Lord's name; serve

the Guru my soul, and keep the company of the servants of God.' (AG, 905)

In the writings of Guru Nanak, this stage of liberation or oneness with God is called *Sach Khand*. *Sach* means true, and *khand* means realm, so '*Sach Khand*' means 'The Realm of Truth'. It is the realm of spiritual ascent, described as the abode of *Nirankar*, the 'Formless One'. *Sach Khand* is not a geographical spot, but the final state of the evolution of human consciousness. Guru Nanak has written that describing *Sach Khand* is like chewing iron (GGS, 8).[39]

'Sach khand vasai Nirankar, kar kar vehai nadhar nihaal Tithai
khand mandal varbhand, Je ko tathai ta ant na ant
Tithai loa loa akar, Jiv jiv hukam tivai tiv kar
Vekhay vigsay kar vichaar, Nanak kathna karara saar'[40]

In order to attain liberation, Sikhism has prescribed the following pursuit:

1. ***Sewa*** **(Service)**: In Sikh doctrine, it is held that selfless service is absolutely necessary for the individual on the path of liberation. Even the tough austerities done by sages are incomplete without *sewa*.

'Sewa kart hoye nihkami; tis kau hot prapat suami (swami).'[41]

---

39. Nanak kathna karaRaa Saar. GGS, 8. http://www.sikhiwiki.org/index.php/Sach_Khand

40. In the realm of Truth, the Formless Lord abides. Having created the creation, He watches over it. By His Glance of Grace, He bestows happiness. There are planets, solar systems, and galaxies. If one speaks of them, there is no limit, no end. There are worlds upon worlds of His Creation. As He commands, so they exist. He watches over all, and contemplating the creation, He rejoices. O Nanak, to describe this is as hard as steel! ||37||, ibid.

41. He who renders service without any desires, does attain to his master, Gill (2015). 'The Language of *Adi Granth*',

'Jangam jodh jati sanyasi, gare poore vichari; bin sewa phal kabuh na pawis sewa karni sari.' [42]
(GGS, 992)

2. ***Gyan* (Wisdom)**: Regular *naam japna* (meditating on God's name), especially in *sangat* (congregation of Sikhs), one attains spiritual wisdom.

'Kabhunsaadh sangat eh paawe, us asthan toh bahar na aawe; Antar hoye giyaan pragaas, us asthan ka nahi binaas.' [43]
(GGS, 278)

3. **Adopting Five Virtues of *Sat* (Truth), *Santokh* (Contentment), *Daya* (Compassion), *Namrata* (Humility), and *Pyar* (Love):** It is prescribed that human beings possessing these qualities build up a character that can attain liberation.

   - ***Sat* (Truth):** ***Gurbani*** (word of Gurus) preaches that truth is one of the most important virtues. Living in accordance with *hukam* (God's will) is truthful living. Truth is not just about speaking truth but also living in line with the true nature of reality. Truthful living for Sikhs includes acting honestly towards others, treating everyone as equals, avoiding criticism, etc.

   - ***Santokh* (Contentment):** Sikh Gurus taught that

---

https://archive.org streamTheLanguageOfTheAdiGranthFollowed ByThePhonetic TranscriptionOf720/Language_B_djvu.txt

42. The perfect guru has given the view that be a man *jangam* (a sect of nomadic Hindu monks), *jodh* (hero/ascetic), *jati* (celibate), *sanyasi* (a class of monks who do not reside among their people and generally spend their lives in solitude and on preaching tours), without service he can never obtain the fruits of his endeavours; service is best kind of act.

43. Sometimes, he (man) gets into *sangat*; he will never return from there (into rebirth). For then he attains the illumination of enlightenment and he attains to the position which is constant.

contentment results in freedom from fear and worry. It is preached that one must accept the circumstances of one's life and submit to the will of God rather than constantly longing or striving to fulfil/satisfy personal desires.

- ***Daya*** **(Compassion)**: *Daya* is a divine quality and has been recognised in other religious traditions as well. Terms like '*dana*' (charity), '*sradha*' (reverence and piety), '*priya vachna*' (sweet speech) used in Hindu scriptures are synonymous with *daya.* So, in Sikh ethics, compassion forms a basic moral quality.

'Keep your heart content and cherish compassion for all beings;
this way alone can your holy vow be fulfilled.'
(GGS, 299)

- ***Namrata*** **(Humility)**: *Namrata* stands for benevolence and humbleness. *Gurbani* promotes *namrata* very strongly; it is stated that a Sikh should always be humble.

- ***Pyar*** **(Love)**: *Gurbani* states that when one's mind is full of love, the person will overlook deficiencies in others and accept them wholeheartedly as a creation of God. Sikhism preaches that human beings should adopt God-like virtues, and God is loving, merciful, full of compassion, and kind. Same qualities are to be adopted by humans.

'Ikas seti ratia na hovi sog santap.'[44]
(GGS, 45)

4. ***Do Away with Haumai*** **(Ego)**: *Haumai*, according to Guru Nanak, is a stage which talks of self-reliance in such a way that makes human beings go ignorant to an extent that they

44. Attuned to the love of the One, there is no sorrow or suffering.

forget their dependence upon God and the ultimate goal of liberation.[45]

> *'One degrades oneself from the Human order because of Haumai.' (AG, 46)*

This *haumai* is an outcome of the attachment to worldly things. Guru Teg Bahadur states that the condition of *haumai* emerges because of wrong attachment by regarding relationships on the earth as eternal and substituting these relations with God. The consequence of *haumai*, as explained by the Gurus, is the possibility of getting reborn into lower forms like animals.

5. ***Detachment from Maya***: *Maya* in Sikhism is the materialistic interpretation of reality, the physical world. As discussed, every aspect is created by God, so it is prescribed that worldly comforts are meant for humans to use and enjoy, but for liberation, one has to be detached from worldly comforts. Unlike Hinduism, Sikhism doesn't preach renunciation of material comforts but preaches that one should be aware of the temporary nature of existence and not be overly attached to material things. The following quotes from *Adi Granth* are noted by Cole and Sambhi to explain the notion of *maya* in Sikhism:

> *'God's omnipotence, though hidden, is the creative force of earth and sky. By the divine might infused within them, they are sustained without pillars. The one created the three world and their binder maya.' (AG, 1037)*

> *'You created the world and put it to work. Giving it the intoxicating herb of worldly love to eat, you have yourself led it astray.' (AG, 138)*

45. Cole, W., & Sambhi, S. (1998). *The Sikhs: Their Religious Beliefs and Practices.* Brighton: Sussex Academic Press.

It is preached that the attachment to *maya* is to be replaced with attachment to God.

Gurmukh vs Mannmukh: In Sikhism, the ideal type is called *gurmukh* (face turned towards the Guru). This term is used frequently in *Gurbani,* implying a God-inspired person who follows the above-discussed virtues prescribed in *Gurbani.* He/she is a person who acts according to the precepts of the Guru. Liberation from the cycle of birth and death is certain for a *gurmukh.* It is explained that the *gurmukh* dwells and meditates upon the name of God, gains stability of mind, '*gurmukhi sagali ganat mitavai.*'[46] (GGS, 942) Freedom from attachment characterises his/her conduct. He is a renouncer in spirit even while carrying out the duties of the householder. The *gurmukh* indulges in the actions dictated by his destiny and yet is not lost in them because spiritual discipline and divine wisdom help him distinguish truly between desired action (*pravrtti*) and renunciation (*nivrtti*) '*Gurmukh parvirat narvirat pachhaṇai.*'[47] (GGS, 941) This ideal type has an equation with the idea of *karma yoga* in Hinduism. That while leading a life of a householder, one can transcend the birth/death cycle by being unattached from material things and performing actions in an unattached manner.

The term used in contrast to *gurmukh* is *mannmukh* (one who has turned his face away from guru). While *gurmukh* is described as an illumined mind, free from ignorance, *mannmukh* is portrayed as an ego-centred person who is confined to evils.

Thus, in Sikhism, liberation is achieved when the cycle of transmigration comes to an end. This stage of liberation is called *Sach Khand.* This stage is attained by living a fearless life, possessing the virtues given in *Gurbani,* serving humanity, meditating on God's name, giving up *haumai,* and detaching from *maya.* The person leading life on these terms is called a *gurmukh,* and liberation is certain for him/her.

---

46. The *gurmukh* erases all accounting.

47. The *gurmukh* knows worldliness and renunciation.

Nirvana and Submerging into Clear Light

Rebirth is certain in Buddhism; it can happen on earth or in spiritual realms, but even being born in higher realms is not the solution because death will eventually occur. Therefore, the permanent solution to this suffering is the release from the cycle of birth and death. It is preached that such release could only be obtained from right practice and meditation, which is possible only if one is born in a human form. This escape is called *Nibbana* (Nirvana), which means non-existence. Buddhist texts explain that Nirvana was the state achieved by Buddha through hard meditative practices. But there is no evidence as to what actually were Buddha's words on Nirvana, and it is believed that he never elaborated about his experience of Nirvana, but preached how to handle this life to attain permanent freedom from suffering. As there is a lack of Buddha's explanation on Nirvana, it has been interpreted in different ways, particularly by Westerners; there are mainly four explanations of Nirvana:

1. ***Nirvana as Annihilation:*** In the translation of the *Lotus Sutra* by Eugène Burnouf (1876), it is quoted that the perfect Buddha, after having performed the totality of obligations, was like a fire of which the fuel is consumed; entirely annihilated in the element of Nirvana in which nothing remains of that which constitutes existence.[48] The analogy of extinguishing fire and a lamp has been used often to explain this aspect of Nirvana. This perspective is also called Nihilism or Nothingness, whereby a person reaches a stage where he has superseded the birth-and-death cycle and nothing is left behind, nor any of the aggregates (material/non-material) cause an effect for further continuity.

48. Dibeltulo Concu, M. (2017). Buddhism, Philosophy, History. On Eugène Burnouf's Simple Sūtras. *Journal of Indian Philosophy*, 45 (3), 473–511.

2. ***Nirvana as Eternal Life:*** Another explanation of Nirvana is that it is not an extinction of the whole existence, but only the extinction of the cravings that produce suffering. Nirvana has been interpreted in terms of subduing all wishes and desires and leading a life neutral to joy and pain, good and evil. From this perspective, Nirvana is a state of blessedness and not a state of non-being. It is said that it is an absolute, eternal state of being that Buddha experienced but could never explain in literal terms.

3. ***An Ethical State in This World:*** Keeping in view that Buddha's teachings were to lead a selfless moral life, another interpretation of Nirvana is calling it a living condition in present life itself, nothing annihilistic or transcendental, not even any kind of blissfulness. It is neither any kind of separate existence in this life nor non-existence after death; rather, it is an ethical state here and now. Proponents of this view offer certain virtues like empathy, detachment, and selfless service as Nirvanic qualities. So they explained that living a selfless moral life is Nirvana. For the people with these qualities, there is nothing to worry about life after death. This connotation of Nirvana is similar to the detached way of life preached in Hinduism and Sikhism.

4. ***A Selfless State of Postmortem Existence:*** This view combines the earlier ones. In this perspective, two stages of Nirvana are explained:

    - ***Nirvana with Remains:*** It is called a stage in this life itself that can be attained by living with virtues of selfless actions, empathy, sympathy, compassion, etc.

    - ***Nirvana without Remains:*** It is explained as existence in a state beyond death, which cannot be adequately described in words, but Buddha and *arhats* experience it. In *Milindapanah,* there is an interesting conversation between King Manender and the monk:

'King to the monk: Does the Buddha still exist?
Monk: Yes.
King: Then, is it possible to point out where he is (here and there)?
Monk: The great fire blazing, will it be possible to point out to a flame which had gone out and say that it was here and there?' [49]

It is explained that on reaching Nirvana, the individual is like a flame that is no longer identifiable and no longer limited to a single wick. The flame is not necessarily destroyed but may actually be expanding by losing its prior individuality. Another analogy of raindrops is used to explain the stage of Nirvana without remains. When raindrops fall in the ocean, they do not lose all existence completely, but lose the prior limitations and characteristics of their separateness from the ocean.

Early school (*Theravada Buddhism*) prescribed Nirvana as an alternative to rebirth and a stage of liberation. But it meant only for *Bhikhus* (monks), who would follow a pursuit prescribed by Buddha himself. He wrote the *Vinaya Pitaka* (the absolute code) for living a disciplined life for *Bhikhus* (monks) and later *Bhikunis* (female monks), as part of his core teachings. The laity could only seek to be reborn as an *arhat* (monk). For the laity, he prescribed the process, which can lead to better rebirths and form a possibility for them to be reborn as *arhats*. The process involved realisation of four noble truths; namely, *dukkha* (suffering, discontent); the cause of *dukkha* is *tanha* (craving) for material and non-material things; the cessation of *dukkha* is the abandonment of that craving; the path that leads to the cessation of *dukkha* and helps in abstaining from craving is the Eightfold Path of right view, right resolve, right speech, right action, right livelihood, right effort, right mindfulness, and right concentration.

Buddha preached that due to ignorance of these truths, the individual remains trapped in the endless cycle of birth, ageing, illness, death, and rebirth.

---

49. Pesala, B. (2001). *The Debate of King Milinda.* Delhi: Motilal Banarsidas.

However, as different schools of thought emerged in Buddhism, the ways to liberate the laity from the birth/death cycles also evolved. Interestingly, the main criticism of the *Theravada* doctrine was that it is confined only to the liberation of monks. The *Mahayana* school came up with the idea of near-Nirvanic fields called *Boddhi fields* or *Buddha lands,* which are free from *dukkha* (sufferings). These realms are the abodes of *Bodhisattvas.*[50] Meditating on them would help the practitioners transcend the birth/death cycle. One such sect in the *Mahayana* school is *Sukhavati* (Pure Land) *Buddhism*. According to this sect, Pure Land (*Sukhavati)* is an abode of *Bodhisattva* Amithabha Buddha (also called Amida/Amitayus/Amituofo Buddha), meaning infinite life. Offering prayers and meditating on his name can make rebirth possible in his realm, which is near Nirvana.

Tibetan Buddhism preaches another way towards attaining liberation, i.e., visualising the Clear Light at the moment of death and submerging into it. This Clear Light takes the consciousness to the *Dharamakya* realm (Buddha Mind), a real and absolutely formless state from where there will be no birth again.[51] Hence, the ultimate goal explained to the practitioners of Tibetan Buddhism is to attain the *Dharamakya* stage after death, from where there is no coming back.

The practitioners of Tibetan Buddhism are trained to experience death with a wholesome mind (alertness) so that they can hold on to the Clear Light that appears like a flash and get absorbed in it. Contemplation of death and being prepared for death at any time is an important teaching given to the practitioners of Tibetan Buddhism. The meditative lessons from the masters to the students involve making their consciousness have a death-like experience of leaving the body for a certain

---

50. In *Mahayana Buddhism*, a person who is able to reach Nirvana but delays doing so through compassion for suffering beings.

51. In *Vajrayana Buddhism*, the Buddha Mind stage is equated to Nirvana.

duration and coming back. Such out-of-body travel experiences are equated to a death-like experience. Such practices make their minds alert in the moments of dying, enabling them to spot the Clear Light. Also, it is preached that being prepared for death enables a person to quickly heal the conflicts in relationships. Since death can arrive unexpectedly, it is important not to delay resolving difficulties and completing unfinished tasks.

Reaching Heaven and *Jannah* Is Equated to Salvation in Christianity and Islam

In Christianity, salvation is explained as being awarded with eternal bliss and a permanent place in heaven on the Day of Judgment after resurrection. In Christianity, living in God's eternal bliss ever after is salvation, i.e., the ultimate liberation of all mankind from sin, forever, that entered the human race with the first man. The only way to salvation is to lead a life in submission to God's love.

Similarly, for Islam, receiving a place in *Jannah* by *Allah* on the day of *Qiyamah* is salvation. The only way to achieve it is to live a life in accordance with the prescribed Islamic code.

Good vs Bad Death

The religious faiths also subscribe to the idea of a good death. Some religions directly categorise a particular kind of death as good and bad, others emphasise that death can be good if the death-related practices prescribed in the sacred texts are performed for the deceased.

Hinduism doesn't directly categorise a particular death as good or bad. However, the *Garuda Purana* elaborates that deaths occurring due to accidents on road/air/water, murders, suicide, etc., are considered untimely and unnatural. Further, certain days are marked as inauspicious, so deaths occurring on these days are not considered good and special rituals are prescribed to deal with them.[52] Hinduism prescribes a series of rituals pertaining to death and dying as mandatory practices to be performed by the kin for the better prospects of the soul after death (elaborated in the next chapter). A few rituals are prescribed for the last phase of the deceased. So, a good death would mean the one that occurs in the surroundings where the family members and kin are available and perform the necessary rituals prescribed for different stages, namely, on death, disposal of corpse, rituals for the afterlife, etc., ensuring the smooth release of the soul and a comfortable afterlife journey.

Sikhism doesn't subscribe to this idea of good or bad death. It is preached that everything happens at the will of God. So, death occurring on any day, anytime and due to any cause is divine *hukam*. The emphasis has been laid on leading a life of a *gurmukh* and dying being unattached from worldly things and relations. Hence, a good death according to Sikhism would be the one that occurs after leading a life devoted to humanity and adopting the five virtues of truth, contentment, compassion, humility, and love in life, surrendering *haumai,* and detaching from *maya*.

Buddhism preaches that all phenomena are temporary, ever-changing, and subject to suffering and rebirth. The ultimate solution to this world of suffering and rebirth is attaining Nirvana (interpreted differently by different scholars). More than death, the emphasis of Buddhist philosophy is to end suffering forever. It is prescribed to lead a life in such a way that leads to rebirth in spiritually higher realms. So, a good death would mean the one that leads to better rebirths. In the *Theravada* school, an ideal death would be the one that leads to the birth of an *arhat* (enlightened one). According to Tibetan Buddhism, dying with a wholesome mind is ideal as it would ensure union with Clear Light and ultimately freedom from the cycles of suffering.

52. 'Funerals', http://www.salagram.net/death-hindu-funerals.html

In Christianity, it is explained that the sacrament of Baptism[53] in childhood establishes a relationship with Jesus. Those who live upto the covenant of love established by Jesus are taken in eternal bliss on the Day of Judgment. Therefore, a good death is that which occurs after leading a life in submission to God's love. In a way, Christian texts explain death as a good event, as it leads the underlying spirit to God's abode. In addition, Christianity preaches that though resurrection is certain, it is advantageous if the death occurs at home, enabling the priest to perform the desired sacraments of Eucharist, Holy Unction, Anointment of the Sick, and the Last Blessings. These practices reassure the deceased of his/her resurrection. Therefore, according to Christianity, the death of a baptised individual is always good as it affirms his/her fate to live forever in eternal bliss.

Islam prescribes *Shahadat* (martyrdom) martyrdom as an ideal death. Unlike other religious faiths, interpreters of Islamic texts recognise honourable types of death as martyrdom. Shaykh Gibril Haddad, in his article, 'Classifications of Martyrs', notes that the person who dies naturally in the cause of *Allah* is a martyr; he who dies of plague is a martyr; he who dies of a stomach disease is a martyr; and he who is drowned or dies because of fire is a martyr. He states that some Islamic scholars believe that one who is crushed in a collapsing building, a woman who dies due to pregnancy, and a woman who dies during delivery are also martyrs. Dying for defending one's property, family, one's faith, and community is also considered martyrdom. It is explained in the Islamic texts that the reward of dying this kind of death is the assurance of *Jannah* (heaven) for the deceased on *Qiyamah.*

Therefore, for Hinduism, a good death is one that occurs at the natural course of time and is dealt with the prescribed rituals. Conversely, deaths that occur due to sudden accidents and

53. It is a ritualistic way to get right with God; accepting Jesus as a Saviour is marked by the sacrament of Baptism, believing that Jesus is Christ.

unanticipated reasons are considered untimely and unnatural. For Buddhism, a good death is one that leads to a better rebirth. Christianity prescribes that the death of a baptised person is good as it ensures an eternal blissful life. Islam, however, specifies certain types of deaths that guarantee a place in heaven. Surprisingly, Islam categorises all kinds of accidental deaths as good deaths that are considered unnatural and untimely in Hinduism. Sikhism believes death occurs at the will of God, so any type of death is good.

Death by Choice: Religious Take on Acts of Suicide and Euthanasia

Suicide and euthanasia are types of death where one's volunteerism in choosing when and how to die is involved.

Hinduism condemns suicide as an evil act when it is committed with a selfish intention. It is preached that human life is so sacred that it is accorded to a soul after many rounds of births and deaths. Human life is an opportunity to attain liberation and transcend the cycle of life and death. So, ending one's life would hamper the spiritual progress of the soul, and the person would be trapped in the *karmic* cycle, even by ending one's life. In Sanskrit, suicide is defined as *atmahatya* (murdering oneself). It is prescribed that each individual is created with certain obligations towards gods, ancestors, family, etc., and these obligations come as the result of *karmic* impressions that the soul is carrying from preceding lives, so by killing oneself, the opportunity for the *karmas* to exhaust is missed.

Thus, *atmahatya* (egoistic suicide), motivated by one's personal interests, is a sinful act with dangerous implications on the fate of the soul. It's written that the person who commits suicide, his/her soul wanders aimlessly until the fixed time span is over, and thereafter experiences the torments in hell and is sent back to earth in a new body to bear the fruits of the remaining *karma*. However, on the other hand, altruistic suicide is permitted in Hinduism. If suicide is committed because of spiritual motivation and done as an act of self-sacrifice or renunciation, then it is considered a great act. In Hindu tradition, it was carried out by *sanyasins* (renouncers) through *agnipravesa* (self-immolation), *prayopavesa* (death by slow starvation), and *samadhi* (sitting in a particular posture for a long time and suspending breath in the state of self-absorption.[54]

In the light of the doctrine of reincarnation and *karma,* euthanasia is also viewed negatively in Hinduism. It is believed that if the person is in an extreme state of pain and irreversible medical condition, it is because of his/her *prarabdha karma*s and therefore must be allowed to bear the fruits of *karma* completely without intervening in the natural process of dying. And, those who participate in the sinful act of euthanasia for someone, their soul will have repercussions of this action in the near future.

Sikhism also rejects both the practices of suicide and euthanasia. It is preached that life is a gift of God, and the timings of birth and death should be left in the hands of God. *Manas Jiwan* (human life) is the topmost position in the evolution ladder and the only opportunity to merge with God. As discussed earlier, in Sikhism, every facet of human life is believed to be happening according to *hukam*, so death also happens at God's will. Sikhism rejects euthanasia and suicide as it is an interference in God's plan. It is preached that one has to accept pleasure, pain, an irreversible state, etc., as a part of His (God's) will. So, individual autonomy to trivialise one's own or someone else's life is not allowed. However, martyrdom, dying for the sake of religious duty, is a welcome move in Sikhism. Guru Gobind Singh, the tenth Guru, created a collective body of initiated Sikhs, the Khalsa Panth. These were the Sikhs who would happily lay down their lives for the sake of others and

---

54. Jayaram, V. (2000). Hinduwebsite.com. Retrieved 13 Novemeber 2019, from hinduwebsite.com: https://www.hinduwebsite.com/hinduism/h_suicide.asp.

fulfil their religious duty. Hence, altruistic suicide is acceptable in Sikhism, too.

Buddhism also condemns the act of suicide and assisting someone in suicide. It is considered an action based on ignorance. Suicide breaches the precepts that Buddha laid out to live life. Buddhism preaches that egoistic suicide is a misguided and futile act. However, dying with the intention to serve others (altruistic suicide) is not considered any kind of offence.

Buddhism is apprehensive about euthanasia, too. It is preached that one can have overwhelming compassion for a sick person, and it is believed that the virtue of compassion for the sick and dying is one of the reasons for starting the Buddhist hospice movement, which gained global popularity in recent years. The rationale behind this movement was to offer a platform for peaceful death to the person who is suffering. As Buddhism believes that thoughts at the moment of death play an important role in deciding the fate of the soul, providing a peaceful environment to the dying is a compassionate act. But assisting a person in committing suicide or killing is seen as breaching the precepts of Buddha.

In most of the Christian denominations, too, death by suicide and euthanasia are considered sins. The religious texts note that one's life is the property of God, and to destroy it is like exercising domination over the property that belongs to God. The individual does not belong to himself, not even to society; he/she belongs to God alone: '*Behold, all souls are mine.*' (Ezekiel 18:4) '*The Lord kills and makes alive; He brings down to Sheol and raise up.*' (Samuel 2:6) Thus, the Lord God is the giver and taker of life.

Christianity also does not favour the practice of euthanasia in the view that all life comes from God as his gift. Human life possesses dignity as God created humans in his own image. This life was created to develop tendencies to love God to the best possible extent and for as long as possible. Again, with the idea that humans were created by God in his own image, and the entire human race evolved from there, all human lives are equally dignified and to be respected. The patients with chronic illness or in a permanent vegetative state are equally human beings, and the very notion that they would be better off when dead is considered a sin. The very idea of euthanasia creates the notion that the body is no longer worthwhile. In addition, Christianity preaches that there shouldn't be any disruption or interruption at the stage of dying, as that is a spiritual process. Hence, suicide and euthanasia are not allowed.

Like the above-discussed religious faiths, Islam also condemns both the acts of euthanasia and suicide. Life is considered sacred, and acts of suicide and euthanasia are viewed as a self-administrated way of ending life against *Allah's* wish. It is only *Allah* who decides the time of death for each individual, and humans have no say in this matter. Thus, human beings cannot attempt to act upon what is primarily *Allah's* domain. This idea applies to acts like suicide, euthanasia (active or passive), homicide, or genocide. Quran notes:

> *'Come, I will rehearse what God hath (really) prohibited you from: Join not anything as equal with Him; be good to your parents; kill not your children on a plea of want; We provide sustenance for you and for them; come not nigh to shameful deeds. Whether open or secret, take not life, which God hath made sacred, except by way of justice and law: thus doth He command you, that ye may learn wisdom.'*[55]

ce, according to Islamic teachings, life is a divine gift that
e lived. Death will occur at God's will, and thus killing
self or someone else is considered a sinful act.

(n.d.). *Rules Related to a Dying Person*. Retrieved 30 May 2020, from
: http://www.sistani.org/english/book/48/2191/

Therefore, all the above religions condemn volunteerism when it comes to dying. Though death is going to happen one day, choosing it at one's own will is a sin and goes against the *karmic* retribution, God's will, and the plan of Jesus. However, altruistic suicide committed for the sake of religious duty or spiritual accomplishment is allowed.

CHAPTER 3

Prescribed Death Practices

Based on their death-related beliefs, all religious faiths prescribe a variety of practices to be followed in the event of death. These practices include rituals to be performed before death (on anticipation of death), at the moment of death, preparation of the body for disposal, disposal of the body, and post-disposal practices. Interestingly, these faiths also list out certain practices which are not to be followed in the event of death. So, popular prescribed and proscribed practices related to death and dying *vis-à-vis* the five religions are discussed in this chapter, taking each of them separately.

Hinduism

With so much variation in sacred texts and their interpretations, and because of Hindus being spread in various geographical locales, an amalgamation of rituals pertaining to death and dying has evolved in Hindu tradition. Though death-related practices evolved mainly during Vedic times, and a few are prevalent even today, most of the practices evolved in the *Dharmashastras* and *Puranas*. *Puranic* rituals, being the latest, have become popular in recent times. The *Garuda Purana* is the guidebook for the laity to deal with the death of their kith and kin. Along with the rituals to be performed for the deceased, the *Garuda Purana* also describes the implications (both positive and negative) for the deceased in the afterlife journey and his/her kin on earth, depending on the extent of conformity and non-conformity to these prescribed practices.

These texts explain *Antyeshti Samskara* (funeral sacrament) as one of the important sacraments amongst the sixteen *samskaras*. In literal terms, *samskaras* are the rites of passage meant for different stages of the life of a Hindu, right from conception till death. *Antyeshti* in Hinduism comprises the following death rituals:

Rituals on the Anticipation of Death and at the Moment of Death

Based on the readings of various scriptures and their commentaries, following are the practices prescribed before death and at the moment of death:

a. **Donations:** For better future prospects of the deceased, Hinduism prescribes the practice of giving donations to the *brahmins*. Amongst these, the gift of a cow is considered most valuable. The cow was called *Vaitarani* (conductor of the dead over the stream of the underworld) in the Vedic times. In the period after 200 A.D., the practice was retained, and the cow was called *Anustarani.* It was either sacrificed or burnt with the corpse, and in the later periods, when cow slaughter was prohibited, the practice of gifting it to the *brahmin* emerged, believing that it would help the deceased in the journey ahead.[1] *Gaudan* (gift of a cow) is done with

1. Pandey, R. (1969). *Hindu Samskaras: Socio-Religious Study of the Hindu Sacraments.* New Delhi: Motilal Banarsi Das.

an ornamented cow to the *panda* (*Vedwa Brahmin*),[2] who would pray that the cow would lead the dying to the next world. The tail of the cow is given in the hands of the deceased, considering that it will assist the dying person in crossing all obstacles in the afterlife journey.[3] Other things that are donated involve essentials like grains, money, sugar, soap, cotton, everyday used articles, a *diya* (an earthen lamp), silver, and a gold coin after being placed on the palm of the deceased.[4] The gift of land to the *brahmin* is also considered meritorious in the afterlife journey for the deceased. The *Garuda Purana* specifies that '*he who donates property will be reborn as a king*' (*Garuda Purana*, II. 30.16)

b. **Laying the Deceased on the Ground:** It is prescribed that a Hindu should not die on a bed or mattress. So when the dying hour approaches, it is essential that a floor is prepared with sandy soil, by smearing cow dung, or by scattering some grass. It is important for a person to die on earth, and he/she should not be suspended between sky and earth. The bed/couch serves as a gap or suspension between the earth and the sky. If the deceased dies on a bed/couch he/she would hang in between. It is believed that between the sky and the earth there is *antariksa* (atmospheric environment), populated by subtle beings, like *pisachas* (demons), *vetalas* (vampires), and the *uragrahas* (nightmares), ready to invade the body, which is still inexperienced of this new aerial condition. Also, if the person dies in the suspended position, the soul on release

2. In Hinduism, priests who perform funeral rites are categorised into different categories of Brahmins, called *Vedwa*, Brahmins, or *Pandas*. They are sacred specialists for performing *Anteyshti samskara*.

3. Singh, D.N. (1999). *Study of Hinduism.* New Delhi: Vikas Publications.

4. Filippi, G.G. (1996). *Mrtyu: Concept of Death in Indian Traditions – Transformation of the Body and Funeral Rites.* New Delhi: D.K. Printworld P Ltd.

finds itself in a *svapnasthana* (dream state) where it has no contact with the ground and is more vulnerable to falling prey to the evil-intended beings. Lying on the ground helps the dying person concentrate on the phenomenon that is going on at the moment of death. It is further prescribed that the deceased should be laid on the ground with his/her head towards the south direction, which is the direction of Yama (God of Death).

c. **Chanting:** Chanting of sacred Vedic mantras or verses from the Ramayana for the deceased is prescribed. Also, there is a tradition of offering water from the Ganges, with *tulsi* (holy basil) leaves and putting it in the mouth of the deceased in his/her last moments. For the elderly, Ganges water with gold and tiny pearls is put in the mouth to ensure a convenient passage in the afterlife journey.[5]

d. **Rituals on Death:** At the moment of death, it is prescribed to close the eyelids of the deceased, put cotton in the nostrils, and cover the body with a white sheet. Immediately lighting an oil lamp and placing it near the body, and keeping it burning continuously, is directed in the *Puranic* texts. At the moment of death and onwards, the house as well as family members of the deceased are struck by impurity, which is called a phase of *asaucha* (nine days for *Brahmins,* twelve days for *Kshatriyas,* fifteen days for *Vaisyas,* and a month for *Sudras*). In the phase of *asaucha*, family members of the deceased are vulnerable to attacks from evil spirits such as *vetalas, pisachas, bhutas,* or living wizards. So there are practices prescribed for the *asauch* phase, discussed in the later section of this chapter.

5. Singh, D.N. (1999). *Study of Hinduism.* New Delhi: Vikas Publications.

Rituals for the Corpse Disposal

The eldest son or the next nearest kin is appointed as the chief mourner. In order to prepare him for performing the rituals, his moustache, beard, and head are shaved, leaving a *bodi* (middle tuft of hair on the head). He bathes and puts on a clean *lungi* (loin cloth).

It is also essential to prepare the corpse; therefore, it is prescribed to wash and clean the dead body, dress it in new clothes, and put some *tulsi* leaves and *Ganga jal* in the mouth. The texts prescribe various protocols for dressing the deceased. The male corpse is dressed in white clothes. A married woman whose husband is alive is dressed in red clothes and bedecked in new bangles, henna, and *bindi* (a symbol of a married woman) on the forehead. For a widow, it is recommended that she should be dressed in clothes of light colour tones. After dressing up, the toes of the deceased are tied, arms are held tightly along the sides, and legs are tied together; thereafter, it is covered with a sheet. In Hinduism, loud cries and weeping are encouraged as they mark the official declaration of death.

Pinda Daan (Rice Balls Donation)

The word '*pińda*' means 'body'. Just before the funeral procession begins, another prescribed practice is offering sweets, made of rice flour, water, and ghee. The practice is prevalent since Vedic times, with the belief that when the *atma* leaves the body and becomes *preta* (the disembodied self), it needs a body *(pinda)* for the journey ahead. These sweet rice balls are offered in the light of giving nourishment to the soul on its journey to become a *pitr* (ancestor). *Pinda daan* is symbolic of nourishing the disembodied *preta* in its afterlife journey. These are offered at different stages during the *Antyeshti* ceremony.

The officiating priest *(panda)* makes these balls, and the first *pinda* is offered to the chest of the deceased or to the floor of the room where death occurred. The bier is then lifted on the shoulders of the four kinsmen of the deceased and taken out of the door of the house, with feet first, and then the second *pinda* is offered at the door of the house from where the body is taken out.[6] The funeral procession is led by the eldest son. Close relatives (only men) follow. The third *pinda* is offered on the way to the road, from where the procession passes by. The fourth *pinda* is offered to the earth of the cremation ground, where the bier is placed.

On reaching the place of cremation, another traditional practice is to lay the corpse on the ground, and the chief mourner, wearing a *janeu* (sacred thread), walks around the corpse, carrying an earthen pot, pouring water from its hole and smashing it towards the head of the deceased. For this practice, I did not find any reference in the sacred literature. However, it persists as tradition. Funtionaries in the cremation grounds explained about this traditional ritual: '*Koi zarurat nahi hai iski vaise, purano mein nahi likha hai, par hum karwa dete hain kyun ki pratha chalti aa rahi hai. Naah karwayen toh log khud hi pooch lete hain*' (This custom is not needed as it is not mentioned in the *Puranas,* but we get it done as it has been going on for a long time. If we don't do it, people themselves ask for it.) There are different stories about this ritual.

The most popular is that breaking the *earthen pot is symbolic of* breaking the relationship with the deceased in this life. Another fable is that when medical science had not developed, before finally cremating the corpse, breaking the pot and creating a sound right near the ears of the deceased was the last attempt to be sure of the death of the deceased.

---

6. It is stated that in Vedic times, the body was carried out from the wall through an opening, and then the second pinda was offered to the spirit at the wall, which was closed again to impede/stop the ghost of the deceased from finding its way back and disturbing the family members. See Filippi, 1996.

Body Disposal: Cremation

In Hinduism, the prescribed method to dispose of the body is the cremation of the corpse on the wooden pyre, although, in early Vedic *Samhitas*, there are hymns that reflect that the corpse is buried.[7] The cremation or burning of the dead body came into practice at a later stage of human civilisation. *Agni* (fire) was considered the messenger of the gods on earth and worked as a carrier of oblations offered to the gods. This principle was applied to human corpses as well. After the person had died, it was thought necessary to send his/her body to Yama (Lord of death). This could have been possible only through the messenger of God, *Agni*. So, after the body was consumed by *Agni* and reduced to ashes, it would indicate that the dead had reached the realm of Lord Yama. Therefore, it indicates that the idea of cremation came into practice when fire worshipping or performing sacrifices became important in the Vedic times. Before that, other practices of body disposal, like leaving the corpses in the open or burial, also prevailed. Another reason for the origin of cremation was the popular belief that the evil spirits mostly originated from the wicked souls of the dead people buried in the earth, so it is essential to completely annihilate the dead remains. Thus, people thought that it was necessary to introduce the system to send the dead to Lord Yama directly through fire. Gradually, it became the most accepted practice amongst Hindus across the globe.

---

7. 'Go to this thy mother, Earth, the widespread delightful Earth, this virgin Earth, is as soft as wool, to the liberal worshipper; may she protect thee from the proximity of *Nirrti*. Earth, rise above him; be attentive to him and comfortable; cover him up, as a mother covers her child with the skirt of her garment. May the earth heaped over him lie light; may thousands of particles (of dust) envelop him; may these mansions distil ghee for him; may they every day be an asylum to him in this world. I heap up the earth around thee placing (upon thee) this clod of earth; may I not be injured; let the *piatra* sustain thy monument; may Yama make thee a dwelling here.' (See: Pandey, R. (1969). *Hindu Samskaras: A Socio-Religious Study of Hindu Sacraments,* New Delhi: Motilal Banarsi Das Publishers, p. 240).

It is prescribed that the pyre is prepared with wooden logs (the purest wood, like sandal, *papal,* and *dak* are recommended). The corpse is placed on the pyre with the head towards the north and the feet facing south. Then the circumambulation around the corpse is made counter-clockwise, with the funeral pyre to one's left. This processional direction is called *prasavya* (prescribed for funeral rites, to honour the ancestors and to heal snake bites). The final fifth *pind* (rice ball) is offered. The shroud is loosened, and the ropes tying the toes together are cut.

Sacred texts also prescribe caste based offerings to the pyre before lighting it. For instance, if the deceased was a *brahmin*, a piece of gold is placed in the hand; if *Kshatriya*, a bow is placed; a jewel in the case of *Vaisyas*. Further, it is prescribed to tear a bit of shroud from the mouth of the corpse and *panchratani* composed of five metals, namely, gold, silver, diamond, sapphire, and pearl, is put in. Also, offering *tulsi* leaves and pieces of sandalwood on the chest of the deceased before the pyre is lit is prescribed in the texts.

In Vedic times, the *anustarani* (cow) sacrifice was performed. In this ritual, the intestines of the sacrificed animal were placed on the corpse's face, and each organ was placed upon the corresponding organ of the deceased.[8] Over the later years, when cow sacrifice was banned, the ritual was replaced by offering different sweets to the body, representing the dismembered parts of the *anustarani* cow. Traditionally, the practice of offering the things used by the deceased to the funeral pyre also prevailed.

In recent times, the traditional practice has been replaced by common utility objects like offering shawls, sheets, money, and sweets before cremation. Usually, these are not burnt with the corpse but given to the crematorium staff who assist in performing the cremation. However, *panchrattan*, *samagri*, and *ghee* (five metals, a mixture of herbs, and clarified butter) are offered and burnt

8. Pandey, R. (1969). Hindu Samskaras: Socio-Religious Study of the Hindu Sacraments. New Delhi: Motilal Banarsi Das.

with the corpse. After the preliminaries are done, the cremation is performed in the light of sacrificial fire (*yajna*). In Hinduism, it is preached that if the corpse is not cremated, the departed soul keeps wandering about for habitation as a *preta* (disembodied spirit).

In Vedic times, there was a custom of having the wife of the deceased lie on the funeral pyre for a moment before making her leave. *Karta* would recite the following hymn from the *Rig-Veda*, addressing the deceased:

> *'O, deceased, your wife desires to be united with you in the future world and is lying with your corpse. She always observed the duties of a faithful wife; concede permission for her to remain in this world and to leave your riches to your descendants.'*
> *(RV. X 187.9)*

Holding the widow's hand and for inviting her down, the following was recited:

> *'Stand up, O woman, you who lie next to the deceased, come to the world of the living, far from your husband, and become the wife of he who will take your hands and will want to marry you.'*
> *(RV.X 18.8)*

When the widow left the pyre, she took a piece of gold or a jewel from her dead husband, symbolic of prosperity for the bereaved kin. This custom was devised to replace the idea of burning widows on the funeral pyre that existed before. However, *sati* or voluntary sacrifice of widows regained popularity in the Smriti phase and remained in practice amongst certain Hindus.

Mid-Cremation Rituals

Hinduism also prescribes practices of *kapalkriya* and *kardena* while the cremation is going on, and the body is half burnt.

- ***Kapalkriya*** **(Smashing the Skull):** After half of the corpse is burnt, another prescribed ritual is *kapalkriya.* It is recommended that the cranial cavity be blown out. The chief mourner is directed to smash the skull with the bamboo stick and then throw that stick over the corpse. The texts offer different explanations for this practice:

    - The life of a man is constituted of ten elements, nine of which cease their functions at death, while the action of the tenth continues for three days after death. '*The seat of this, the tenth element, is in the skull, which is accordingly smashed in order to set it free*'.

    - Some aspect of consciousness is still believed to be sustaining, and it is released after smashing the skull. Therefore, *kapalkriya* is performed to permit the exit of the last *prana* (breath) from the body, the *dhananjayavayu.*

    - The deceased no longer belongs to any friends or relatives. *kapalkriya* indicates the detachment of living with the dead.

    - The breaking of the skull also prevents its misuse for some occult practices which are prevalent in Hinduism. The *pandas* working at the cremation grounds were also asked about the rationale of this practice. In their words, '*Yeh toh bahut zaruri hai, nahi toh khopri aise hi reh jaaye toh galat istemaal hota hai.*' (This is a very important ritual; the skull is likely to be misused if not broken fully.) '*Upar ki cheezein chipak jaati hain khopri ko.*' (Other worldly beings take over the half/burnt skull.)

Thus, the texts and the functionaries at cremation grounds both portray *kapalkriya* as a necessary practice in the *Antyeshti* ceremony.

- *Rite of Kardena:* After the *kapalkriya,* this rite is performed in which the participants (gathering) take a piece of fuel and offer it into the pyre, and a cry of mourning is raised in chorus. This is the last offering given to the pyre. Thereafter, it is prescribed that the mourners return and bathe. In earlier times, it would happen at the river en route. In some places, there is a tradition of bathing anywhere outside the home. In modern times, most of the mourners wash their hands and feet at the facilities provided at the cremation grounds and bathe in their house after returning.

Post-Cremation Practices

In Hinduism, certain practices are prescribed to be followed after cremation. These include the rituals meant for the smooth afterlife journey of the deceased; to deal with *asaucha* (impurity) caused due to death; and practices to revere the ancestors.

1. ***Practices Prescribed for Asaucha* (Impurity):** In Hinduism, the moment of death initiates the phase of *asaucha.* During this phase, the householders where the death has occurred are vulnerable to the ill effects of the pollution caused by death. Different texts have prescribed various practices as preventive measures for the same. For instance, before stepping inside the home, the mourners have to touch the stone, fire, cow dung, grain, *til*-seed (sesame), oil, and water as a mark to purify themselves from the pollution caused by death. Some texts also refer to the chewing of *neem* leaves, inhaling smoke of certain pieces of wood, etc., as purifiers. The practice of bathing after cremation is also interpreted as cleansing of mourners, particularly the chief mourner, due to the pollution caused by death.

This period of *asaucha* ranges from ten to fifteen days, or even a month from the date of the death, depending upon the deceased's caste, mainly based on the observance of the rules of purity and pollution in different castes. Also, the intensity of pollution caused by the death of men/women varies according to their marital status. The texts elaborate both the prescriptive and proscriptive norms to be observed in this phase of *asaucha*. The proscriptions include forgoing or abstaining from routine activities like cutting hair and beard, reciting specific *mantras* and prayers, avoiding social life, not washing, not combing the hair, not having sex, etc. Prescriptive norms include sitting and sleeping on floor mats rather than beds, eating only outsourced food (supplied by relatives or friends), eating just once a day, and exhibiting feelings of grief and sorrow. Observing these rules also marks the mourning of death.

2. ***Recitation of Garuda Purana***: Immediately after the day of cremation till the *asaucha* period is on, it is prescribed that the *brahmin* is invited at home, and *Preta Manjari,* the section of the *Garuda Purana* dedicated to the journey of the soul in the afterlife, is read for the bereaved.

3. ***Asthi-Sanchayana / Phoolchugna* (Collection of Bones) – Third Day After Death**: Another prescribed practice after cremation is the collection of unburnt bones. There is no unanimity on which day after the death this has to be performed; certain texts specify the thirteenth or fifteenth day after cremation, while others state the third, fifth, or seventh day after cremation. However, the most popular practice is collecting bones on the third day after death. In order to collect bones, it is prescribed that the ashes are first sprinkled with milk and water, and the bones separated using a *Udambara* stick. In the Vedic literature (the *Taittiriya* branch of the *Yajur-Veda),* there are instances of women doing this ceremony, preferably the senior wife of the deceased. In those times, the collected bones were cleaned and washed, deposited in an urn, and buried. In the case of the deceased who used to perform Vedic sacrifices, the bones were burnt again. The plausible reason behind burning the bones again or burying

them deep in the earth was the belief that the dead are supposed to take on a new shape in the other world, for which it becomes necessary that every part of the material body is sent to the next world either by burning or through burial.

However, in *Puranic* literature, this practice of *asti-sanchayana* changed. It is prescribed that the collection of bones has to be done by the chief mourner. It is recommended that he first pick up three bones, only using the thumb and the little finger, and then all present collect the remaining bones in an urn or vase. In *Puranic* texts, the Vedic practice of burying these ashes got replaced by immersing them in flowing water. In the *Smriti* phase of Hinduism, the sanctity of rivers increased. Lord Shiva is perceived as the deity for destruction, and in *Puranic* stories, the Ganges is supposed to have originated from Shiva's hair, so the tradition of the immersion of ashes in the rivers, particularly in the Ganges, evolved, perceiving that it would be meritorious for the dead and would help him/her gain liberation. Eventually, places like Haridwar, Varanasi, or Prayag in Allahabad, where the Ganges flows, became the hubs for *asti-visarjan* (immersion of ashes).

> *'The virtuous one, whose bone floats on the water of the Ganges, never returns from Brahmaloka to the world of the mortals. Those whose bones are thrown into the Ganges by men live in heaven for thousands of Yugas.'*[9]

Sraddha Rites

As discussed earlier, the practice of *pinda daan* evolved in Vedic times with the idea to nourish the disembodied self in its afterlife

9. 'The *Anteyeshti Samskara*', *http://www.salagram.net/antyeshti-ceremonies-functions.htm*

journey. *Sraddha* rites are carried out in phases, beginning with the *pinda daan* on the day of death itself.[10] After that, the following series of *sraddhas* are prescribed in Hindu texts:

a. ***Nav*** (New)-***Sraddha***: Ten days after death, it is prescribed to perform a *pinda daan* with the idea of constructing a suitable body for the subtle essence that leaves after death. It is performed by the chief mourner with the assistance of a priest at the river banks. The site is preferred to be far from cremation grounds. The *brahmin* begins by announcing that the reason for this rite which is to provide the deceased with a temporary body. Then a subtle trail is drawn along the north-west and south-east direction on which ten sweet balls made of rice flour, sesame seeds, sugar, milk, yoghurt, butter, and ghee are placed. An invocation is repeated while placing each sweet ball on the trail:

    - *First:* May this form the head;
    - *Second*: May this form the neck and the shoulders;
    - *Third*: May this form the heart and the chest;
    - *Fourth*: May this form the back;
    - *Fifth*: May this form the stomach and the abdomen;
    - *Sixth*: Groin;
    - *Seventh*: Intestines;
    - *Eight*: Legs upto knees;
    - *Ninth:* Ankles and feet;
    - *Tenth*: While laying the tenth, the priest, followed by

10. Bowker, J. (1993). *The Meanings of Death.* Cambridge, USA: Cambridge University Press.

> the relatives of the deceased, collectively say: '*May this offering creates nourishment and satisfies hunger and thirst.*'

Thereafter, the *pindas* are divided into four sections. Water is poured on the *pindas*, and a long cotton thread is placed upon it—a symbol of weaving together all parts. It is preached that now the subtle body will receive water for the first time. Water is made to drip from a shell (*sankha*)—ritually and symbolically connected with the uterus. This ritual is equated to the embryonic formation of the subtle body. It is a symbol of the notion that at that moment, the 'disembodied one' becomes an 'embryo' ready to be born as an ancestor. The ritual is concluded by throwing those sweets (balls) into the river and offering food to *brahmin,* hay (*chaara*) to the cows, and *roti* (Indian bread) to the dogs (representatives of the infernal gods). This rite is considered impure *sraddha* as its purpose is only the formation of some kind of subtle body for the essence left after death for the journey ahead. It is explained that these offerings ensure that the deceased gets food and water while crossing sixteen tormenting phases towards Yama's abode. These sixteen balls in total include five/six offered on death. The irony of doing it on the tenth day is symbolic of the gestation period of nine solar months (or ten lunar months); one day is equated with one lunar month.

It is prescribed that if *nav-sraddha* is not performed, the disembodied soul turns into a *pisacha* (ghost) that wanders here and there. This *pisacha,* in need of a body, desperately secures the necessary organs by penetrating into the living bodies to satisfy its thirst and hunger. The easier targets of the *pisacha* are the mentally ill, bodies of sleeping persons, foetuses in the womb, infants, etc.

b. ***Ekadasa*** **(Eleventh)** ***Sraddha***: On the completion of *nav-sraddhas*, the *ekadasa sraddha* is performed on the eleventh day after death. This *sraddha* is meant to make *preta* reach the *pitrlok* (join ancestors). On the riverbank, after ritualistically cleaning the place by the priest, a little earth is dug in which some durva[11] grass is laid, eleven *pindas* are kept, thread is placed on them (symbolic of unifying principle), and water and milk are offered through a seashell. After offering prayers for *preta*, these are thrown in the river or fed to a cow. Further, after purification of the chief mourner (having bath or dip), again *panca sraddha* is done in a similar way, and prayers are offered that the deceased may no longer linger on the embryonic stage of *preta* and soon become *pitr.* Followed by this, a series of prayers is offered for the smooth journey of the *preta*.

The ancient ritual *vrsotsarga* (setting a bull free) has significance for the smooth journey of a *preta* towards *pitrlok*. In earlier times, sacrificing a cow at the cremation site was meant to help the *preta* on the journey ahead, and then it transformed into the idea of releasing a cow (*vrsotsarga*). These days, the *vrsotsarga* ritual is replaced by donating the cow in the name of the deceased.

The eleventh-day ritual is concluded by offering food to the *brahmins*.

c. ***The Twelfth Day Sapindikarana (Samyojna Sraddha)***: These rites are meant to celebrate the arrival of *preta* at the *pitrlok*. Fifteen *pindas* are offered again on the riverbank. In *Sapindikarana* rite, it is assumed that the deceased has arrived at *pitrlok* amongst ancestors. Thus ancestors' presence is acknowledged in this rite. Five *brahmins* participate in this ritual: three representing the father, grandfather, and the great grandfather of the new *pitr,* and the other two represent the witness gods. The deceased (the new *pitr*) is represented by a bunch of *durva* grass tied together. The *brahmins* are fed with boiled rice and vegetables, followed by another round of *daan*, where the chief mourner mixes the rice with usual ingredients and divides it into two parts;

11. Special grass used in Hindu sacred ceremonies.

one part is made into a large *pinda,* and the other half is divided into three *pindas* of usual dimensions. The first and the biggest *pinda* is offered to the deceased and rest three to his ancestors (with whom the deceased is supposed to unite). After the usual practice of keeping them in a furrow, the largest one is divided into three and merged with other three, indicating that the deceased is finally assimilated to the ancestors. The ritual is concluded by offering alms to the priests. '*At this point, the ancestor is called with the new name as he is born in the pitrloka; Sharma for Brahmin caste; Verma for Ksatriya; Gupta for Vaisya, and Dasa for the Shudra caste.*'

Thus, according to the Hindu sacred texts, *pindas* are offered for the *preta* to be born as a *pitr*. If this is not performed, the *preta* can become a *pisacha* that can intrude human bodies to fulfil its cravings for body, food, and water. According to the *Puranic* texts, *sraddha* rites are important to help the deceased reach *Yamlok* (the realm of Yama) smoothly, and *pindas* provide the necessary nourishment to the soul at different stopovers in the journey.

d. **Thirteenth Day *(Kiryakaram):* Restoration of Routine and End of Mourning:** To mark the end of the mourning phase, the last ritual is performed on the thirteenth day of the death. The *karta* (chief mourner) performs *kiryakaram* with the assistance of the *panda.* Gods and goddesses are offered prayers and are symbolically invited onto the ground. Offerings of boiled rice, fruits, vegetables, and sweets are made. A widow is made to accept the life of resignation from now on. The ceremony officially marks the end of the pollution phase, and the routine of life begins. The thirteenth day also symbolises continuity, and ritualistically, the responsibility of the deceased is passed on to the heirs. A *pagri* (turban) is tied to the heir, and the ceremony is called *rasam pagri.* Thirteen to seventeen *brahmins* are fed with a wholesome meal. Utility articles like bed, utensils, clothes, and money are donated to the *panda* (chief priest who assisted throughout). Relatives and friends join for a collective meal.

Death-Related Practices Prescribed for Special Cases

Hindu sacred texts have prescribed different practices in the event of the death of special cases like children (below the age of 14), sages, kin dying at a distance, and accidental deaths.

For children, it is prescribed that they do not require the material necessities in the next world, as they have lived for a very short span on earth, and they are not accustomed to those. Therefore, *sraddhas* and *pinda daan* are omitted for children (boys uninitiated/girls before puberty). Their innocent lives do not inflict so much impurity; so purification rituals are also not required. Burial is the prescribed method to dispose of their bodies. Abortive children are also to be buried. *Smriti* texts also approve air burial and water burial for children.

The *Antyeshti* ceremony for the ascetics and saints is also different. It is believed that sages give up on all worldly attachments and are enlightened beings, so they attain *moksha* after death. Hence, rituals meant for the afterlife journey of the soul are not required for them. The oldest reference to dealing with the dead bodies of the ascetics is found in the *Sruti* texts like the *Taittiriya Aranyaka* and the *Baudhayana Grhyasutra*. The prescribed *Antyeshti* for ascetics in these texts is laying the body in a ditch, placing the begging bowl on one's belly, and placing the *kamandalu* (pot) with water on one's right hand. The ditch is covered with earth, and a mound is raised with the idea of protecting it from animals. The post-cremation ceremonies are prohibited in the case of *sanyasis* (sages). The last rites for saints are completed with the grand feast without any mourning.

In the later years, amongst certain sects, water burial for the *sadhus* is also a prescribed practice. A few texts also hold that the soul of a great ascetic is released through a point called *Brahmarandhra* (a minute opening in the crown of the head) that ensures *moksha*. Hence, they do not require any rituals for the afterlife journey.

In Hindu texts, attention is given to those who die at distant places, away from home, and the corpse is not found. It is prescribed that it is essential that the corpse is located for *Antyeshti*. However, if the corpse is not found, it is prescribed that at least thirty bones are brought, and post-cremation rituals are performed. If bones are also not available, then, considering the direction in which death has occurred, it is prescribed that the effigy of a person is made, and with other essentials, the cremation is performed.

In earlier Hindu texts, it is stated that those who die because of accidents, killed by weapons, choked by poison, drowned in water, fallen from a mountain top or tree, etc., cannot be accorded a place in *pitrlok*, so the rites meant for the afterlife journey go futile. However, in *Smriti* texts, it is prescribed that *Antyeshti* has to be performed in these cases also with certain *prayaschittas* (preventive rituals). Hence, accidental deaths are considered unnatural and untimely deaths in Hinduism.

In addition, *Manusmriti* prescribes certain habits as anti-social, so people who indulge in those habits are considered *patitas* (fallen). They are also denied funeral ceremonies because, being anti–social elements, they do not deserve the privilege of receiving the last *samskara* and a place in *pitrloka* like others who have lived a life in conformity to *dharma*.

Also, for the elderly who die leaving sons, grandsons, and great-grandsons, it is prescribed that they are offered silver coins on the bier (copper if poor), marking the celebration of their longevity.

In Hinduism, there is a belief that dying on certain days is a bad omen. There is a phase called *panchak* (five days), identified with specific lunar positions of *nakshatras* (constellations). This period is considered inauspicious for dying. The underlying belief for the phase of *panchak* is that anything that occurs during this period will recur at least five times. So death in this period might lead to the death of other surviving members of the family. So symbolically, while cremating the dead body of the deceased who died in the days of *panchak*, it is prescribed that the idols of *durva* grass are made, one for each of the remaining days of the *panchak*, and are burnt with the dead. At some places, dolls made up of cow dung are burnt along with the corpse. Also, death occurring during a solar or lunar eclipse is considered inauspicious, and in such cases, prayers for *grah shanti* (improving planetary positions) are performed.

Practices for Revering Ancestors

1. **Annual Commemoration** ***(Barsi/Barsodhi/Titthi)*****:** On the completion of one year of death, the date decided according to the lunar calendar, the death anniversary is marked by family/kin by gathering for a collective meal and feeding *brahmins* and the poor.

2. **Fortnight Commemoration for All Ancestors:** As ancestors have an important place in Hinduism, so, in general, all ancestors of the family are revered and remembered (ritualistically) for a particular period in the month. According to the Hindu calendar, every year, the month of *Bhadra* (September–October), *Krishna paksha* (dark moonlit), and *Ashwin* (October) are believed to be the most auspicious days for revering ancestors. On these specific days, *brahmins* are offered food, perceiving that it will benefit the ancestors. In *Smriti* texts, like *Manusmriti*, epics like Mahabharata and in different *Puranas,* this practice has been given due importance. It is preached in Hinduism that performing these rites would

gain many merits, and not doing so could result in serious repercussions for one's own life. Different ways of ancestor worship are prescribed, like *pinda daan*, feeding *brahmins*, libations of water, milk, and vegetables, etc. Interestingly, on the days meant for revering the ancestors, it is preached that other Hindu *samskars* like initiation, marriage, etc., are not to be celebrated.

Sikhism

Sikhism evolved during the times when other religions like Hinduism and Islam were prevalent in India. Both these religions preached a ritualistic pattern to worship God and also prescribed specific rites for different aspects of life, including rites of passage. However, Guru Nanak and his successors rejected the ritualistic ways prescribed in these religious faiths to revere God and developed a different pursuit to reach God by meditating on his name, singing praises, serving humanity, etc. Guru Nanak and the later Gurus never endorsed any kind of rituals for any aspect of life, and it is evident from the following verses in *Adi Granth*:

> *'If they happen to know the nature of God, they will realise that all rites and beliefs are futile.'*
> *(AG, 470)*
> *'Rituals and ceremonies are chains of the mind.'*
> *(AG, 635)*
>
> *'Cursed be the ritual that makes us forget the Loved One.'*
> *(AG, 590)*
>
> *'Let compassion be your mosque, faith your prayer carpet, and righteousness your Qur'an. Let modesty be your circumcision and uprightness your fasting. Thus, you will become a true Muslim.'*
> *(AG: 140)*

Similarly, in the event of death, the prescribed rituals in Islam and Hinduism, prevalent in those times, were rejected by Guru Nanak and other Gurus. Particularly, the Hindu rituals discussed above, prescribed for the afterlife journey of the soul, are condemned by Sikh Gurus. There is a composition in Guru Granth Sahib, explaining that Nanak emphasised reciting the Lord's name for better prospects of the soul's journey after death over the rituals prevalent in those times.

> *'The one Name is my lamp. I have put the oil of suffering into it. Its flame has dried up this oil, and I have escaped my meeting with the Messenger of Death. O people, do not make fun of me. Thousands of wooden logs, piled up together, need only a tiny flame to burn. The Lord is my festive dish of rice balls and leafy plate; the True Name of the Creator is my funeral ceremony. Here and hereafter in the past and in the future, this is my support. The Lord's praise is my river Ganges and my city of Benares; my soul takes a sacred cleansing bath there. That becomes my true cleansing bath if night and day I enshrine love for you. The rice balls are offered to the gods and the dead ancestors, but it is the brahmins who eat them. Oh Nanak, the rice balls of the Lord are a gift, which is never exhausted.' (GGS: 358)*[12]

Thus, Guru Nanak rejected the afterlife rituals prescribed in Hinduism and emphasised acquiring the qualities of *gurmukh*. Instead of rituals for the betterment of the soul, he preferred meditation on God's name for the liberation of the soul. It is also stated that Nanak was not adamant on the body disposal method prescribed by any religion. In Sikh texts, there is a *sakhi* (story) explaining the same:

12. Myrvold, K. (2006). 'Sikhism and Death'. In K. Garces-Foley, *Death and Religion in a Changing World* (pp. 178–206). New York: Routledge.

> *'When it became apparent that Guru Nanak Dev ji's end was impending, his Hindu and Muslim disciples started an argument over claiming the guru's body for funeral rites. The Muslims wished to bury him according to their customs, while the Hindus wished to cremate his body according to their beliefs. To settle the matter, Guru Nanak Dev himself was consulted. He explained to them the idea of Jyotijot; that only his mortal body would expire, but that light which illumined him was divine light, and would pass to his successor. The Guru requested his devotees to bring flowers and instructed the Hindus to place flowers on his right side and the Muslims to place flowers on his left side. He told them that permission for funeral rites would be determined by whichever set of flowers remained fresh throughout the night. Then Guru Nanak requested the devotees to recite the prayers (Sohila and Japji). After the prayers, the Guru told them to cover his head and body in a sheet, and then he instructed everyone to leave him. With his last breath, Guru Nanak infused his spiritual light/jot into his successor second Guru, Angad Dev. The devotees returned the next morning. They carefully lifted and removed the sheet which had been placed over the Guru's body. All were amazed to discover that no trace at all remained of Guru Nanak Dev Ji's mortal body. Flowers that they kept on both sides remained; these flowers did not wither at all.'*

Death-Related Practices Prescribed/Proscribed in *Rehat Maryada*

As discussed, from its very inception, Sikhism did not fix any rigid rituals pertaining to death and dying. However, *Rehat Maryada*,[13] the book of Sikh code, prescribes certain practices to be followed in the event of death.

---

13. 'Sikh *Rehat Maryada*', *http://www.gurunanakdarbar.net/sikhrehatmaryada.pdf*

1. **Dying and on Death:** It is prescribed that on the anticipation of death, only *Gurbani* should be recited or the word '*Waheguru*' should be chanted by his/her side, which shall help in inducing a mood of resignation to God's will. On death, the survivors must not grieve or raise a hue and cry or indulge in breast-beating. Also, singing of '*Kirtan Sohila*'[14] is prescribed when the person is dying or has already died. *Bhai Gurdas* (1551–1636) explains that *gurmukhs* do not weep on the occasion of death, but rather recite '*Kirtan Sohila*'.[15]

2. ***Antim Ishnan*** **(Last Bath):** The washing of the corpse is called *antim ishnan.* It symbolises ritualistic purification of the body before it is offered to fire. It is prescribed that the dead body should be bathed and dressed in clean clothes. The Sikh symbols of *kanga* (wooden comb), *kachha* (cotton underwear), *karha* (steel bracelet), and *kirpan* (steel sword), if worn by the deceased, should not be taken off. For dressing, there are no prescriptions found in *Rehat Maryada*, but the traditional practice is to dress the deceased in new clothes. Men, in particular, are shrouded in white and women (married) are adorned in bright colours as a bride. Perhaps, these ways have been adopted from Hinduism, as when Sikhism evolved, most of the adherents were Hindu converts. Thereafter, the body has to be put on a plank.

3. ***Antim Ardas*** **(Last Prayer):** After the body is prepared, *ardas* about its being taken away for disposal is offered. It is prescribed that the hearse should be lifted after the recitation of *ardas* and taken to the cremation ground; hymns that induce a feeling of detachment should be recited. After reaching the cremation grounds, again reciting *ardas* is prescribed.

---

14. 'Kirtan Sohila' is a prescribed pre-sleep, night scriptural prayer.

15. Singh, J. (1998). *Varan Bhai Gurdas: Text, Transliteration, and Translation* (Vols. 1–2). New Delhi: Vision Venture.

4. ***Antim Sanskar* (Cremation):** According to *Rehat Maryada*, cremation is the prescribed method for the deceased of all age groups. However, where arrangements for cremation cannot be made, the body can be immersed in flowing water or disposed of in any other manner. For cremation, the dead body should be placed on the pyre, and the son or any other relation or friend of the deceased should light the pyre. For the congregation, it is prescribed that they should sit at a reasonable distance and listen to *kirtan* or collectively sing hymns, particularly detachment-inducing ones. When the pyre is fully aflame, it is prescribed to recite the '*Kirtan Sohila.*

5. ***Post-Cremation Path*:** After the cremation, it is prescribed that the congregation, on reaching home, should commence with a reading of the Guru Granth Sahib. It can be done at home or in a nearby gurudwara, and after reciting the six stanzas of the 'Anand Sahib',[16] the *ardas* is offered and *karhah prashad* (sacred pudding) is distributed.

6. ***Collection of Ashes*:** When the pyre is burnt out, the whole of the ashes (including burnt bones) are collected and immersed in the flowing water anywhere or buried at the cremation site only. Raising a monument in the memory of the deceased at the place where his dead body is cremated is forbidden in Sikhism.

7. ***Bhog* (Culmination of the Funeral Rites):** The tenth day after death is marked as the last day for mourning. Reading of the Guru Granth Sahib that commenced on the day of death should be completed on the tenth day. If the reading cannot be completed on the tenth day, some other day may be appointed for the conclusion of the reading. It is prescribed that the reading of the Guru Granth Sahib should be carried out by the

16. 'Anand Sahib' is a hymn of bliss, recited prior to offering *ardas*.

kin of the deceased and members of the community. If possible, it is prescribed to recite *kirtan* also. It is categorically specified that nothing in the context of a funeral is to be performed after the tenth day.

Proscriptions in *Rehat Maryada*

In *Rehat Maryada*, the following rituals peculiar to the Hindu tradition have been sternly proscribed:

a. **Not Placing the Body on the Floor:** It is proscribed that the body of a dying or dead person, if it is on a cot, must not be taken off the cot and put on the floor.

b. **No Lamp Lighting:** *Rehat Maryada* notes, '*nor must a lit lamp be placed beside*'. In Sikhism, keeping an oil lamp lit after death in the belief that it will light the path of the deceased is rejected.

c. ***No Donations***: Sikhism proscribes donations of cows, in particular, which is a prescribed practice in Hinduism.

d. ***No Adhmarg***: The ceremony of breaking the pot used for bathing the dead body amid doleful cries halfway towards the cremation ground is prohibited in Sikhism.

e. ***No Organised Lamentation by Women:*** Organised lamentation by women or sitting on a straw mat in mourning for a certain period is prohibited.

f. ***No Picking of Bones from the Ashes:*** Picking of the unburnt bones from the ashes of the pyre for immersing in the river, at Patalpuri (at Kiratpur), at Kartarpur Sahib or at any other such place is also proscribed in *Rehat Maryada*.

g. ***No Kapalkriya:*** Piercing the skull while the pyre is burning with a rod or something else is rejected in Sikhism. It is categorically specified that the *kapalkriya* is contrary to the Guru's tenets.

h. ***No Pinda Daan:*** The ritual of donating sweets made of rice flour, oat flour, or solidified milk *(khoa)* for ten days after death is also proscribed.

i. ***No Kirya:*** Practices of concluding the funeral proceedings ritualistically, serving meals to *brahmins* and making offerings in the name of *sraddha* are proscribed in *Rehat Maryada*.

Although Rehat Maryada has prescribed a few practices and categorically rejected some of the funeral rites practiced in Hinduism, however, scholars have documented the following other rituals prevalent in Sikh tradition:

1. ***Modha Dena*** **(Participation in Carrying the Bier)**: The bier is carried by the sons and brothers of the deceased, led by the chief mourner, the eldest son. Only male acquaintances of the deceased participate in this ritual. This practice has its roots in the law of inheritance (*mitakshara*) in Hinduism. Because according to these rules, only male *sapindas* (descendants) were given the right to inherit the ancestral property, so they would shoulder the bier of the deceased.[17] Interestingly, *Rehat Maryada* does not describe this aspect, neither prescribed nor proscribed.

2. ***Dhamalak Bhanana*** **(Breaking of the Earthern Pot)**: This practice is a similar version of *adhmarg*, i.e. rejected in *Rehat Maryada*, but still popular amongst Sikhs. When the funeral procession arrives near the cremation ground, the chief mourner makes the round of the bier with an earthen pot full of water in hand. While moving, he keeps pouring the water. On completion of the round, the pot is thrown

17. Erasmo, M. (2019). *Death: Antiquity and Its Legacy (Ancients and Moderns).* London: I.B. Tauris.

by force, and thereafter, the procession proceeds for the next rite of *ardas.*[18]

3. *Custom of Pagri* **(Ritualistic Transfer of Paternal Authority):** Again, this ritual has been borrowed from the ancient Hindu tradition. It is through the rite of *pagri* that the son inherits his father's status and becomes the head of the household. The ceremony begins after the culmination of *bhog*. The chief mourner/eldest son/performer of all rites receives a turban in front of Guru Granth Sahib. This is symbolic of getting a new status of being the head of the household after his father.

4. **Immersing of Ashes at Patalpuri, Kiratpur Sahib:** *Rehat Maryada* did not make any compulsion on doing this; rather, it has been rejected. But this place is very popular amongst adherents of Sikhism for the immersion of ashes in the river. It has historical significance. Guru Hargobind (1595–1644) established the village, Kiratpur, around the Sutlej River, so on his death, his body was cremated here, and the bones were consigned to the Sutlej. And, the remains of Guru Har Krishan were similarly immersed here. Further, it is stated that Baba Sunder (grandson of Guru Amardas) was instructed, along with other disciples, by Guru Amardas on the procedures to be followed after his death, and he mentioned that his ashes/bone remains were to be immersed here. From here, the tradition of immersing ashes in the waters flowing at Kiratpur started. gurudwara was constructed in the 1970s. The prevailing custom is that before the ashes are immersed, the name of the deceased is entered in the gurudwara register. Thereafter, over a bridge, the ashes are immersed in the flowing river. Then, after a bath and cleansing at the river itself, the kin pray at the gurudwara, and an *ardas* in the name of the deceased is

18. Kalsi, S.S. (1994). Sikhism. In J. Holm, & J. Bowker, *Rites of Passage* (pp. 138–156). London: Printer Publishers.

offered. And donations in cash and utensils, in particular, are made, and *langar* (collective meal) is partaken. The practice is called *phull pauna* (immersing of flowers).[19] The certificate of *phull pauna* is issued by the Gurdwara authorities, and the kin collect it in a week's time from Anandpur Sahib.[20]

Thus, according to Sikhism, death occurs at the will of God; therefore, it has to be accepted with humility and resignation. Sikhism prescribes a non-ritualistic and flexible pursuit to be followed at the moment of death and the disposal of the corpse. The ultimate goal for the present life is to attain liberation, and that is possible only by leading a life of a *gurmukh,* by possessing the virtues of humanity, truthfulness, contentment, compassion, humility, and surrendering the ego, when alive. And once dead, no amount of ritual can affect the fate. The soul is going to come back to life, if not liberated.

Buddhism

The early schools of thought, particularly *Theravada Buddhism*, preach that if Nirvana is not attained, rebirth is bound to happen. Like Sikhism, *Theravada Buddhism* also doesn't subscribe to any afterlife journey; hence, the death-related practices prescribed in this school are also meant only for the disposal of the body in a less-ritualistic manner. However, as Buddhism evolved, the idea of the underlying-self wandering in its disembodied state emerged, and this led to the evolution of complex death-related practices. Different schools of Buddhism prescribe practices to be followed for preparing oneself for death (contemplation of one's own death). *The Tibetan Book of the Dead* has laid out a course of

19. The metaphor of flowers is used for the left bones and ashes of the deceased.

20. Another major gurudwara in the region; details from Kiratpur are sent to Anandpur Sahib weekly, and from there certificates are issued.

rituals to be followed right at the moment of death, disposal of the body, and post-disposal practices.

Contemplation on Death

Contemplation on death is given much emphasis in Buddhism, right from the *Theravada* doctrine to later schools of thought. *Maranasatti Sutta* (Mindfulness of Death) is the sacred text of the *Theravada* school that focuses on the importance of giving attention to one's death while being alive. Instead of avoiding the topic, one is encouraged to confront it as directly as possible and to recognise that death is inherent in life. The Buddhist practitioners argue that there are other benefits of contemplation of death beyond preparing oneself for death. For instance, it makes an individual prioritise their goals and makes the practitioner content with the accomplishments in life. It is believed that without mindfulness of death, whatever *dharma* (religion) one practices, it will be superficial. Confronting death directly overcomes one's fears, dislikes, and confusion around death and ensures a deep sense of peace and well-being.

All schools of thought prescribe different ways for the same, like in the *Theravada* doctrine, teachers instruct practitioners to maintain death as a constant companion. One way to do this is to wear a *mala* or Buddhist prayer beads made of bone, each bead is sculpted in the shape of a skull. In the *sutta* (discourse) on the Four Foundations of Mindfulness, the monks are guided to meditate on the corpse and its different stages of decay to contemplate death.[21] It is prescribed that one can see the actual corpse or can imagine it. The idea is to remind oneself that, like this corpse, one's own body also has the nature to decay.

---

21. Thera, N. (Ed.). (1994). *The Foundations of Mindfulness Satipatthana Sutta.* Retrieved 20 April 2020, from www.accesstoinsight.org: https://accesstoinsight.org/lib/authors/nyanasatta/wheel019.html

Tibetan Buddhism takes it further. The meditative lessons from the masters to the students involve making their consciousness have a death-like experience of leaving the body for a certain duration and coming back. Also, as discussed earlier, Tibetan Buddhism prescribes dying alert, so in the meditation lessons given to the practitioners, the ability to concentrate well is emphasised. Sand *mandala* (rangoli) making and ritualistically destroying it on completion is another practice that inculcates better concentration; destruction of a beautiful self-made *mandala* is a symbolic reminder of temporary life.

Death-Related Practices Prescribed in *Bardo Thodol (The Tibetan Book of the Dead)*

Bardo Thodol prescribes the following death-related practices:

1. **On Death:** When it is realised that all the events of the process of death (discussed in the previous chapter) have occurred, the face of the deceased is covered with the white cloth, and nobody is supposed to touch the body till the consciousness or the *bardo* body has not separated from the corpse. Assuming that this separation takes about three to four days, the body is kept intact.

2. ***Hpho-bo* Service:** The priest or lama who assists in extracting the consciousness is called *hpho-bo.* On arrival at the place of death, he sits near the head of the deceased. All doors and windows of the room are closed, and the kin are not supposed to be inside. Absolute silence is required for performing this service. The chants of the *hpho-bo* guide the consciousness about the directions to be followed. In the case of accidental deaths or in the event that the dead body is not retrieved, the *hpho-bo* does this service by hypothetically assuming the dead body. He visualises the body of the deceased and performs the ceremony for about an hour.

3. **Death Horoscope:** While the *hpho-bo*'s service is going on, another lama, *tsi-pa* (astrologer lama), is engaged to make a death horoscope. Based on the moment of the death of the deceased, it is determined who can touch the corpse and who cannot. An auspicious time for body disposal and the rites to be performed for the departed is calculated. Considering the minimum time taken by the consciousness to depart from the body, the auspicious date for disposing of the body is usually three to four days after the death.

4. **Treatment with Corpse During This Phase:** The corpse is tied up in a sitting posture, just like ancient mummies found in the graves. It is called the embryonic posture, symbolic of how life began in the form of an embryo; the next life beyond this should also begin like that. After resting in this posture, the corpse is placed in the corner of the room, and the mourners and visitors are allowed to enter. All these days, till the corpse is at home, all meals are offered to the deceased and thrown away subsequently.

5. **Funeral Procession:** As per the auspicious date and time, found by *tsi-pa,* the officiating lama assists in the removal of the corpse from the house. The use of caskets or coffins is avoided. The corpse is laid upon its back on a sheet or a piece of cloth spread over a framework made of bamboo and is taken out. In areas where Tibetan Buddhism is practised sternly, the corpse is carried in the embryonic posture itself. Thereafter, led by the chief lama, the funeral procession begins. Other lamas also follow the procession. The chanting of verses goes on throughout the procession, and various musical instruments like ringing bells, drums, and trumpets made of human thigh bone are played.

6. **Cremation:** The wooden pyre is set in the place of cremation. Mourners and relatives bring refreshment, out of which some is offered to the funeral pyre and the remaining is taken by

the lamas. The funeral pyre is perceived as being dedicated to *Dhayani Buddha Amitabha* (an image of Buddha). As the fire rises, fragrant oils, sandalwood, and incense sticks are offered. After the cremation, the remains are collected by the lamas, crushed and mixed with clay, and *stupa*-like forms are sculpted from it and placed on the higher hill tops or caves.[22]

7. ***Mtshan-Spyang/Spyang-Pu or Chang-Ku* (Effigy of the Body):** After the disposal of the body, an effigy of the deceased is prepared, dressing a stool, a block of wood, or any other suitable material. This effigy is offered food (all meals) for 49 days.

8. **Reading *Bardo Thodol:*** Whilst other funeral rites are going on, the recitation of *The Tibetan Book of the Dead* begins on the day of death itself by the lamas all day and night, till the corpse is disposed. It is believed that the more the number of lamas, the better the service. In some families, this ritual is performed in the monastery where the deceased used to pray. After the disposal of the body, *spang-pu*, is perceived as deceased, and the recitation of *Bardo Thodol* continues for 49 days.

9. **Conclusion of Funeral Rites:** After the completion of reading *The Tibetan Book of the Dead* in 49 days, the final farewell is bid to the departed by burning *spang-pu.* The ashes collected this time are mixed with clay, and miniature *stupas* called *sa-tschha* are formed out of it and placed in the open areas, like a hedge

---

22. In Tibetan Buddhism, in areas where enough firewood is not available, forest burial and cave burials are the alternative choices adopted for body disposal. The earth burial is not recommended because of the belief that the consciousness has the capacity to wander without a body in the intermediate stage and might get back into its dead body and become a vampire. This is perceived as a very dangerous phenomenon. So cremation is the most suitable method. However, if it can't happen, sky and cave burials are opted but after three to four days, when the flesh is consumed by the birds, the leftover is collected and crushed further, mixed with clay or some other edible stuff like flour, and balls are made out of it; it is again thrown out in forests or caves so that they are also consumed by the birds.

along the hills and caves, etc. These can be retained by the family as a memory of the deceased and placed in the altar of the home. This marks the end of funeral rites in Tibetan Buddhism.

Thus, in Tibetan Buddhism, very intricate death-related practices are prescribed. Believing that the consciousness in its disembodied state is vulnerable to distractions, right from the moment of death till final disposal and even after that, it is the prerogative of lamas to ensure the smooth transition of consciousness from the physical body to its new birth. The prescribed rituals are meant so that the deceased sails through the intermediary phase smoothly and gets a good rebirth.

Christianity

In almost all the denominations of Christianity, one of the duties of the church is to express communion with the deceased and the bereaved family. In Christian tradition, a variety of practices pertaining to death and dying prevail. In Roman Catholicism, the rituals are very intricately prescribed with very minute detail in terms of the role of the priest, protocols on their costumes, colours of robes, etc. In other denominations like Protestantism and sects that emerged thereafter, the rigid patterns of dealing with death do not prevail. So, in this book, I have listed out the major ones, gathered from the sacred texts and heard from the priests in different churches in Chandigarh.

Practices on Anticipation of Death

In Christianity, there are seven sacraments prescribed in almost all the denominations, namely, Baptism, Confirmation, Eucharist, Holy Orders, Holy Unction, Marriage, and Penance.[23] Out of

23. 'The Seven Sacraments', http://www.jesuschristsavior.net/Sacraments.html

these, a few are prescribed for the deceased on the anticipation of death. With Baptism itself, Christians are given assurance by the church that every individual who is baptised will be taken by Christ in his grace and will surely get a place in heaven. So, Christians die with this assurance that death is the beginning of their eternal life with God. However, Sacraments of Penance, Eucharist, Anointing of the Sick, and the Last Blessing (particularly in Roman Catholicism) are prescribed for the deceased on the anticipation of death. These are meant to prepare the dying person's soul for death.

- **Sacrament of Penance (Confession)/Absolution**: This ritual is meant for the forgiveness of sins. Theologians believe that Christ instituted the priesthood for two primary functions: to forgive sins and to administer the sacrament of Eucharist. This forgiveness of sins is done through the ritual of confession. It is one of the important sacraments in Christianity (across all denominations). An underlying biblical teaching is that if humans have to experience salvation, they must repent and believe that confession offers a means of reconciliation with God. It is considered to be the first step towards the priestly assistance for the dying. The Roman Ritual (I, cap. iv, 8) indicates that the priest is supposed to draw upon all the resources of his prudence and charity to obtain a confession from the sick person (Deathbed Confessions and Conversions). However, if the deceased is not in a condition to speak for him/herself, the priest offers prayers requesting forgiveness for the sins of the deceased from God. The idea is to give assurance to the dying that his/her sins are forgiven.
- ***Eucharist or Holy Communion* (*Viaticum* in Latin)**: Eucharist is connected to the death of Christ, and the ritual is a symbol of being witness to Christ's death. In the New Testament, the event of the Last Supper of Jesus is documented, where, before his day of trial, Jesus offered a piece of bread and shared from

his wine with his disciples, calling it his blood and flesh. This event is the origin of the Eucharist ritual. It is noted in the texts that when Christ instituted the Holy Eucharist, in the presence of apostles, he took bread, blessed and broke it, and gave it to his apostles, and said:

"'All of you drink of this; for this is My blood of the new covenant which is being shed for many unto the forgiveness of sins;"

Finally, He gave His apostles the commission, "Do this in remembrance of Me."'
(Matthew 26:27)

Since then, and with the manifestation of the church (all major denominations and sects), the Eucharist is an inevitable part of the church's liturgy. It is believed that priests exercise their power to change bread and wine into the body and blood of Christ by repeating, at the Consecration of the Mass, the above-quoted words of Christ. It is prescribed that the sacrament be done for the ill or dying person as well. After the confession, the reception of the Holy Eucharist is done for the dying person by the priest. Eucharist for the deceased is carried out carefully, and all efforts are made to awaken the deceased to participate and receive the last communion.

- **Anointing of the Sick/Extreme Unction/Holy Unction:** When a Christian is very sick, the priest anoints the person with oil in a special ritual of healing called Anointing of the Sick. This sacrament is administered to the sick, the dying, and to those who are terminally ill or are about to undergo surgery, for the recovery of their health and for spiritual strength. The ritual is meant for not just physical healing but also for mental and spiritual healing. It is believed that this sacrament was instituted by Christ and later proclaimed by St James. It is done by anointing the deceased with blessed oil accompanied by prayer.

Only a priest can validly administer it. Through this sacrament, the church continues the healing ministry of Jesus. In the past, this sacrament was often kept strictly for those close to death. In more recent years, the church has encouraged greater use of this sacrament for illness, which is not necessarily life-threatening. Particularly for the dying, this is carried out along with confession and reception of the Eucharist. While performing the ritual, Psalms from the Bible are read. According to the Latin church, anointment is essential for the five sense organs: the eyes, ears, nostrils, mouth, and hands, but there is diversity in custom in different schools of Christianity.

- **Apostolic Benediction or the Last Blessing:** After Holy Unction, the prescribed practice for the dying is the last blessing. This rite involves the chanting of the Holy name of Jesus, at least mentally, by the deceased. This is seen as a gesture of resignation by the dying person. It is an expression of willingness to accept one's sufferings in reparation for sins and submitting humbly, entirely to the will of God.

These practices are prescribed when the death of the person is anticipated. However, in the cases where the deceased has lost consciousness due to an accident, seizures, etc., conditional forgiveness is imparted, the Eucharist is omitted, and Extreme Unction and Last Blessings are given by the priest. It is prescribed that in cases when the deceased is unable to make a confession, Extreme Unction may prove to be the most effective means of alleviation.

According to the theologian Rev. Father Juan Bautista Ferreres, in recent times, due to prolonged hospitalisation and use of life support systems, it is not possible to determine the considerable time before the moment of death to carry out these rituals for the dying. So, absolution and Extreme Unction can even be given after the deceased has been declared dead. The most important prerequisite for carrying out these rites is assurance that the deceased was baptised. If not, then the priest is supposed to administer Baptism as well (Ferreres, J.B., 1906)[24]. Therefore, in Christianity, the sacraments for the dying are carried out in all conditions, and it's the prerogative of the church to provide assistance to the deceased in the last hours of life.

Practices Prescribed on Death

Immediately after death, the priest is called to recite a prayer called the 'Recommendation of Departing Soul'. However, in the absence of a priest, it is recommended that these prayers be recited by the family members and friends present at the time of death. The Holy Name of Jesus is recited, and the following verses are whispered in the ear of the deceased:

> *'Into thy hands, Lord, I commend my spirit;'*
> *'O Lord, Jesus Christ spirit, receive my spirit;'*
> *'Holy Mary, pray for me;' and*
> *'Mary Mother of grace, Mother of mercy, do thou protect me from the enemy and receive me at the hour of my death.'*[25]

Body Preparation

Washing of the corpse is a mandatory practice prescribed for preparing the body. As discussed earlier, in Christianity, the body is also given equal importance as the soul, so there are certain peculiarities prescribed for the dressing of the corpse. For the laity, it is recommended that the deceased's body be dressed in a decent outfit (new or the favourite clothes of the deceased). The body is decked up neatly. In Western societies, even the embalming of the

---

24. Ferreres, J. B. (1906). Death Real and Apparent in Relation to the Sacraments: A Physiologico-Theological Study . Miami: Hardpress Publishing.

25. 'Preparation for Death', http://www.newadvent.org/cathen/04660c.htm

body is prevalent. The idea is to make the corpse look good. Also, putting up the cross on the deceased and lighting a candle in front is a mandate. However, in the event of the death of the clergy, it is prescribed that they have to be attired in their religious costume and adorned with vestments (liturgical garments) according to their designation in the church's hierarchy. The body is placed in the coffin, and the face is not covered until burial.

Rites Observed at church

After the body is ready, the next step is taking the body to the church. In Roman Catholicism, it is prescribed that the parish[26] priest go to the house of the deceased with clerics carrying a cross and the stoup of holy water. Before the coffin is removed from the house, holy water is sprinkled on it and prayers are offered. Then the procession leaves for the church. Black is the colour code prescribed for mourning. So the clergy assisting in the process wear black gowns. Behind the priest, the coffin is carried by the bearers, or it may be drawn on the hearse. Mourners carry the lighted candles. Prayers are recited as the procession moves. The coffin is placed on a pedestal, and the candles are lit around. For the laity, the prescribed direction is facing towards the altar (feet pointing towards the altar), just like they sit in the church while praying. The clergy and the bishops are laid in the opposite direction from the layperson. The underlying idea seems to be that the bishop (or priest) in death should occupy the same position in the church as while alive, i.e., facing his people whom he taught and addressed in the church. The mourners observe the deceased, and collective prayers are recited. This service is called a vigil or wake.

26. Parish is the territorial division of a church. The Christians residing in a particular area register with the church in the territory, and the priest in that church is responsible for offering pastoral care to the members in that very territory.

Exequial Mass: The Mass[27] of Christian Burial

According to the funeral liturgy, the Mass in the presence of the body of the deceased is held in the church. In this Mass, the priest provides the full meaning of the Eucharist sacrifice of Jesus Christ. Here, the family is consoled and reminded that the deceased, who was baptised in Christ, still lives on and there is assurance of his/her resurrection. Then the congregation is asked to offer tributes to the deceased, and the Mass concludes with the final blessing. This ceremony is called the Exequial Mass.[28] Thereafter, the body is sprinkled with holy water and is ready to be taken to the funeral grounds.

Body Disposal and the Practices at the Graveyard

In biblical tradition, different methods of disposing of dead bodies have prevailed. There is evidence of cremation and sky burials. The preferred method in ancient Israel was earth burial, but that was a custom, not a commandment.[29] However, certain elements in the scripture point out that burial in the earth was the most accepted practice of body disposal. A very popular one is: God said to Adam some 6,000 years ago: '*For dust you are, and to dust you will return*' (Genesis 3:19). In early biblical scriptures, many instances of earth burial are mentioned. Abraham, the first biblical

---

27. Mass is the central act of worship in the life of a Catholic. Going to Mass is about spending time with God, but also receiving his grace (inner strength to live the Christian life). The name 'Mass' comes from the final blessing said by the priest in Latin '*Itemissaes*' meaning 'to send out' as Jesus Christ sent his disciples out to the world to take his teaching to them. http://www.thepapalvisit.org.uk/The-Catholic-Faith/FAQ-on-Faith/1-10/What-is-a-Catholic-Mass

28. An Exequial Mass is the Mass directly connected with the obsequies and is celebrated on the day of death or the day of burial. http://www.sspx-uk.com/index.php?option=com_content&view=article&id=91&Itemid=77

29. 'What Does the Bible Say About the Cremation of a Dead Body?' http://www.truthortradition.com/articles/what-does-the-bible-say-about-the-cremation-of-a-dead-body

patriarch, went to a great deal of trouble to buy a cave for burying his beloved wife, Sarah (Genesis 23:3–20). Later, his sons, Isaac and Ishmael, also buried their father alongside Sarah, and that became the family grave for the Old Testament patriarchs and matriarchs. The Israeli and Judah kings were buried along with their ancestors.

In the New Testament also, there is mention of the burial of John the Baptist, Lazarus, Stephen, and of the Lord Jesus. As the core tenet of Christianity is the idea of the resurrection of Jesus from his grave, so burial in the earth became the accepted way to dispose of the dead in Christian tradition. The burial law of the church indicates that every individual has the right to choose the burial grounds where they wish to have their mortal remains interred. One can express the desire in the will, or even the testimony of a near kin or confessor.[30] It is acceptable to know the desire of the deceased. However, in the event of no such desire expressed by the deceased, the person is entitled to be buried in his/her parish's burial grounds. It has also been stated that in earlier times, the clergy/priests/cardinals/bishops were privileged to be buried within the boundaries of the church. Before placing the body in the grave, the following rites are performed:

1. **Absolution:** Reciting special prayers for the forgiveness of sins is called the absolution rite. After the Mass in the church is over, the congregation proceeds towards the graveyard, where the rite of absolution is performed. Certain prayers to pardon the deceased are recited over the corpse before it is laid in the grave. Reciting these prayers before burial is considered obligatory and meant not to be omitted. The following prayer is recited:

   'O God, Whose attribute it is always to have mercy and to spare, we humbly present our prayers to Thee for the soul of Thy servant N,

30. The priest who hears confessions.

which Thou has this day called out of this world, beseeching Thee not to deliver it into the hands of the enemy, nor to forget it forever, but to command Thy holy angels to receive it, and to bear it into paradise; that as it has believed and hoped in Thee it may be delivered from the pains of hell and inherit eternal life through Christ our Lord. Amen.'[31]

Thereafter, the priest makes the round of the coffin and sprinkles holy water. After the absolution, the body is carried to the grave, and as the procession moves along, the verses are chanted. There exists a variety of verses in different denominations and sects; however, the following are the popular ones:

'For as much as it has pleased Almighty God to take out of this world the soul of__________, we therefore commit his/her body to the ground, earth to earth, ashes to ashes, dust to dust, looking for that blessed hope when the Lord Himself shall descend from heaven with a shout, with the voice of the archangel, and with the trump of God, and the dead in Christ shall rise first. Then we, which are alive and remain, shall be caught up together with them in the clouds to meet the Lord in the air, and so shall we ever be with the Lord, wherefore comfort ye one another with these words.'[32]

2. **Blessing of the *Sepulchrum* (Tomb):** The next prescribed practice is the blessing of the tomb; mandatory if the grave is dug for the first time and not used before. The following verse is recited:

'"I am the resurrection and the life," saith the Lord;
he that believeth in me, though he were dead, yet shall he live:
overliveth and believeth in me shall never die.
I know that my Redeemer liveth.'[33]

---

31. 'Christian Burial', http://www.newadvent.org/cathen/03071a.htm
32. https://bible.org/article/committals-grave-site
33. Allien, T. (1797). *The Book of Common Prayer.* New York.

3. **Lowering the Body and the Final Petition:** After blessing the grave, the most solemn rite is lowering the coffin into it. One more time, holy water is sprinkled, and the following is recited:

   'We therefore commit (his/her) body to the ground;
   earth to earth, ashes to ashes, dust to dust;
   in the sure and certain hope of the Resurrection to eternal life.'

There is the tradition of covering the coffin and the face of the deceased after lowering the body in the grave (precisely done by the son or a close kin) and of throwing some dust/mud into the coffin while reciting a short prayer for the deceased. The grave is covered, and the flowers and wreaths[34] are offered.

Memorials

Christianity prescribes following memorial practices to be observed after a few days of burial.

1. ***Requiem Mass*** **(Memorials)**: In Christian tradition, the third, seventh, thirtieth, and fortieth days after burial are marked for holding a memorial service for the deceased. There is slight variation in specifying the days, like in Roman Catholics it's these days, somewhere its third and the thirtieth, and for others it is seventh and the fortieth; however, the rationale is that these days are symbolically linked to the day of the burial of the Christ, the day of his rising again (resurrection), and he being seen by disciples upto forty days before he ascended to heaven. The Mass for the dead is celebrated on all these days at the parish church. It is sung with the opening line, '*Give them eternal rest, O Lord*'. The special set of prayers and

34. Wreath is a circular flower bouquet. In Christianity, it is a symbol of eternal life, representing the beginning of a new eternal life after physical death.

verses is recited, called observing the 'Office of the Dead' in liturgical language. Collective meals are shared in the memory of the deceased. Friends and family visit the grave and offer flowers. Other than these days, the Requiem Mass is held on the annual death anniversaries (especially the first), birthdays, or other special days related to the deceased.

2. **All Saints' Day:** In the Catholic church, 1st November is marked as All Saints' Day. It is a solemn Holy day, dedicated to the saints of the church who have reached heaven. It is prescribed that it's a Holy Day of Obligation.[35] It was instituted in Rome before 373 C.E. The celebrations vary in different cultures, like a feast in the church, celebrations at home, visiting the graves and offering flowers and candles, etc.

3. **All Souls' Day:** Since the early eleventh century, in Christian tradition, in various denominations, particularly amongst Roman Catholics, Eastern Orthodoxy, and a few other denominations, the next day after All Saints' Day, i.e., 2nd November, is observed to remember and commemorate all dead souls. The celebration is associated with the doctrine that the souls of the faithful who at death have not been cleansed from the temporal punishment due to venial (not seriously too wrong) sins and from attachment to mortal sins, could not attain the bliss of heaven. So, through the prayers on this day, an attempt is made to help them attain full sanctification and moral perfection. This rite is prescribed for those Christian denominations, particularly Roman Catholics, who believe in Purgatory. Amongst the Protestant denominations, this day is celebrated in a secular light and not a religious obligation because of their disbelief in Purgatory.

---

35. A feast on which the faithful are obliged to hear Mass and abstain from servile work. In Christianity, days like Easter Sunday, Christmas, All Saints' Day, etc., are Holy Days of Obligation.

Therefore, in Christianity, in the event of death, the prescribed practices include blessing the dying by the sacraments of penance, Holy Unction, and Eucharist. The common prescribed practices amongst all denominations range from the preparation of the body, Mass at the church, final burial, and memorials. In all these phases, the priest of the parish's church has a very important role to play; both performing the prescribed rites for the deceased and giving moral support to the bereaved. Interestingly, the use of the word 'celebration' in the context of death is often found in the Christian texts. This indicates that death is not to be mourned. It appears that Christianity preaches the celebration of death as it is the beginning of the eternal life of their loved ones.

Islam

Islam also prescribes a variety of death-related practices, ranging from the moment of anticipation of death till the final disposal. Islam also preaches to its followers that they should always remember death in their everyday lives. It is one such religious faith that prescribes that the present life is a preparation for eternal life. Sayyid Muhammad Rizvi, in his article on 'What You Should Do Just Before Death', and Muhammad Husein Kermali, in his work on 'Burial Rituals', elaborate on the following death-related practices prescribed in Islam:

1. **Life in Preparation for Death:** Islam preaches that the present life is to be devoted to the preparation of eternal life after death. So, preparing for death is a lifetime job. Every individual is accountable for his/her deeds in the eyes of the Almighty. So, one must try to fulfil one's obligations towards the 'Creator' (*Allah*) and lead life as prescribed in the Quran. Remembering death in daily life activities is encouraged in Islamic teachings. Prophet Muhammad has preached that one should always be reminded of his/her death and life must be lived like a traveller passing through. Visiting the graves frequently is encouraged

so that one is reminded of one's end always. The Prophet spoke often of death, and the Quran is filled with warnings of the dangers of ignoring one's mortality and of not preparing for death before it is too late. Attending funerals is not considered a morbid exercise; in fact, Muslims are encouraged to do the same. Also, in Islam, it is necessary to include the subject of death in regular discussions. Muhammad said, '*Make much mention of the destroyer of delights, which is death.*'

Islam does not preach monastic life, but it's encouraged to be devoted to *Allah* while leading a life of a householder. Getting married and having children are considered *Allah's* blessings. Prophet, too, was a married man. But, while living as a householder, specific religious duties are considered mandatory. For instance, offering five daily prayers is a mandatory practice that actually reflects the different stages of a man's life, reminding him/her of the end. A good Muslim doesn't have to renounce the materialistic world but should lead a life dedicated towards the five pillars of Islam. Therefore, in Islam, present life is considered an important part in the journey of the *ruh* (spirit) that transits with death and ends with the permanent settlement in either *Jannah* (heaven) or *Jahannum* (hell).

2. ***Al-Wasiyya* (Islamic Will)**: In Islam, making a Will is prescribed as a religious obligation for Muslims. It is preached that before death, a Muslim must perform certain duties, namely, payment of his/her debts, if any, and execution of his/her Will.

> '*It is the duty of a Muslim who has anything to bequeath not to let two nights pass without writing a will about it.*'[36]

Islam prescribes the following points to be kept in consideration while making a Will:

36. Noted in Sahih Al-Bukhari (one of the six Hadiths of Sunnis).

- In order to return the debts, one has to write clearly what was borrowed from whom, enabling the executor of the Will to return it to the rightful owner.

- In Islam, two-thirds of one's property has to be given to the legal heirs, and within that, the fixation of shares for all heirs is defined. However, for the remaining one-third, the individual can exercise his/her discretion. So, while making a will, it is directed that one must clearly state any charity or donations one wishes to make with that one-third of the property.

- While writing the Will, Islam permits one to include any religious obligations which one could not fulfil and wants to be done by others. For instance, prayers, if any, fasting, *hajj* (pilgrimage), etc. For the same, it is required by the deceased to specify from where to take the expenses for these religious obligations that he/she wishes to be fulfilled after death.

- Lastly, it is also directed that in the Will, one must mention notes asking for forgiveness from brethren, for whatever wrong one may have done in his/her lifetime.

Thus, it appears that Islam preaches very practical guidelines for the deceased and also for the bereaved as part of religious duty itself. It is encouraged that one must express one's wishes clearly, so that there is no confusion left afterwards, and the deceased dies in a peaceful state of mind.

Practices on the Anticipation of Death *(Ehtezar)* and at the Moment of Death

Before Death

When death is anticipated and the deceased may or may not be in the state of *saqaratul mawt* (intensive pain), it is recommended that the *muhtadar* (dying person) be laid in such a position that if he/she were to sit, he/she would face the direction of Mecca (called *Qiblah*). Also, it is recommended that the dying person should be moved to his/her usual place of prayer in the home, only if it does not cause any kind of pain or inconvenience. Also, making him/her recite the *Shahadah* (testimony of faith) is prescribed. In this declaration, a dying person reaffirms his faith in *Allah* and Prophet Muhammad:

> *'I have accepted Allah as the Lord; Muhammad as the Prophet; Islam as the religion; Quran as the book of God; Ka'bah as Qiblah.*
>
> *And I believe that surely the Hour of Doom will come in which there is no doubt; and that Allah will resurrect all those who are in their graves. And I believe that the reckoning of our deeds is the truth; Paradise is the truth, and Hell is the truth.'*[37]

Further, it is advised that the deceased should recite *surahs* and *ayats* from the Quran. It is believed that it helps to ease the moments of *saqarat* (pain) and helps in relieving the dying from the pangs of death.

On Death

Soon after the death, the following steps are recommended in Islam:

- Close the eyelids and mouth of the dead person; the two jaws are to be tied with a cloth strip around the head, so that the mouth does not open.
- Straighten the arms and legs of the deceased; two toes are to

37. Rizvi, S.M. (n.d.). *What You Should Do Just Before Death.* Retrieved 2 June 2020, from www.al-islam.org: https://www.al-islam.org/articles/what-you-should-do-just-death-sayyid-muhammad-rizvi

be tied together, and the arms are to be placed on the two sides of the body.

- The dead body has to be shrouded in a clean sheet, preferably white in colour.
- Switch on the light in the room where the body is kept.
- *Wali* (next kin), if absent, has to be informed immediately. *Wali,* or the personal representative appointed by the deceased in the will, is responsible for all after-death rituals.
- *Ayats* from the Quran are to be recited until the body is taken for cleaning.

3. **Practices for the Preparation of the Dead Body for Final Disposal:** According to *Sharia,* there are four important stages in after-death rituals, namely, *Ghusl* (washing), *Kafan* (shrouding), *Salatul Mayyit or Namaz-e-Janaza* (funeral prayer), and *Dafan* (burial). Certain elements in these rituals are considered as *wajib* (obligatory acts), and some are considered as *mustahab* (recommended acts).

Ghusl-e-Mayyit (Ritual to Wash the Corpse)

Giving three *ghusls* (washing three times) to a Muslim's dead body is considered *wajib* in *Islam.* However, before beginning the bath in the ritualistic manner, it is mandatory to remove all dirt and oily substances, if any, from the body of the deceased. If there is any *najasat* (urine, stool, blood, etc.) on any part of the body, it is obligatory to remove it before the ghusl. Bathing of the corpse is done in three steps; firstly, a very small quantity of *sidr (berry or lotus leaves)* is added to the water and the body is cleansed with it; secondly, water is mixed with camphor and again the body is washed; and thirdly, the body is finally cleaned with clear water.

The important aspect while performing *ghusl* on the corpse is that, at every step, before commencing, the performer has to make a *neeyat (*an intention to do an act for *Allah)* and declare that he/she is performing *ghusl* with *sidr*, camphor, and water. *Neeyat bandhna* is considered an important aspect for all religious acts in Islam. For instance, while performing the *ghusl,* the performer says, *'I am washing this body with camphor water Wajib Qurbatan Ilallah.'*[38] Thereafter, the body is gently dried with a clean towel. Also, certain precautions are recommended while performing *ghusl* on the dead body:

a. It is considered mandatory that those who are bathing the dead body must have performed *Mase Mayyit* (an act of bathing themselves before touching the body). If that cannot happen, it is recommended that the person performing *ghusl* should make *wudhu* (the act of ablution done before prayers).

b. It is compulsory to cover the body, particularly the *auwra* (private parts) with a sheet or any other kind of cover while washing. It is *haraam* (sinful act) to look at the private parts of a *mayyit* (dead body).

c. The recommended method for washing the body is *ghusl tartibi*, which means bathing in a sequence from head to neck and the right side of the body first and then the left side. *ghusl irtimsi* (immersion of the body into a river, pool, etc.) is forbidden.

d. It is recommended that during the *ghusl,* the body must be laid in the direction that his/her soles must face *Qiblah*.

e. The person giving *ghusl* should be a Muslim, preferably a *Shia Ithna-Asheri* (adult, sane, and should know the basic,

38. Kermali, M.H. (n.d.). *Burial Rituals.* Retrieved 23 March 2020, from www.al-islam.org: https://www.al-islam.org/printpdf/book/export/html/17906

essential rules of *ghusl)*. He/she should belong to the same gender as the deceased.

f. While performing *ghusl,* it is recommended to recite *surah/ ayats* of the Quran and *dua* (prayer) for the *marhum* (deceased) rather than keeping quiet or chatting.

g. It is considered *haraam* to take any remuneration for giving *ghusl.* If any remuneration is paid and the person receives it as an earning, *ghusl* will be *batil* (void). The person who gives *ghusl* to the dead body should keep the *neeyat* of *Qurbatan Ilallah* (obedience to and for the pleasure of *Allah*) while performing this act.

h. Water should not be *mudhaf* (have changed its smell and colour) when mixed with *sidr* and camphor.

i. In some writings, the use of perfumes after *ghusl* is also mentioned.

j. It is also specified that in case water is not available or the body has open and bleeding wounds or is partially crushed, or any other valid reason for abstaining from using water, then three *Tayammums* (Islamic act of dry ablution using sand and dust) should be given. The person performing this rite is supposed to strike his palms on the earth and then wipe them on the face and the back of the deceased. If possible, one must use the hands of *mayyit* (dead body) to perform *Tayammum.*

Kafan-e-Mayyit (Shrouding the Corpse)

The second step in body preparation is *kafan* (*wajib* act). It refers to shrouding or systematically wrapping the body with three obligatory clothes for men and five obligatory clothes for women. As a precaution, it is mentioned that each of the three pieces of cloth used for the *kafan* should not be transparent so that the body becomes visible. The following pieces of *kafan* are considered mandatory:

a. ***Loin Cloth* (*Lungi*)**: It is an apron-like cloth worn around the waist. It is meant to cover from the navel to the foot; even better if it covers the body from the chest to the feet.

b. ***Tunic Shirt:*** It is a piece of cloth that covers the body from the shoulders to the knees, preferably even to the ankles.

c. ***Inner Wrapper* (Sheet Cover)**: A large sheet of cloth that covers the entire body. As a precaution, it should be long and wide enough so that the front and the back parts overlap, and the top and the bottom ends can be tied with a string.

Other than these three, an additional two pieces are recommended to cover the head and neck of the female deceased. A turban is another piece of clothing that is recommended to cover the head of males. The outer wrapper sheet for both males and females is an additional recommended piece for the *kafan.* It is suggested that the colour of the *kafan* be white. The process of wrapping, reciting the *surahs,* or *ayats* from the Quran is recommended. Lastly, both ends of the *kafan*, over the head and below the toes, are knotted.

Though the *kafan* covers the deceased fully, a provision is kept that the face is visible. However, only restricted people are allowed to see the face. If the deceased is female, all women can see, and only those men who are not eligible to marry that woman as per Islamic law are allowed; vice versa for men. Islam propounds that the body, after shrouding, is *pak* (pure), so any kind of impurity, if it occurs, must be removed, even if noticed in the grave. For instance, if the body is discharging waste matter (*najasat*), special precautions are to be taken while shrouding.

After the shrouding process is over, the body is laid in such a position that the right shoulder should face the *Qiblah*, implying that the deceased is ready to undergo the next step of *Salatul Mayyit* (funeral prayer).[39]

Salatul Mayyit or Namaz-e-Janaza (Funeral Prayer)

Funeral prayer is the next obligatory act. It is mandatory to perform *Namaz-e-Janaza* for the deceased of any age who used to pray in his/her lifetime and understood *mummaiz* (could distinguish good deeds from bad). It is recommended to perform *Namaz-e-Janaza* in the mosque and not in the graveyard or at home. Customarily, the *janaza* (funeral procession) proceeds towards the *kabristan* (graveyard) and halts at a nearby mosque to perform the funeral prayer. For carrying the dead body, the use of a coffin is forbidden in Islam, except for certain conditions, like accidental cases when the body is damaged. In normal conditions, the bed for carrying the body is sourced from the mosques.

The bier carrying the body is laid before the congregation, with its face towards the *Qiblah*. According to the Quran, performing the funeral prayer for the dead is one of the religious obligations of the Muslim community. *Namaz-e-Janaza* is performed with a specific method which is different from the routine *namaz*. Unlike the routine *namaz,* it is done in the standing posture. *ruku* (bowing) and *sajdah* (prostrating) are not allowed. However, for people participating in the congregation, it is compulsory to perform *wudhu* (ablution) in the same way as they do for their routine prayers. The *imam* (priest) stands right in the front, reciting loudly, and all others stand in rows and repeat the recitation after *imam*. After making *neeyat,* the prayer begins. It comprises five *takbirs* (saying *Allah hu Akbar*) followed by *duas* (prayers) for the deceased. These prayers are different for males, females, and children (below thirteen years of age).

---

39. Kermali, M. H. (n.d.). Burial Rituals. Retrieved March 23, 2020, from www.al-islam.org: https://www.al-islam.org/printpdf/book/export/html/17906

In interpretations of Islamic writings, there are opposing opinions on women's participation in funeral prayer. On the pretext of the right of the deceased on his/her Muslim brethren to perform *dua* for him/her, one school permits women to participate in it. However, in the pre-Islamic era, there were rituals of widows' chest-beating and tearing. Due to these women's participation in the funeral processions is restricted. But in the cases where *Namaz-e-Janaza* is read at home, women are allowed to participate.[40]

Dafan (Burial)

Dafan (burial) is the last *wajib* (obligatory) act meant for disposing of the body. It is mandatory to bury the body in a Muslim graveyard only. The body on the bier is placed, and a grave is dug nearby. Three times, the body is moved slowly to the grave; after pausing for a few seconds, it is kept back on the ground and lifted again. At the fourth time, it is finally lowered into the grave and is put to rest on its right side with the face towards the *Qiblah*. After the body has been laid in the grave, the tied ends of the *kafan* are unfastened, and some earth is put under the cheek of the *mayyit*. An earthen pillow is made with earth under the head to rest it a little above the ground.

Talqin (teach or explain a point) is then recited. In the Arabic language, the deceased is told about the two angels, *Munkar* and *Nakir*, who will visit the grave and will ask a few questions, and the deceased is supposed to give the correct answers. Those correct answers are also whispered for the deceased. Wooden planks are laid over the body, the grave is closed, and a mound of earth is formed. Islam discourages constructing a tomb over the grave.

---

40. https://www.al-islam.org/burial-rituals-muhammadhusein-kermali/after-death-rituals#method-namaz-e-mayyit

Post-Burial Practices

The literature did not reflect on any fixed practices to be performed after burial. However, in Islamic tradition, some post-burial practices are observed, and certain restrictions are maintained.

1. ***Salat-ul-Wahshat* (Prayer After Burial):** This *namaz is* performed usually on the first night of the burial between the routine evening (after sunset) and the night prayer. After the prayers, a *dua* is recited for the forgiveness and peace of the departed soul.[41]

2. **No Exhumation of Grave:** It is considered *haraam* (offence) to open the grave of a Muslim. However, there is no objection to doing so if the dead body has decayed. Digging up or destroying the graves of the descendants of *imams*, the martyrs, and the pious persons is considered *haraam,* even if they are very old.[42]

3. **Condolences:** It is recommended, in fact, considered as a religious, moral, and social duty of *mu'minin* (believers) that condolences are conveyed to the family of the deceased after the burial. With regard to the bereaved family, it is important that they should bear the loss with patience by often reciting verses from the Quran. Praying, paying s*adaqa* (alms) to the poor, and remembering the *marhum/marhuma* (deceased) in dua are the prevalent ways to remember the deceased.

4. **Visiting Graveyards:** Islam encourages visiting graveyards as a reminder of one's own death. Women are also allowed to visit the graves. But, there are certain principles for visiting the grave: (a) one should remember death and visualise oneself as lying in the grave; (b) worldly talks, jokes, and laughs should be avoided and, instead, recitation of the *surahs* of the

41. 'Rules for *Namaz-e-Mayyit*', http://www.islamic-laws.com/namazmayyit.htm

42. 'Rules Related to a Dying Person', http://www.sistani.org/english/book/48/2191/

Quran and *duas* for the dead buried in the cemetery should be practiced; (c) eating and drinking in the cemetery should be avoided; (d) it is recommended to visit either on Thursday or Friday.

Therefore, Islam prescribes a very detailed and rigid pattern to be followed in the event of death. Death is given so much importance in Islam that present life is perceived as the only opportunity to prepare for the post-death eternal life. The materialistic gains or losses of the present life are of no importance for deciding one's fate after death. Much focus has been given to conforming to the righteous code of conduct prescribed in their sacred texts. Practices like daily prayers, visiting graveyards, participating in funeral prayers, etc., are also the mediums that make an individual contemplate on his/her death and the life afterwards. A dead body is considered as *pak* (pure). Hence, Islam rules out any pollution caused by death. Rituals pertaining to death are portrayed as noble acts to be commenced with proper precautions by the learned people of the community.

Thus, across all five religions, death is far more than a biological event—it is a sacred transition shaped by diverse theological beliefs. Each tradition prescribes specific practices to guide the soul or consciousness after death, reflecting deeper views on the afterlife, rebirth, or liberation. While Hinduism and Tibetan Buddhism focus on assisting the soul through a complex post-death journey, Sikhism emphasises faith and remembrance over rituals. For Christianity (largely, across all denominations), the inevitable event of death offers a certainty to live ever after with God in his eternal bliss. The believers will be rewarded with eternal life, and non-believers will be accorded eternal damnation. Islam views death as a pivotal moment leading to eternal accountability. While for some religions, the presence of a corpse creates impurity, for others, after death, the being is in its purest state. Some believe that it is a pause in the endless life cycles; others preach that it is the end of life on the earthly plane and the beginning of life in some new plane, from where there is no coming back. These varied beliefs not only shape death rituals but also profoundly influence how followers live, preparing for what lies beyond t his life.

CHAPTER 4

Perceptions of Death and Its Related Aspects

In the light of the death philosophy of Hinduism, Sikhism, Buddhism, Christianity, and Islam, I interacted with the people following these religious faiths about their experience of dealing with the death of their loved ones. It was done with the technicalities of social science research. The profiles of the participants, the questions asked, and tabulated data of their responses can be found in Annexures A and B of the book (pages 255, 261). Through their personal stories and reflections, the chapter delves into how beliefs and practices shape people's perceptions of death, their grieving processes, and the meanings they derive from loss. By comparing the experiences of the bereaved across these five religious traditions, we gain insight into the diverse ways death impacts our lives and how different belief systems offer unique perspectives on coping with it. I also explored how closely their views on death and the related aspects align with the death philosophies of the religion they follow.

To begin with, to know how religiously inclined they are and how they practice their religious ways in daily life, I asked them how often they visited their place of worship (temple, gurudwara, monastery, church, and mosque)—whether daily, weekly, or just occasionally. Interesting patterns emerged.

Among Hindus, most described themselves as occasional temple-goers. Out of 60 respondents, 40 (about two-thirds) said they visit the temple only once in a while. A smaller proportion of 12 participants stated that they go weekly, and just eight said they make daily visits. A similar trend appeared among Sikhs. Every Sikh respondent reported going to the gurudwara, yet most (69%) said they visit only occasionally. Nine said they go every day, and six go weekly. For Buddhists, too, the majority—17 out of 22—said they visit their temple occasionally. Five said they go daily. Some explained that in Chandigarh, there aren't any monasteries and only one small temple, so they visit more regularly when they're back in their hometowns. The Christian respondents showed a slightly different pattern. Half of them said they attend church weekly, mainly for Mass. Roman Catholics usually go on Sundays, while Protestants and their sub-groups attend on Saturdays or Fridays, depending on their church. Ten respondents said they go to church daily, while only five described themselves as occasional visitors. In short, regular church-going is an important part of life for most Christians in our sample. For Muslims, prayer (*salat*) is central—it's one of the five pillars of Islam. The expectation is to pray five times a day, and 13 of the thirty-six male respondents said they do so at the mosque. One of them explained: '*A man's prayer is only counted when offered in the mosque.*' Ten others said they visit the mosque weekly, mainly for Friday prayers, while six go on special occasions like Eid or during Ramadan. Interestingly, the seven respondents who said they don't visit mosques at all were women. They explained that their tradition doesn't require or permit them to pray in mosques, but they still perform their five daily prayers at home.

About their daily prayer routines at home, among Hindus, prayer was woven into the household in many ways. Two-thirds of them said they pray more than once a day—most often twice, usually in the morning and evening. The forms of prayer varied: some read from prayer books, others lit lamps, and many joined their families in the evening *aarti*. A smaller group prayed just once a day, and a handful admitted they didn't follow a fixed routine at all.

'Chalte-firte path kar lete hain; jab mann karta hai; kabhi subah kar liya, kabhi raat ko,' (We pray casually while going about our day; whenever we feel like it; sometimes in the morning, sometimes at night)—a response that stood out amongst the Sikhs. About a third, however, said they make it a point to pray more than once daily, often reciting a *path* in both the morning and evening.

Buddhists stood out for their regularity. All of them prayed at home, and most—18 out of 22—said they pray several times a day, sometimes twice, sometimes even thrice. Their practices include lighting lamps before their deities and chanting Buddhist mantras. Only a small number said they limit themselves to a single prayer a day. Clearly, prayer is a central part of their everyday rhythm. Christians also described prayer as an important part of family life. The majority said they gather once a day, often in the evening before bedtime, for a family prayer. A smaller group said they pray twice daily, while a few explained that they don't have a set routine but remember God whenever they feel like. Muslims, unsurprisingly, were the most regular in prayer. Most of the respondents—an overwhelming majority—said they offer the five daily prayers as prescribed. A few said they pray less frequently, choosing instead to focus on Fridays, or to pray more intensively during Ramadan.

Looking at the bigger picture, nearly everyone reported some level of connection to their place of worship, whether daily, weekly, or occasionally. The most frequent daily visitors tended to be older people. The only group not visiting their place of worship were Muslim women, but that was because they were following their religious guidelines only. And, every single respondent said they pray at home, even if they confessed not to sticking to a strict schedule. Hence, all of them showed conviction towards their religious faith.

Fear of Death

People sometimes express fear of death, called thanatophobia.[1] For Sigmund Freud, this fear is not for one's own death: '*Our own death is indeed quite unimaginable, and whenever I make the attempt to imagine it I... really survive as spectators.... At bottom nobody believes in his own death, or to put the same thing in a different way, in the unconscious, every one of us is convinced of his own immortality*'.[2] He says that what one fears is not actually death, because while living, one has never died; there are some other hidden fears that manifest as fear of death.

However, another notable author, Ernest Becker, in his book *The Denial of Death*, contests Freudian thought and explains that death anxiety is real. Fear pertaining to death is a deep source of concern for people that generates many phobias in everyday life. He adds that people tend to deal with this death anxiety by attempting to deny death in their regular behaviour. Amongst important functions of society, one is to strengthen its individuals against death-related anxiety. Therefore, societies develop certain practices that contribute to death denial. Use of flowers for decorating the funerals, embalming, advanced medical systems, insurance schemes, etc., are some of the methods devised in modern societies to help people feel that there is no fear. Had there been no mechanism for the denial of death, the normalcy in society and its normal functioning would not have sustained.

---

1. The term 'thanatophobia' is derived from the Greek death God Thanatos.

2. Freud, S. (1953). *The Standard Edition of the Complete Psychological Works of Sigmund Freud* (Vol. 4). (pp 304) London: Hogarth Press.

Therefore, for Becker, death induces fear, and to deal with the fear, people deny death.[3]

Robert Kastenbaum, another famous psychologist, has opposing views from both Freud and Becker. He states that it is not that people always fear death or that death anxiety is always very high. All the fears, as well as joys, are influenced by the social learning experiences. Individuals may fear or may not fear death. It depends on what kind of social environment they have been socialised in. The fears also have the imprints of socio-historical circumstances.[4] For instance, the fear of death was prevalent in many preliterate societies throughout the world. In nineteenth-century Europe and America, the fear of being buried alive was widespread. In modern times, the fear of dying or being trapped in a persistent vegetative state or suffering from prolonged illness before death is expressed by people. Hence, for Kastenbaum, there is no standard version of fear of death; one's fears and anxieties pertaining to death are manifested from the social conditions and might change with time. However, looking at the prescribed death beliefs of various religious faiths, it appears that these faiths portray death as not the ultimate end of existence and assure some sort of continuity of life. These faiths prescribe that death has to be accepted as part of life and not be feared. With this backdrop, participants' fear of death was gauged. Respondents from different faiths were asked three questions: 'Do you fear your own death? Do you fear the death of a loved one? And do you participate in activities that put your life at risk?'

A majority of Hindu respondents said they were not particularly afraid of their own death. Yet, when it came to the thought of losing a loved one, nearly everyone admitted to being deeply fearful. When the discussion shifted to risky activities—things that could endanger life—only 40% said they sometimes

---

3. Becker, E. (1973). *The Denial of Death.* New York: Free Press.

4. Kastenbaum, R. (2000). *The Psychology of Death* (3rd ed.). NewYork: Springer.

took part in them, and most of these were younger people. Even then, many clarified that they usually weigh the risks and take safety precautions before doing anything dangerous. One man, for instance, shared that he once enjoyed fast driving, but after his father's death, he became too fearful and gave it up.

Sikh respondents spoke about death with remarkable boldness and simplicity. As prescribed in the Sikh religious texts, their words carried a tone of acceptance, even fearlessness '*Marna tan hai hi, darna kya fer?*' (Death is certain; what is there to fear about?); '*Bura lagega, par darr nahi hai*' (I will feel bad, but I am not afraid of it); '*Na, Waheguru jad marji bula len*' (Not scared at all, God can call me any time); '*Bas nam japp de hoye jaiye*' (I wish I could die chanting God's name); '*Darr nahi lagda par apne jande ne dukh hunda hai*' (I am not scared, but it is painful to see our loved ones dying). Also, many participants across different age groups even shared stories of the life-risking adventures they had taken on, almost an indicator that, though death is inevitable, they lead lives to the fullest.

Buddhist respondents admitted that they feared their own death and were also afraid of losing a loved one. '*Koi nahi marna chahta*' (Nobody wants to die); another confessed, '*Aisi baat karna bhi accha nahi lagta, hai na?*' (We don't even like talking about death, right?). And most of them said, '*Darr toh hai maut ka.*' (Yes, I am scared of death). Interestingly, despite their fear of death, most of them enjoy participating in activities that involve thrill and risk to life. When asked how they justify this contradiction, one respondent said, 'I like the thrill in life, but I don't want to die.' This stance is primarily because most of them come from the upper Himalayan region, where even daily chores involve a great deal of risk. Buddhist philosophy teaches that impermanence is a fundamental truth of life and that fear of death comes from failing to accept this impermanence. Remembering death and practising mindfulness on mortality are central practices across all Buddhist traditions.

Yet, our respondents' views didn't seem to echo these teachings. On probing further, it became clear that many of them were not fully aware of Buddhism's core ideas about death. Instead, because they are now living in a Hindu-dominated region, their understanding is shaped more by Hindu beliefs about the afterlife and rebirth. In other words, in a plural society, the dominant religion often leaves its imprint—even on how minorities think about something as universal as death.

The largest number (74%) of Christian respondents do not fear death. They opined that death is a reality of life, so they are not afraid. A few of them said that they fear death. One of them said, '*I am afraid because death is tragic and relatives and friends will be sad to see me dead, but, at the same time, I am also not afraid because I believe in Jesus Christ and I believe that after death, I will go to heaven with Christ.*' Another one said, '*My death would be a process towards eternal life of the soul, but dying can be unpleasant as it is associated with suffering, so I am afraid.*' Also, the largest number of respondents (60%) like to participate in the activities where the risk to life is involved. However, a few elderly respondents who spoke of not fearing death said they intentionally don't risk their lives. One elderly woman respondent, when quizzed about her interest in adventurous activities, uprightly said, '*It is suicidal! I pray for those who do it.*' On the whole, their responses were totally aligned with their religious philosophy. They seem to be assured to a great extent that death will lead them to a blissful, eternal life. A very large number (70%) 21 out of 36 Christian respondents also do not fear the death of their loved ones. This implies that their bold approach towards death is driven by their religious teachings. They were confident that they would be granted eternal bliss after resurrection, as they had been baptised in Christ's name.

It was fascinating to find that none of the Muslim respondents feared their own death. As some put it: 'What's there to be afraid of?', 'One day we all have to die', and 'There's nothing fearful about going to God's abode'. Yet, nine admitted they feared losing their loved ones, especially parents. They explained that it is not fear per se but the pain of loss that worries them.

Interestingly, unlike others, Muslim respondents showed no hesitation in discussing death. From childhood, daily prayers remind them of mortality—the five daily *namaz* symbolise life's journey from birth to death, while references to *Qiyamah* (the Day of Judgment) are common in everyday conversation. However, not fearing death didn't translate into reckless behaviour. Most of them avoid risky activities, explaining that life is God's gift and must be lived responsibly. As one said, 'Not fearing death doesn't mean I should jump into a crevasse. God has given us life and shown us the right way to live it.' Only ten, mostly younger, respondents enjoyed adventure and risk-taking. Overall, Muslim respondents appeared fearless about death itself but cautious about life, guided strongly by Islamic teachings that emphasise living righteously in preparation for the Day of Judgment.

Looking across the responses, a clear pattern emerges: Hindus and Buddhists tend to fear death, while Christians, Muslims, and Sikhs appear more accepting of it. For Hindus and Buddhists, the idea of an uncertain afterlife seems central to this fear. Both traditions speak of the soul's journey after death—Hinduism describes a wandering spirit that can even trouble the living, while Buddhism speaks of a transitional state that may be difficult or traumatic for the deceased. Since the next life's form or destination is unclear, uncertainty itself fuels anxiety. Interestingly, many Buddhists we spoke to seemed more influenced by Hindu ideas than by Buddhist teachings, which may explain why their fears echoed Hindu beliefs.

In contrast, Christians and Muslims expressed less fear of death. Their scriptures emphasise that there is no return to earthly life; the soul's fate is sealed, often with the hope of eternal peace in God's presence. This certainty offers reassurance. Similarly, Sikh respondents were largely fearless. For them, death is simply God's will, with no prolonged afterlife journey—*Akalpurkh* (God) has already determined the soul's destiny.

These findings echo Kastenbaum's view that fear of death is deeply shaped by one's social environment. Religious orientation, being such a vital part of that environment, provides either certainty or uncertainty—and with it, either peace or fear.

Death as a Theme of Discussion

The modernisation phase brought about huge transformations in society. Technological developments, speedy growth of capitalism, abundance of material comforts, and social security systems like insurance made people perceive that they had emerged stronger and that their daily life was secure. Processes of nature like ageing and death became a threat to this taken-for-granted ontological security.[5] In modern times, death recedes further and further from day-to-day human experience.[6] Johnson, in his article, 'Denial: The American Way of Death', notes: '*Modern America appears to be preoccupied with the preservation of youth and beauty, which is catered to by the plastic surgeon. Society seems content to cling to the illusion that life can last forever.*'[7] These statements coincide with the sequestration of death approach, which emphasises that, in modern times, death is a sequestrated and hidden phenomenon, not likely to be included in everyday experience. Even sociological studies in modernity

---

5. Giddens (1991) notes that the purchasing of ontological security through institutions and routines protects us from direct contact with madness, criminality, and death. By ontological security, he refers to the sense of order and continuity in relation to the events in which human beings participate and the experiences they have, in their day-to-day lives.

6. Moore, C.C., & Williamson, J.B. (2003). The Universal Fear of Death and the Cultural Response. In C.D. Bryant, *Handbook of Death and Dying*. Thousand Oaks, California: Sage.

7. Johnson, J.A. (16 November 2004). *Denial: The American Way of Death*. Retrieved 2 June 2020, from www.orthodoxytoday.org: http://www.orthodoxytoday.org/articles4/JohnsonDeath.php

contribute to the sequestration of death as they present it as a morbid and negative phenomenon.[8] Thus, in contemporary times, predominantly in Western societies, the natural reality of death doesn't fit into the meaningful and fulfilling part of social life, and is therefore bracketed and sidelined from everyday routine affairs. On the other hand, largely, all religions preach contemplation on death and prescribe various methods for the same. To explore whether the respondents discuss death or like to sequestrate it from everyday life affairs, they were asked whether they discuss death quite often, rarely, never, or on the occasion of someone's death.

'*Hai toh bahut* depressing *hi kyun baat karna.*' (It is very depressing, so why discuss?); '*Dil ghabrata hai soch ke bhi.*' (My heart sinks, even thinking about it.); '*Veham karte hain ghar mein.*' (Considered as superstitious in the family.), '*Sham ko aisi baatein nahi karte.*' (I don't talk about such things in the evenings.); 'TV *pe bhi kuch aaye aisa toh band kar dete hai.*' (We switch off the TV if something of this sort is telecast.); and '*Aisi baatein kaun karta hai!*' (Who talks about such topics!). These were the prominent responses from the Hindu respondents when they were quizzed about how often they talk about death. Most of them said that death is only discussed on the occasion of someone's death. While interacting with me, most of the Hindu respondents sobbed. A few also had goose bumps, and most of them even questioned me regarding my choice of such an area of research! Thus, it appears that the Hindu respondents avoid discussing death. For them, death is perceived as a negative subject and is sequestrated from everyday life. Not just sequestration, in Hinduism, avoidance of death is also shaped by the idea of *asauch* (ritual pollution) associated with death. This belief also explains why many Hindu respondents refrain from discussing the subject, as the notion of pollution attached to death creates a sense of discomfort.

---

8. Willmott, H. (2000). Death. So What? Sociology, Sequestration, and Emancipation. *The Sociological Review,* 48 (4), 649–665.

Among Sikh participants, too, death is rarely a subject of regular reflection. Although they may not openly fear it, most tend to ponder death only when confronted with someone's passing. This suggests that their perceptions do not fully align with the prescribed death beliefs in the Sikh texts; they, too, appear to sequestrate it.

Buddhism emphasises regular contemplation on death as a core tenet. Yet, when asked about it, one Buddhist woman responded, '*Koi nahi marna chahta, fir aisi baat kyun karni hai na?*' (Nobody wants to die, so why talk about such things?). Amongst Buddhist respondents, too, death is mostly a denied subject. They also reflect upon death only on the occasion of someone's death. During interviews, those who avoided the topic also appeared hesitant when speaking about the loss of their kin. This indicates that their perceptions diverge from the Buddhist teaching of death contemplation; they, too, tend to sequestrate death.

In Christianity, importance is given to remembering death in everyday life. In their sermons, Christian priests preach about remembering the event of the death and resurrection of Christ, and this is echoed in the responses of our participants. Most of the Christian respondents (80%) discuss death frequently, often linking it to daily prayers that recall Christ's sacrifice. Several explained that death is an undeniable reality, while one noted, 'A Christian believes in eternal life with God in heaven, so death has to be welcomed.' Only two respondents said they rarely discuss death, one admitting, 'I feel unhappy to talk about death because it is tragic.' Four others said they speak of it only during funerals; one reflected, 'I am reminded of my death whenever I visit the graveyard, but once I leave, I forget again.'

Notably, unlike respondents of other faiths, Christian respondents (men and women) showed no uneasiness while discussing the subject. Although all had witnessed the death of a near kin, talking about death didn't appear to be disturbing. For them, death is not a negative phenomenon but a passage to eternal life, aligning closely with Christian teachings. Interestingly, this is contrary to the sequestration of death approach that emerged in Western countries that are predominantly Christian societies.

Among the Muslim respondents, the majority said they often talk about death, describing it as '*Yeh toh sachai hai*' (It is the truth) and '*Is mein kuch* negative *nahi hai*' (There is nothing negative about it). A few revealed that they are reminded of death in their daily prayers, as in Islam, the five-time *namaz* (prayer) indicates the different phases of life from birth to death. One respondent noted that the thought of the Day of Judgment frequently brings death to mind. Several of them said they contemplate death only during the funerals. Nevertheless, the largest proportion of Muslims reported remembering death regularly, reflecting the teachings of Islamic texts.

Good Death and Preferred Place for Death

Different religions define a 'good death' in varying ways—some emphasise the manner of dying, while others view it as one that occurs naturally at home, surrounded by family and rituals. In modern times, however, death most often takes place in hospitals.[9] To explore this shift, respondents were asked whether their idea of a good death aligns with their religious teachings, and whether they would prefer to die at home, in a hospital, or elsewhere.

Hinduism does not explicitly categorise death as good or bad, but stresses the performance of prescribed rituals at the time of death for a better afterlife. On the idea of good death, common responses from most of the Hindu respondents were: 'Good death is disease-free death'; 'Dying at an appropriate age is good death'; 'Death after fulfilling all responsibilities is good'; 'Pain-free and sudden death is a good death'; etc. On the preferred place for

---

9. Elias, N. (2001). *The Loneliness of the Dying.* New York: Continuum. Nuland, S.B. (1994). *How We Die: Reflections on Life's Final Chapter.* New York: Vintage.

death, a large majority (87%) chose 'home', aligning with the idea of good death prescribed in Hinduism. However, the reasons for this preference were: 'At home, it would be pain-free death'; 'I would like to die in sleep as it would be less troublesome'; 'Sudden death is a good death'; 'I want to die without any suffering'; and 'Dying at home amongst loved ones is comfortable'. The remaining seven respondents expressed that they would prefer the hospital as the place of death. Their responses were: 'Death *toh* hospital *mein hi hoti hai, bimar padenge toh wahin leke jayenge*' (Death obviously happens at the hospital because when I will fall ill, I will be taken there only); 'There, one doesn't feel the physical pain'; 'The family members also don't suffer seeing their near ones in pain'. One respondent said that at the hospital, it will be easier for the doctors to take the organs that can be of some help, as she wished to donate all the organs that can be used after death. These responses came mostly from younger participants (20–30 years). Thus, while some preferences for hospital reflect secular motives, the majority's preference for home often reflects a wish for personal comfort rather than religious orientation. This suggests that Hindu respondents' perceptions of a 'good death' lean more toward material comfort than the scriptural emphasis on ritual performance.

Sikhism doesn't subscribe to the idea of good or bad death, though martyrdom for the cause of humanity, on religious duty, serving others, etc., is appreciated. Moreover, Sikhism prescribes that death occurring at any place can be ideal, if it comes after leading a life with contemplation on God's name and possessing virtues of truthfulness, humility, contentment, etc. Contrary to religious beliefs, the first thing that emerged amongst Sikh respondents was that they believed in the concept of a good death. Common responses on their idea of good death from most of them were, 'Dying at an age when free from all responsibilities'; 'Dying without pain is good'; 'Dying after the age of 80'; 'Dying in sleep'; 'Dying healthy without ailments is ideal'; 'After settling family'; *ghoomte-firte* (casually, hale and hearty); 'Dying sudden'; 'Disease-free'; etc. One respondent said, '*Path karde-karde chale jaiye*' (Death while praying is ideal); another said '*Sewa karde hoye marr jaiye*' (Death while serving others). Therefore, the responses of the majority suggest that, similar to Hindus, Sikh respondents' perceptions of a good death are also shaped more by material comforts than by religious teachings. Further, most of them (85%) preferred to die at home, citing reasons such as being surrounded by loved ones, dying in sleep, or experiencing a healthy and peaceful end. Six respondents (13%) chose hospitals, reasoning that medical support there could ensure a less painful death. Overall, the preference for home reflects a desire for comfort rather than alignment with Sikhism's core teaching of detachment from material ties and relations. This suggests that Sikh respondents' perceptions of a 'good death' are also inclined towards personal comfort rather than by religious ideals.

According to Buddhism, a good death means dying with the thoughts that lead to a rebirth in spiritually higher realms. Tibetan Buddhism, in particular, prescribes good death as dying in a wholesome mind (alert) so that consciousness can visualise the Clear Light and submerge into it, bringing an end to the birth-death cycle. However, in the phase of modernisation, death has shifted to hospitals. A deceased in the last phase of life is sometimes lying unconscious in well-equipped hospital settings, not even in a condition to comprehend the unknown surroundings, let alone dying in a 'wholesome mind'.

When asked about their idea of an ideal death and preferred place for dying, Buddhist respondents also largely framed their views around material goals. Common answers included: '*Saare kaam khatam hone ke baad*' (After finishing all tasks), '*Bacche* set *ho jayen*' (Once the children are settled), 'Free *ho jayen uske baad* death *aaye toh achi hai*' (After being free from worldly responsibilities), as well as dying healthy, without prolonged illness, or through a sudden, painless death. Notably, none of the responses reflected spiritual aspirations, such as dying with wholesome thoughts or attaining a rebirth in higher realms, as prescribed in Buddhist teachings. Regarding the place of death, most of them preferred to die at home, mainly for reasons of comfort. Three chose hospitals; one explained that unconscious death there would spare them pain—directly opposing the Buddhist emphasis on maintaining a 'wholesome mind' at death. Another respondent wished to die in the hills during an expedition, while one woman simply said, 'Death *achi nahi lagti, kahin pe bhi na aaye*' (I don't like death, so I wish it never comes, anywhere). These responses suggest that, like others Buddhist participants' views on good death were also shaped more by worldly concerns and personal comfort rather than by spiritual ideals, reflecting an underlying attitude of non-acceptance of death.

Christianity preaches that death in itself is good because it is only death that will lead them to an eternal, blissful life. However, getting baptised in Christ is of utmost importance for assurance of attaining bliss after death. Practices prescribed before dying, like anointment of the dying, Eucharist, etc., are considered important as a symbolic reassurance of resurrection to the deceased. Therefore, for Christianity, any death would be good if the deceased is baptised in Christ and whatever he/she does in life is for the love of God. Getting the opportunity to get prescribed sacraments performed while dying works like a cherry on the cake. While most of the Christian respondents also pointed towards material comforts, a few had a religious inclination too. The common responses from the former category were, 'Pain-free sudden death is good'; 'Death without suffering and prolonged illness'; '*Chalte-firte, bina sewa ke*' (Hale and hearty without being dependent upon others); 'Dying in sleep'; '*Bina bimaar huye*' (Without falling ill). One respondent said, 'Society *ke liye kuch acha karke jaana*' (Good death would be one that comes after contributing something better for society). A few of them said that a good death would be dying on a 'Holy Day',[10] and a few also said that they wished they could receive the last blessings before death.

On their preferred place of death, most of them (90%) wished to die at home; nobody preferred the hospital. The reasons given by most of them were that at home they will have their family around; the priest can come to bless; and 'Hospital *mein marne se pehle bahut kharcha hota hai, gharpe hi theek hai*' (The treatments at hospitals, prior to death are very expensive, so it is better to die at home); etc. One respondent expressed a wish to die in a church. Among those who selected 'Can't say', the common replies were: '*Jab marna hai toh kahin bhi mar jao, kya farak padhta hai*' (When one has to die, it can be anywhere, it doesn't matter), and 'I never thought about it, so don't know'. Thus, on the idea of a good death and preferred place of dying, Christian respondents' views reflect two tendencies: for some, the comfort and convenience of dying at home; for others, the desire to receive prescribed religious sacraments before death.

Unlike other faiths, Islam explicitly identifies *Shahadat* (martyrdom) as a good death—occurring in war, accidents, or while on religious duty. Among respondents, however, many associated a good death with comfort: dying at the right age, after fulfilling duties, in good health, without suffering, or in sleep. A few, though, linked it to spiritual ideals, such as dying in prayer, after completing *hajj*, or in a mosque. One young respondent strikingly said she wished to die in an accident: '*Mujhe toh Shahadat chaiye. Us se gunnah maaf hote hain aur seedha jannat milti hai!*' ('I want martyrdom, because it forgives sins and leads straight to heaven'). On the preferred place of death, the majority chose home, citing comfort. Seven, however, expressed

10. In Christianity, significant events in Christ's life are celebrated as Holy Days like Good Friday (he was crucified), Easter Sunday (he was risen from the grave), Christmas (his birthday), etc.

religious preferences, including dying in a mosque, during *hajj*, in an accident, or simply '*Allah jahan chahe*' (wherever God wills). Thus, while many Muslim participants also framed good death in terms of comfort and home, a strong religious inclination was also evident among some, reflecting both worldly concerns and deep religious aspirations.

Interestingly, on the idea of good death, there is unanimity amongst the respondents of all religious faiths. For most of them, irrespective of gender, age, class, and education, a good death is one that occurs after the accomplishment of material desires. Likewise, the largest number in all the categories prefer home as a place of death because of the comforts of dying at home.

Perceptions on Doctrine of the Afterlife Journey and Existence of Other Realms

As previously discussed, these religious traditions prescribe that the physical body ceases to exist, while the disembodied self embarks on a journey. They also hold that there are other realms beyond the earthly plane. Participants from all faiths were asked whether they believe in the afterlife journey of the soul, consciousness, spirit (or *ruh*), and the existence of otherworldly realms as described in the faith they follow.

Hinduism prescribes that after death, the soul, based on the *karmic* impressions it has gathered in the previous life, halts at temporary realms (physical worlds other than earth), heaven, or hell. The largest proportion (70%) of Hindu respondents stated that they do not believe in the existence of heaven and hell. The common responses were: 'All pleasures and pains are in this life only'; 'No one knows what happens beyond'; 'Who has seen it?'; 'Nine months in the womb is hell, as that is such a suffocating time for the soul'; etc. These responses indicate that the perceptions of Hindu respondents on this aspect do not correspond to the prescribed beliefs in Hindu religious texts. Interestingly, there appears to be a contradiction in their perceptions; most of them fear death, and perhaps due to the uncertainty attached to the fate of the deceased after death, but at the same time, they also do not believe in the afterlife journey prescribed in their sacred texts.

In Sikhism, heaven and hell are described as states of consciousness and not as real realms. The largest majority of 93% do not believe in the existence of heaven and hell. The instant response from most of them was, '*Sab kuch eithe hi hai!*' (Everything is here only). These perceptions of the Sikh participants fully align with the Sikh doctrine.

Buddhism prescribes that just like the earth, there are other realms of existence in this large universe. For instance, the *Theravada* doctrine talks about realms like *arupadhatu* (Godly, immaterial and formless realm) and *rupa dhatu* (ghostly realm with form but only subtle matter), where, like earth, living beings are subject, to life and death. In Tibetan Buddhism, too, other than this material realm (*nirmanakaya*), *dharmakaya* (Buddha Mind), and *sambhogakaya* (spiritual realm) also exist. All Buddhist respondents believe in the existence of other realms. In their words: '*Marne ke baad aatma jaata hai*' (The soul goes there after death); '*Swarg or nark hota hai*' (heaven and hell exist); '*Jaise aap mein swarg hota hai vaise hamare mein bhi karam ke hisab se milta hai*' (Like in Hinduism, we too have heaven where we reach according to our deeds). For them, other realms do not exist in parallel but are different abodes where disembodied souls/spirits go after death. Thus, their views were found to be inclined towards Hindu beliefs and were not aligned with Buddhist sacred texts.

Most of the denominations in Christianity prescribe the existence of an afterlife and realms of heaven and hell as the final destinations for the soul. It is prescribed that those who are baptised in Christ's name are awarded with a blissful life in heaven. Roman Catholicism, in particular, also propagates the existence of Purgatory, an intermediary phase, where souls are sent temporarily for cleansing of venial sins. As prescribed in their texts, all Christian respondents believe in the afterlife and the existence of heaven and hell as final destinations for the soul. Common responses from most of them were: '*Swarg yeshu ka ghar hai*' (Heaven is God's home); '*Ache kaam karne waalon ko woh khud lene aate hain aur apne ghar rakhte hain*' (God comes himself and takes those who do good deeds along with Him to His home); '*Bure kaam, maar-dhaad karne waalon ko nark milta hai*' (Those who do bad deeds and commit violence go to hell); 'Hell is a real place where wicked people suffer the wrath of God, and who believe in Jesus Christ go to heaven'; 'Life in heaven is with Jesus and opposite to it is hell'; 'Heaven is a home of God and hell is devil's home'; 'Heaven is where God is and hell is the realm away from God'; etc.

On Purgatory, while the Protestant respondents denied the existence of any such realm, Catholics and a few respondents from other sects stated that they believe in the existence of a temporary phase where sinful souls are sent for cleansing of sins, but ultimately they also ascend to heaven. Their responses reflected their conviction that heaven is a realm of God, where souls who are submitted to Jesus are ascended, whereas hell is a place meant for punishment for the souls who are unfaithful to Jesus. It was very interesting to observe that while answering this question, respondents across all age groups, income categories, educational qualifications, and denominations sounded assured that they will be going to heaven because they have submitted to Christ. Thus, it can be inferred that Christian respondents on this aspect of death are very religious and their perceptions are fully in line with their religious doctrine on the afterlife.

Like Christianity, the sacred texts of Islam also explain heaven and hell as realistic realms. On the Day of Judgment, all souls will be raised from their graves, and their final fate will be decided. They will be given either heaven as a reward for their deeds or hell as eternal punishment. All Muslim respondents believe in the existence of heaven and hell as separate realms that will be awarded to them after death as permanent destinations. In the words of a few: '*Sab ka hisaab hoga aur Allah faisla sunayega*' (Every person will be held accountable and God will announce the final fate); '*Qayamat ke din ya toh jannat milegi, ya jahannum*' (On the Day of Judgment, either I will be given heaven or hell); and '*Kafiron ke liye toh pakka jahannum hai*' (Those who don't abide by God's command will certainly be sent to hell). Thus, perceptions of Muslim respondents on the doctrine of the existence of heaven and hell exactly correspond to the prescribed death beliefs in their sacred texts.

Perceptions on Reincarnation/Transmigration and Resurrection

Hinduism views death not as an end, but as the doorway to another beginning. Unless the soul is ultimately absorbed into *Brahmand* (the eternal universe), it is believed to pause briefly in heaven or hell before taking birth again—either in a human body (reincarnation) or in another form of life (transmigration). Among our respondents, 77% affirmed their belief in rebirth, a conviction voiced most strongly by middle-aged participants. Many explained that this belief had been ingrained since childhood through teachings, stories, and religious practices. Interestingly, a few went beyond doctrine to share personal experiences. One respondent pointed to a mark on his arm, describing it as a scar carried from a previous life. He recalled that, as a child, he would speak vividly about places remembered from that earlier existence. At the same time, younger participants were more sceptical. To them, reincarnation sounded like a tale rather than truth, something unproven and lacking evidence. Still, given that the majority endorsed it, the perception of Hindu respondents broadly aligns with the traditional doctrine of rebirth.

Like Hinduism, Sikhism also preaches that death is an opportunity for the human soul to ascend further and unite with

God; however, if that doesn't happen, the soul is reborn in the human form or in another life form. The largest proportion of (73%) Sikh respondents do not believe in the doctrine of rebirth. The outright responses were: '*Kise pata?*' (Who knows?); '*Kabhi nahi dekha*' (Never seen it); '*Sab aithe hi mukjaanda*' (Everything ends here only); '*Kahaniyaan hain sab*' (All are stories); and 'Proof *toh nahi hai*' (There is no proof). However, a fair number of respondents said that they believe in the rebirth of the soul. Some of them narrated their own experiences about it. Nonetheless, Sikh respondents diverged from the prescribed doctrine of transmigration in Sikhism.

Buddhism, though diverse in its schools of thought, upholds the doctrine of rebirth. In *Theravāda*, the idea of a permanent self is rejected; instead, it is taught that a stream of consciousness continues after death. Tibetan Buddhism, by contrast, affirms the existence of an underlying soul that undergoes rebirth. When asked about their own beliefs, all Buddhist respondents affirmed faith in rebirth. Pressed further on *who* or *what* is reborn, most replied '*atma*' (soul), while one admitted uncertainty but maintained that 'something' is reborn. This indicates that the early Buddhist doctrine of 'no-self' (*anatta*) is not widely embraced in practice. Since most respondents identified with the Tibetan tradition, their views reflected that school's teaching—belief in a soul and its cycles of birth. On this aspect, then, the perceptions of Buddhist respondents closely matched the Tibetan doctrine of death and rebirth, but their narratives were more inclined towards the Hindu version of reincarnation.

Among Christian and Muslim respondents, belief in the afterlife was already evident from their earlier responses. Both groups expressed firm conviction that, as prescribed in their scriptures, God will one day descend to earth and the dead will rise from their graves. When asked directly about the doctrine of resurrection, all respondents affirmed their belief. Their responses not only reinforced their faith in resurrection but also highlighted how closely their perceptions align with the prescribed death beliefs of their respective religions.

Perceptions on the Role of Deeds in Deciding Fate After Death

The doctrine of *karma* (action) forms the central theme in Hinduism. It is very strongly preached in Hindu Texts that it is only the *karmic* impressions that regulate and decide the fate of the soul after death, and also are the deciding factor for its reincarnation. Hinduism propounds that *karmas* are so powerful that they cannot be worn out unless they fructify. The Hindu respondents' perceptions on the doctrine of *karma* were gathered by asking whether they believe that the *karma* of the present life affects the fate of the soul after death.

The majority of the Hindu respondents (63%) do not believe that *karma* affects the fate of the soul after death. Nevertheless, quite a few respondents said that they believe in the law of cause and effect; actions do fructify, but in this life only and not beyond.

Like Hinduism, Sikhism also propounds the thesis that the soul carries the impressions of the actions performed in the present life to the next life. It is the *karma* of the past life that determines the favourable or unfavourable conditions in the present life. However, Sikhism prescribes that with contemplation on God's name and leading a life of a *gurmukh,* the impact of *karma* can be nullified. The large majority (82%) of Sikh participants showed stronger divergence by disbelieving in the doctrine of *karma.* However, most of them said that *karmas* do affect, but only in this life and not after death.

While *karma* remains a central theological principle in Hinduism and Sikhism, respondents from both communities largely confine its effects to this life, signalling a shift from doctrinal to experiential and rational understandings.

Buddhism emphasises that deeds performed by the deceased do impact his/her fate after death, but indirectly, with the dying person's final thoughts playing an important role. A person with wrong *karmas,* if practising mindfulness/meditation, can hold on to the right thoughts at the moment of death, and will be born in better circumstances. So, when Buddhist respondents were asked whether they believed that *karmas* impact their fate after death, the vast majority believed that *karmas* affect the fate of the soul after death. A few of them mentioned that practices like releasing birds and animals are considered beneficial after death, so at times they do it. Interestingly, none of them opined that the role of the thoughts of a dying person can be a factor influencing the next birth of the soul. Instead, their views reflected a Hindu-like understanding of *karma* and rebirth, likely influenced by living in a Hindu-majority setting.

Christianity emphasises leading a life in submission and love for God for better prospects in the afterlife. In order to understand the respondents' perceptions on the same, they were asked whether they felt that deeds played an important role in deciding the fate after death. While the largest number (63%) do not believe that deeds affect the fate after death, at the same time, 11 (37%) respondents do believe that deeds affect the fate after death. Those who disagreed maintained that actions have consequences only in this life, not beyond death. In their words: 'The way to heaven and eternal life is only through Jesus'; 'Righteous deeds are meant to exhibit one's love for Jesus'; 'Even wrong deeds are forgiven; just love God'; 'I try to do righteous actions for my own satisfaction and not for assuring a place in heaven'; 'I try to perform good deeds not to earn any brownie points after death but to exhibit my love for God, who did so much for the whole mankind'; and one very elaborate response was, *'I am careful for not deviating from God's ways but being human, I commit sins but I also ask for forgiveness from God. He is a loving Father, always ready to forgive us and not like a policeman who is always trying to catch us for doing wrong and punishing us.'* Therefore, for most of them, love for God is more important than deeds in deciding one's fate after death. This indicates that their perceptions wholly match the prescribed death beliefs in Christian texts.

Islam strongly preaches that the soul's eternal fate rests solely in God's judgment, determined by the actions performed during earthly life. Islamic law prescribes a righteous path for every aspect of living, promising eternal reward for those who follow it and punishment for those who stray. When Muslim respondents were asked about this belief, every one of them affirmed it. Most emphasised that *Allah* judges human deeds, sending sinners to hell and true believers to heaven. Some added that divine evaluation is not confined to the Day of Judgment—God continually observes and assesses human actions. Respondents also noted that deeds bear consequences both in this life and the next.

At the same time, many acknowledged the human struggle to live sin-free. As one respondent candidly admitted: '*Pata hai gunnah hai, fir bhi jhooth bol dete hain kai baar*' (I know lying is a sin, yet I still end up lying sometimes).

Overall, Christian and Muslim respondents, irrespective of gender, age, education, and class, were fully convinced by the criterion defined in their texts for better prospects after death. They also try to conform to the prescribed ways for their fate after death. The perceptions of Hindu and Sikh respondents are slightly varied from their prescribed texts; they do believe in *karma,* but are not convinced by the belief that *karma* fructifies after death. Buddhist respondents believe that *karmas* affect the fate of the deceased, but they didn't mention the importance of thoughts in determining the fate after death as prescribed in Buddhist texts.

Perceptions on Organ Donation and Whole Body Donation

Organ donation refers to the act of donating one's functional body organs to the needy after death. With so much advancement in medical technology and the approval of the brain-dead criterion as the indicator of death, organ donation has become a popular trend in recent times. In 1994, the Government of India passed the Transplantation of Human Organs Act, which legalised the procurement of organs (eyes, heart, lungs, pancreas, liver) from brain-dead patients.[11] Since then, in Chandigarh, organ donation is encouraged by medical institutions. Another trend that gained popularity in the twentieth century is donating the body to medical institutions for research and medical education instead of disposing of it in a religious way.

These practices, though popular in Western countries, do not fall in line with religious doctrines. Mostly, these religions prescribe disposal of the body either through burial or cremation for the better prospects of the deceased and bereaved. Also, any kind of tampering with the corpse is absolutely forbidden. So, with such religious orientation and socialisation, deciding to donate the organs after death and pledging the body to the medical institution is clearly an indicator of change. Respondents' perceptions on the same were studied by asking them: a) whether they are aware of these practices; and b) whether they are willing to go for these options.

'*Bachpan se yahi pata hai ki jala dete hain, kahin rakh lenge toh darr sa rahega.*' (Since childhood, it has been taught that bodies are cremated; it is scary thinking that the body is still there after death); 'Family *ko lagega abhi bhi hain*' (Family members will not be able to comprehend that the person is gone till the body is not disposed of)*;* '*Atma bhatkegi*' (The soul will wander)*;* '*Mukti nahi hogi*' (One won't be able to get *moksha*); and '*Mein kar bhi doon, par family nahi manegi*' (Even if I do it, my family will not let it happen). These were the responses of most of the Hindu respondents, explaining their apprehensions about pledging the

11. 'Organ Donation Registers Four-Fold Increase at PGI', *The Tribune* Dated 27 November 2015, http://www.tribuneindia.com/news/chandigarh/community/organ-donation-registers-four-fold-increase-at-pgi/163562.html

body to medical institutions. The vast majority of 93% Hindu respondents were aware of the concept of organ donation (mostly about eyes) after death, and five out of those said that they had already pledged their eyes. Further, while the largest proportion (68%) was aware of the whole body donation concept, only two of them were positive about pledging the body for medical research than disposing of it in the religiously prescribed way.

96% of the Sikh respondents were aware of the concept of organ donation after death and were in favour of donating organs; however, here again, most of them knew about eye donation in particular; two of them confirmed that they had already pledged their eyes. However, on the idea of whole body donation, while a large proportion (65%) of our Sikh respondents was aware of the concept, only three respondents were positive about pledging their bodies for medical research rather than disposing of the body in the religiously prescribed way. One respondent in particular said that he was thinking along those lines, but was not sure about it.

On probing the reasons for reluctance for this practice, they said: '*Vaise tan mitti hai, par jala hi dena theek lagda hai*' (Although, mortal remains are just dust, but cremation appears to be the appropriate way); '*Mein tan kardan par ghardeyan ne nahi manna*' (I would do it but the family members will not be convinced); '*Yeh toh hum pe* depend *nahi karta, peeche* family *jo reh jayegi unke upar hai ki kya karna hai*' (It doesn't depend upon the deceased's choice, it is on the kin to decide what to do with the corpse); and one respondent humorously said, '*Maran toh baad tan chadd deyo!*' (Spare the person after death at least).

Almost all Buddhist respondents were aware of the concept of organ donation after death, eye donation, in particular, and were willing to donate their eyes. But most of them were unaware of the concept of pledging the body to science. In the Tibetan School of thought, complete disposal of the body is given importance for the better prospects of consciousness. Therefore, it appeared that their perceptions on this aspect match the prescribed death beliefs in Tibetan Buddhism.

Prompt responses from Christian respondents on their unwillingness to pledge the body for donation: 'Jesus *humein kabar se uthaynege*' (Jesus will wake us from the grave); 'This body belongs to God, it shouldn't be spoiled'; 'Dust has to go back to dust'; 'Body has to sleep in peace'; 'Angels will come to meet in the grave'; etc. One respondent very firmly said, '*Woh* medical *kaamon ke liye toh un bicharon ki le jaate hain, jinki* body *ko koi apna lene nahi aata*' (For medical purposes, those bodies are taken that are abandoned, and no one from the family and near kin comes to receive it). Most of them stated that they will be able to rise again with their bodies only if they are in the grave after death.

All Christian respondents were aware of the concept of organ donation, and many of them were willing to donate. However, even more than half of them knew about the cadaver donation but were unwilling to do so because, for them, mortal remains must go in the grave for them to be raised for eternal life.

Muslim respondents expressed unwillingness for both practices. They said, '*Yeh sharir Allah ki amanat hai, waise hi vapis jayega*' (This body belongs to the God, so it has to go back as it is); and '*Sharir Allah ki den hai, bina ched chad ke vaise hi jaana chaiye*' (This body is a gift from God and should go back without any tampering); '*Yeh toh* body *ki* insult *karne jaisa hai*' (This is an insult of the body); 'Death *ke sameh pe sharir bahut pak hota hai, usko dafnana hi sahi hai*' (After death, the body is very pure; burying it is the correct way); and '*Qayamat ke roz sab ruhon ko qabar se uthaya jayega, isliye dafan zaruri hai*' (On the Day of Judgment all souls will be risen from the graves so burial is important).

Overall, Hindu, Sikh, and Buddhist respondents are willing to practice organ donation. However, at the same time, they are apprehensive about whole body donation for medical purposes and are inclined to the disposal of the body in the religiously prescribed manner. The plausible reason could be the uncertainty regarding the fate after death. They are convinced by the religious socialisation that it is important to dispose of the complete body and nothing should remain. There is a contradiction in their perceptions; while a large number of both Hindu and Sikh respondents said that they do not believe in the afterlife journey and realms of heaven and hell, despite that, they are not convinced of the whole body donation practice and prefer to dispose of the body in a religious way only. This indicates their deep-rooted faith in their religious teachings, which doesn't let them follow the secular practice of whole body donation.

Further, Christian respondents are willing to donate organs in order to help somebody, which can be a way to showcase one's love for Jesus. They are unwilling to donate the whole body because there is a strong conviction that Jesus will raise them one day from their graves. Till then, the body has to sleep in the grave. Muslims rule out both these practices as they believe that the entire body is a gift from *Allah*, and it has to be returned with full fidelity. In terms of their profiles, education, income, sect, age, etc., this does not seem to be the influencing factor in their perceptions. Across these variations, their conviction in their religious belief is similarly placed; strong and invincible!

Preference for Any Alternate Method for Body Disposal Other Than That Prescribed by Religion

These religious faiths prescribe cremation or interment as the righteous method to dispose of the body. However, in modern times, alternatives to these conventional practices are emerging. One alternative, which is gaining popularity these days, is electric cremation. Keeping in view the environmental hazards caused by burning the corpses, the use of crematoria became very popular in Western countries. In India, it came into practice in January

1989 as a part of the Ganga Action Plan. Respondents were asked whether they would prefer any alternate method other than the one prescribed in their religion to dispose of the body.

Only 25% Hindu respondents were willing to use an electric crematorium instead of a conventional wooden pyre. A few of them said: 'It is better as it is environment-friendly'; 'One doesn't have to see the loved ones burning'; 'Cremation on a wooden pyre creates a bad odour'; 'It is very economical'; etc.

Anteyshti is amongst the important sacraments prescribed for a Hindu in the sacred texts. The ritual of *kapalkriya* and making offerings while the pyre is lit are mandatory practices in Hinduism. An electric crematorium doesn't facilitate performing any of those. This is plausibly the reason that most of the Hindu respondents preferred religiously prescribed conventional cremation over an electric crematorium. The functionaries of cremation grounds verified that the use of an electric crematorium in their premises is minimal compared to conventional cremation. Mostly abandoned and unclaimed bodies are burnt electronically because this is very frugal as compared to the conventional process.

Shockingly, a large proportion of the Sikh respondents (71%) also preferred the conventional method of cremation on a wooden pyre. Amongst Hindu and Sikh respondents, mostly those who preferred electric crematoria were the young respondents, falling in the age group of 20–30 years. Though *kapalkriya* is discouraged in *Rehat Maryada*, still, Sikh respondents hesitate to use an electric crematorium.

The majority of the Buddhist respondents (77%) also preferred the traditional wooden pyre. They said that they prefer cremation on a wooden pyre because this is the method used traditionally, even in their villages, so they want to stick to it. In the words of a few respondents: '*Gaun mein jaise hota hai, wahi theek hai*' (The way it is done in villages appears to be correct); '*Jahan lakdi nahi mile wahan toh kuch aur socho hai, yahan toh lakdi hai*' (When firewood is not available, then one can think of something else, here there is so much wood). However, five respondents preferred alternative ways of body disposal. While four of them said they would prefer an electric crematorium, one of them said, 'Body dispose *kardo kaise bhi, mujhe toh kutte bahut pasand hain, mera sharir toh kutton ko kaat ke khila dena*' (Just dispose of the body anyhow. I love dogs and would prefer that my dead body be served to dogs). Interestingly, Buddhism doesn't prescribe any fixed practice of body disposal, but the cremation on a wooden pyre is a prevalent method in recent times in the Buddhist regions in India. Therefore, they prefer cremation on the pyre to conform to the tradition.

For 93% Christian respondents, burial as prescribed in their religion is the preferred choice. Only two respondents were willing to use an electric crematorium. One of them said that in the coming times, like in Western countries, there will be no land left for burials; then cremation will be the only option, so it's better to do it electrically. Another respondent said, 'Donation of the body is better than both'. However, considering the responses of most of them, it appears that when it comes to the disposal of the body, Christian respondents are highly religious and they believe that Christ will awaken them from their graves.

Lastly, looking at the response of our Muslim respondents, it is clear that their perceptions of the method of body disposal are intensely religious. All of them prefer burial as the method of body disposal. Most of them shared that '*Qayamat ke din kabaron mein se sab ko nikala jayega*' (On the Day of Judgment, the bodies will be raised from the graves).

Preference for Post-Cremation/Burial Rituals and Religiously Prescribed Ways of Mourning

All the religious faiths prescribe certain practices to be followed after the body is disposed of. These include the practices meant to help the deceased in their afterlife journey, mourning the death, doing away with the impurity caused by death, remembering the deceased in a ritualistic way, etc. Respondents were asked whether they think performing these prescribed post-cremation/burial practices is important for them.

Hinduism

In all the categories of the prescribed post-death rituals, a vast majority felt that these are important. I got a variety of reasons for their willingness to perform these rites. For instance, '*Agar na karo toh atma ki gati nahi hoti*' (The soul doesn't ascend further, if these are not done)*; 'Agar yeh naah karo toh mare huye wapas aa jate hain*' (If these rites are not performed, the dead come back)*; 'Pinda daan karne se kehte hain ki aage kasht nahi hota*' (*Pinda daan,* they say, leads to a pain-free life ahead for the deceased)*; 'Na karo toh atma bhatakti hai*' (If not done, the soul wanders and haunts)*; 'Hamare kaam safal nahi hote*' (Not doing these may lead to obstacles in our life); '*Kehte hain panditon ko khilane se unhe pahunch jaata hai*' (It is said that food offered to *brahmins* reaches the deceased)*; 'Saddiyon se chalta aa raha hai, kuch toh hota hoga*' (These are age old rituals; there must be something beneficial); and '*Tassali hoti hai ki yahan se nipat gaya sabh kuch ab*' (These practices give a psychological satisfaction that the deceased has completed this life). These responses point towards the religious bent of the respondents. However, it appears that they do not know the meanings prescribed in the religious texts, but they blindly trust whatever has been heard or witnessed and fear the ill effects that may happen if not done.

Some of the responses point towards the notion that doing these rites is important for Hindu respondents because of social obligation, like: '*Lok ki ki kehnge? Apne maa baap layi ehna vi nahi kitta?*' (What will people say? The children couldn't even do this much for the parents?)*; 'Samaaj mein chal raha hai toh nibhana padhta hai*' (Whatever is prevalent in society has to be conformed to)*;* 'Urbanites are still not that rigid but in villages, if in the event of death, ritualistically food is not offered to the *brahmins* (*bramhbhoj*), other villagers boycott the family and don't even visit that home'; 'I personally dislike it, but if I wouldn't have done this, people would have said that because she is a daughter, she didn't do these rituals for parents; had there been a son, he would have done them'; 'One has to do many things because one lives in society'; '*Mann pe bhoj rehta hai na karo toh*' (It is psychologically discomforting, if not practiced).

Interestingly, it was found that most of the respondents were not aware of the religious meaning (explained in the prescribed section) behind the *pinda daan* and *sraddha* rites. Some perceive that it is important either because they are scared of any ill-effects that may affect the deceased or the kin for not doing them, and others are apprehensive about their social image that may suffer because of not performing the rites.

A few, who perceived that the rites should not be held, opined that the ashes can just be buried in the cremation grounds or somewhere else, as immersing them in water causes pollution. In the light of *pinda daan* and holding memorials, a few respondents highlighted the financial aspect. They said that doing those rituals in Haridwar, Pheowa, etc., is very expensive and appears to be a waste of money; instead of feeding *pandits,* it is better to feed the poor and donate it to the needy. A few also shared that memorials don't appear to be doing any good to the deceased or the family; it is just a gathering collected for a formality, and expensive meals are just a way to show off. These responses point towards the slight deviation from the religious beliefs in the perceptions of a few respondents.

But looking at the responses of the majority, it can be said that most of the Hindus prefer to conform to the traditionally prevalent post-cremation practices. But the rationale for doing so is not only religious, it is also psychological (fear) and social (conforming to the societal norms).

Sikhism

In Sikhism, the *Rehat Maryada* prescribes certain post-cremation practices, and a few practices are prevalent in the Sikh tradition. 87% of the respondents approve the practice of immersing ashes in Patalpuri at Kiratpur Sahib, even when it is not a compulsion in *Rehat Maryada*. Some prominent responses were: '*Jo baniya hoya hai, na karo tan veham hunda*' (It gives an uneasy feeling, if the ongoing tradition is not followed); 'It gives a sense of satisfaction'; 'It gives a feeling that now the person is gone'.

There is another traditional practice of donating utensils and money at Kiratpur Sahib, though not mentioned in the *Rehat Maryada*. 78% Sikh respondents favour this practice. In the words of a few: '*Hunda tan kuch nahi, apni mann di tassali hundi hai*' (There is nothing concrete about it, just the psychological satisfaction); '*Oh mangde nahi kuch, jo dena de diyo*' (The personnel at gurdwara don't ask for anything; give whatever you feel like); '*Jithe ehna kar de haan, Gurdware ch de deyo ki farak pehnda hai?*' (Where I spend so much on other things, if I give little at the gurdwara, how does that matter?); '*Hun ehni door ja kuch naah diyo channga nahi lagda*' (I go so far to immerse ashes, it doesn't feel good if something is not donated there); '*Kehnde ne atma aandi hai wapas, oh de naah de bartan honge tan langar chakkhlugi*' (It is said that the soul might visit back, so if utensils in his/her name are donated, it might eat *langar*). This indicates that for Sikh respondents, conforming to the tradition is more important than following the prescribed code in the *Rehat Maryada*.

The vast majority believes in holding a *path* after cremation as prescribed in the *Rehat Maryada*. Some of them explained that holding *path* and reciting *kirtan* is an ideal way to remember the dead; a few also opined that it gives them strength to bear the loss. Similarly, concluding the mourning on the tenth day and holding *bhog* has also been preferred by most of the respondents. As prescribed in Sikhism, reciting God's name in all situations is preferred by most of the Sikh respondents. Thus, Sikh respondents prefer to follow the traditional way not only because of religious reasons but also for the psychological satisfaction that they get by conforming to the tradition. Their perceptions match the prescribed post-death practices, and they also believe in following the traditionally prevalent practices, even the ones that the texts do not endorse.

Buddhism, Christianity, and Islam

Buddhism, particularly the Tibetan school, prescribes specific days (third, seventh, fourteenth, and forty-ninth) after death for holding a memorial service. On these days, *bardo* body (consciousness) enters a new stage on the way to the next birth. Respondents' perceptions on the same were studied by asking them whether they feel these are important or not. Almost all of them felt that it was important to perform post-cremation memorials as prescribed in the religious texts. Only two respondents had a different view. One said that it doesn't matter; a loved one can be remembered in any way, even without holding memorials, and another said, '*Kya zaroorat hai itna kharcha karneki; apne pe kharcha kar lo, marne waale ki jagah*' (There is no need to spend on such rituals, better to spend on oneself than on the one who has died).

Further, in Christian tradition, after burial, specific memorial services are prevalent. Respondents were asked whether they felt it was important for them to hold ritualistic memorials or if they would prefer some other way to remember the deceased. A vast majority (73%) of Christian respondents do not prefer to hold religiously prescribed memorials. It was interesting to hear from many of them that death has to be celebrated with friends and kin. A few of them said that loved ones can be remembered happily anyway. Some interesting responses were: 'Remember them in prayers'; 'Cook the food that they liked'; 'Sing songs of their choice'; etc. Their responses also reaffirm the earlier findings that Christian respondents do not fear death.

As discussed earlier, Islam doesn't prescribe any fixed rituals to be observed after burial for mourning, but traditionally, practices like visiting the graves, reciting *dua* (prayers) for the deceased, visiting the bereaved family to offer condolences, widows abstaining from meeting people other than family members, etc., are prevalent. Hence, our Muslim respondents were asked whether they preferred to hold those practices or would like to remember the deceased or celebrate death in their own way. 83% respondents prefer to mourn death according to the traditionally prevalent ways only. Six of them feel that following these practices is not important; the deceased can be remembered in any way. They also explained that once the burial is done, nothing else matters. Therefore, looking at the responses of the majority, it can be said that our Muslim respondents are largely religious about this aspect of death, and their perceptions fall in line with the prevalent religious tradition.

Therefore, it can be said that, except for Christian respondents, all others believe that it is essential to adhere to the post-cremation/burial practices prevalent traditionally and prescribed in their sacred texts. However, Hindu respondents in particular do not favour these practices only because they are religious, but because they prefer to conform to the tradition, and a few of them fear the unprecedented implications that may occur to the deceased and themselves for not doing the desired rituals. Sikh respondents, too, appear to be conformists. Despite the fact that Sikhism, being a liberal religion, has not laid out any compulsory post-cremation practices, it was found that most of the Sikh respondents feel that it is important to adhere to the traditionally prevalent practices.

Again, there is duality in the responses of Hindu and Sikh respondents. Though they claim that they don't believe in the afterlife journey and realms like heaven and hell, they very strongly believe in performing the post-cremation rituals meant for a smooth afterlife journey.

Buddhist respondents believe that performing post-cremation memorials is important because not performing might impact the afterlife journey of the deceased, implying religious inclination in their perceptions. Muslims, however, feel it is important to perform the traditionally prevalent post-burial practices because, for them, abiding by the religiously prescribed code in every aspect of life is of the utmost importance.

Views on Suicide and Euthanasia

As discussed earlier, religions condemn these two practices as sinful acts. It is preached that the inevitable reality of death is pre-destined; so ending life by one's own choice is not encouraged in any of these religious faiths. Highlighting that in the phase of modernisation, people have liberal attitudes towards contemporary death issues—people belonging to various denominations in Christianity were found to be more aware and supportive of the right-to-die and death with dignity movements that stemmed from the increasing ability to technologically prolong life and the dying process.[12] A study conducted by the National Opinion Research Center in 1985 revealed that 80% believed that suicide or euthanasia was 'ok'. Our respondents' perceptions of both of these practices were studied.

In all the major religious faiths, altruistic suicide is approved, but egoistic suicide is considered a sinful act. Respondents were asked whether they perceive suicide as a sin or if they feel that it is acceptable in certain circumstances.

Almost all of the Hindu respondents, most of the Sikh respondents (87%), all Buddhist, Christian, and Muslim respondents consider suicide as a sinful act. Most of them called it an act of cowardice. A few Christian respondents elaborated that life is given once by God; ending it at one's own will is an

12. Kearl, M.C. (1989). *Endings: A Sociology of Death and Dying.* New York: Oxford University Press.

aberrant sin for which there is no forgiveness. From many Muslim respondents, the prompt response was, '*Yeh toh bahut bada gunah hai!*' (This is a severe sin). Only six Sikh respondents (13%) were liberal enough to say that they believe that it is acceptable in certain circumstances.

Euthanasia is legally permissible in several countries, and India has taken cautious steps in this direction, too. In 2011, the Supreme Court legalised passive euthanasia, allowing the withdrawal of artificial life support for patients in a persistent vegetative state. Building on that, in 2018, the court delivered a landmark verdict, recognising advance medical directives, commonly known as 'living wills'. It held that the right to live with dignity under Article 21 of the Constitution inherently includes the right to die with dignity.

Respondents across the faiths were asked whether they considered it a sin and an anti-religious practice, or if they felt that it should be allowed if the deceased is in extreme health crises and there are no chances of recovery, or if it should be allowed because at that stage one's working organs can be used for others.

72% of Hindu respondents believe that euthanasia should be allowed if there are no chances of recovery and if it releases the deceased from pain and provides relief to family members. Only 26% believe that it is a sin. One respondent stated that it is easier said than done; in her words: '*If I think for others, I would say switch off the ventilator; however, if I have to do it for someone close to me, I will have the hope of his/her recovery till the end.*' This reflects the emotional sensitivity linked with the practice of euthanasia.

Interestingly, all Sikh respondents believe that euthanasia should be allowed. 80% feel that it should be allowed if the person is so unwell and the chances of recovery are nil. The remaining 20% favour this practice because they feel that euthanasia will let the working organs of the deceased be used for others.

Further, all Buddhist respondents condemn euthanasia as a sinful act. 90% Christian respondents also believe that euthanasia is a sinful act. They said, *'Death is only in the hands of God; humans should not intervene in God's plan.'* Almost all the Muslim respondents (97%) reject euthanasia, calling it an anti-religious practice. Most of them justified their answer by stating that one's life is only in the hands of *Allah*; human beings cannot decide about someone's death; they can only pray for the other person (*Hum sirf dua kar sakte hain, jaan nahi leh sakte!*).

Overall, it appears that on the act of euthanasia, the Hindu and Sikh respondents keep a liberal view, indicating that their perceptions on this aspect do not align with prescribed religious beliefs in their sacred texts, matching Kearl's observation that people in the late 1980s have adopted a liberal view on aspects like euthanasia. However, all Buddhist, Christian, and Muslim respondents perceive the practice of euthanasia as a sinful act.

The Gist of Perception of Death

Across faiths, people's perceptions of death often mirror their religious teachings, yet not always. Hindus revealed a paradox: while many dismiss doctrines of the afterlife and karma, they still conform to the prescribed death rituals, often out of social compulsion. Their views also showed a rational side—supporting organ donation, a 'comfortable death' as a good death, and openness to euthanasia. Sikhs, reflecting their faith's liberal ethos, mostly denied the afterlife, karma, and rebirth. Still, tradition pulls them back—many conform to post-cremation practices and hesitate about whole-body donation. Buddhists leaned strongly on religious beliefs, though often blending them with Hindu ideas. They feared death's uncertainty, affirmed rebirth, favoured wooden pyres, and rejected euthanasia, while modestly supporting organ donation. Christians stayed closest to doctrine—believing in resurrection, heaven, and hell, and favouring burial. They opposed suicide and euthanasia, yet accepted organ donation and redefined good death in more personal terms. Muslims were the most aligned with their texts—firm in belief in the afterlife, resurrection, heaven, and hell. Burial and post-burial practices were seen as essential, while organ donation, euthanasia, and suicide were firmly rejected. Overall, Hindus appeared conflicted, Sikhs selectively liberal, Buddhists religious with Hindu influences, while Christians and Muslims were firmly rooted in their doctrines.

CHAPTER 5

Death Practices and the Paradoxical Situation

Analysis of respondents' perceptions across different faiths reveals that most individuals interpret death and its associated aspects through the lens of their religious beliefs. To better understand how these perceptions align with real-life experiences, participants were asked to reflect on the actual practices they carried out upon the death of a close family member. This allowed for an examination of the extent to which these practices conformed to the tenets of their respective religions. Additionally, the study seeks to highlight the gap—if any—between modern individuals' beliefs about death and the practices they ultimately follow. Accordingly, this chapter explores whether the death-related rituals observed by the respondents align with their religious teachings and personal perceptions of death. Specific focus is given to areas such as death planning and the practices undertaken before, during, and after death. Supporting data can be found in **Annexure C** of the book (page no. 272).

Planning About Death: Will-Writing or Sharing of Last Wishes

Will-writing is an appropriate way to plan for one's death. It was explored whether or not planning for death is a popular practice amongst the respondents. Specifically, on two aspects: a) whether the deceased members of the respondents' families had left behind a Will; and b) whether witnessing such a death prompted them to create their own Wills. The aim was not limited to understanding just the intentions about bequeathal of their assets, but also any personal wishes or rituals they wanted to be performed.

Will-Making Among Respondents' Deceased Kin

Among the deceased kin of Hindu (75%), Sikh (84%), Buddhist (91%), and Christian (83%) respondents, the majority had neither written a Will nor verbally expressed their last wishes. This was true even in cases where death was anticipated and the individual had endured a prolonged illness. Some respondents admitted feeling guilty for not recognising subtle signs that their loved ones may have given in their final moments. One woman recalled how her mother, perhaps sensing the end was near, tried to indicate in the hospital that she wished to return home for her last moments. Focused on continuing medical treatment, the daughter could not fulfil this unspoken desire, and her mother passed away in the hospital. Another respondent, whose father had not left a Will, reflected, '*Kaash Will kar li hoti, ab bahut dhakke khaane padte hain... maine apni mother ki toh karwa di hai, iss* incident *ke baad*' (I wish he had written a Will; now it is very difficult to resolve many matters. After this incident, I have made sure to get my mother's will prepared).

One informant, recalling the sudden death of his mother, shared: 'She got up in the morning and began her routine *path* (prayers). Perhaps sensing some uneasiness, she suddenly called me and said: *"mein ja rahi haan, panj paudiyan kartiyan, baki khatam kar dena"* (I am going, I have completed the beginning verses of the prayer, please finish the rest). Before we could grasp what she meant, she collapsed and passed away.' Another respondent noted that while his father had not made a Will, he did express a wish that his eyes be donated after his death. A woman respondent, speaking of her late mother, said that although her mother had written a Will long ago to record her possessions, she would often remind the family verbally: '*Mere marre te roti changgi khilayin*' (On my death, serve a good feast).

Such experiences highlight that, despite awareness of approaching death, Will was not made—pointing to a broader lack of planning for death.

Interestingly, Islam prescribes Will-writing as a religious duty for Muslims. Yet, in the majority of cases (75%), no Will was made. Only in four cases did respondents confirm that the deceased had left one. When probed deeper about not following this practice, which is also prescribed in their religion, most of them said that a Will is necessary when there is some debt to be cleared by the dying person; in the absence of a written Will, it is customary to announce the matter to the congregation: if any debt is owed, the creditor may forgive it (*karza maaf karna*); otherwise, the responsibility to repay falls upon the heirs. According to respondents, this practice was followed as they believed '*Ruh ko Allah ke ghar bina kisi bojh ke bhejna hota hai*' (The soul should be sent to God's abode free from burdens). With respect to property inheritance, respondents emphasised that *Sharia* (Islamic law) already stipulates fixed shares for heirs, so it is not important to write about it.

Writing of Will by the Respondents

Respondents were also asked whether, after witnessing death in their families, they had made a Will or shared their wishes in any form with friends or kin. Among Hindus, only one respondent had written her wishes, saved them on her personal computer, and informed her son. However, 90% Hindu respondents admitted they had neither written nor verbally expressed their wishes regarding their own death. Only a few mentioned that, after experiencing death in the family, they often reflect on these matters and start sharing their wishes with the family members. Among Sikh respondents, only four respondents had documented or verbally shared their desires. Three had prepared a legal Will, while one reported discussing his belongings and succession with his son. The majority (91%) had taken no step in this direction. When asked why, common responses from both Hindu and Sikh respondents included: 'It never occurred to us', 'Never thought on these lines', 'Not yet done', 'Might do it in a few years', and, particularly among women, 'Possess nothing to be written in a Will'. One elderly respondent remarked, 'Hajje bahut time peya saada, haje kitthe jaana' (We still have plenty of time; we are not going anywhere). None of the Buddhist respondents had taken any steps toward Will-making. On probing further, they explained that property is expected to pass automatically from fathers to sons, while several women noted that they had no property in their own names to bequeath. Among Christians, only one respondent had made such arrangements. She explained: '*Likha kuch nahi hai, lekin apne beton ko bol ke rakha hai ke dono bahuon ke liye Jewellery kahan rakhi hai aur meri death pe kaunsi Prayers zaroor karna*' (I have not written anything, but I have told my sons where the jewellery for their wives is kept and which prayers should be recited upon my death). Those who had not made Wills mostly said they did not own anything that could be passed on. Their responses suggest that Will-making was understood primarily as a matter of distributing material assets, rather than a way to express wishes regarding the body, rituals, or ceremonies. In the case of Muslim respondents, only three (8%) had prepared Wills, while most reported taking no steps to plan for death. They felt it was 'too early' to make a Will. Despite Islamic texts prescribing the practice, Will-making was not common among them. The two main reasons cited were: a) Wills are seen as necessary only when one has outstanding debts, and b) many felt that their time of death had not yet come.

Therefore, planning for death in terms of leaving a will is uncommon across all religious faiths. Although respondents acknowledge the certainty of death, most are reluctant to prepare for it—even after witnessing the death of a close relative. Thus, these results do not align with studies about the growing trend of death planning in contemporary societies.

Practices Before Death

As discussed in the earlier chapters, different religions prescribe a range of practices to deal with death. The rituals begin in the final moments of life, on the anticipation of death. Hence, the respondents were asked whether they followed those practices or not.

Hinduism

On anticipation of death, Hinduism prescribes practices like giving donations in the name of the deceased, particularly a cow, food to *brahmins*, cash and kind, etc. Other practices include laying the dying person on the floor, giving *Ganga jal* and *tulsi* leaves to the dying, reciting some prayers/*mantras*, etc.

When the respondents were asked whether or not these practices were performed for their dying kin, it was found that only in nine (15%) cases, due to prolonged illness and on the anticipation of death, the donations were given. Most of them said that cash and food were donated in the temple. Only one *brahmin* respondent had donated the amount equivalent to the value of a cow, as suggested by their family *purohit*, for the peaceful release of the soul of the deceased and the journey afterwards, indicating a religious bent of mind. One respondent explained that her father had the routine practice of donating funds to an organisation working for the education of poor children, so that was done as his routine activity, even when he was in his last stage. However, in the majority (85%) of the cases, no donations were done prior to death. On probing the reasons for the same, most of them stated: 'Death occurred in a hospital'; 'They never thought about it'; 'Didn't get time for all this'; 'Donations were given after death'; etc.

With regard to the shifting of the dying on the floor, it was found that in none of the cases was the dying person laid on the floor. For those who died in the hospital, it was understandably not possible. However, even for those who were at home and the death was anticipated, respondents stated that it was done only after death. Most of them said, '*Woh toh baad mein utaarte hain na neeche?*' (Aren't they taken down later?) This implies that not laying the dying on the floor was not because of any intention of not following the religious way, but because they had believed from the tradition that the body is laid on the floor after death. Further, in a larger number (60%) of the cases, *Ganga jal* and *tulsi* leaves were not given to the dying. Largely, these were the cases where death wasn't anticipated, and it happened in the hospital. However, 40% respondents confirmed giving *Ganga jal* and *tulsi* leaves to the dying because death occurred at home. One respondent said that she managed to give her mother *Ganga jal* during the last minutes, even when she was in the hospital, and this gave her some sense of satisfaction. From the responses, it appears that this could not happen mainly because of the hospitalisation of the deceased in the last stage.

Regarding recitation of prayers or chanting of *mantras*, it was found that in most (78%) of the cases, it wasn't done. Even those (22%) who confirmed that it was done, no single prayer, *mantra*, or pattern was found in their responses. One respondent stated that her husband was in extreme pain, so all her prayers were for his relief. Another respondent stated that, as the death of her mother was anticipated, she used to recite the *Bhagavad Gita* for her in her last days. Another common response from those who said they prayed was that they were praying to have the strength to bear that situation while they were having their loved ones in ICUs. One respondent remorsefully said, 'I wanted to sit and pray calmly for my father, but there was so much chaos in the hospital that we were confused and panicked. I wish instead of running around, we could have silently sat and prayed.'

Thus, amongst Hindu respondents, no fixed practices were performed for the dying. Largely, prayers were offered for reasons other than religion, for instance, to gain strength for oneself rather than praying for the afterlife of the deceased. Not performing certain rituals like laying the dying on the floor cannot straight away be called the result of not being religious. Rather, it happened, perhaps because of not knowing exactly about the prescribed practices due to variations in Hinduism and in a few cases (where death occurred in a hospital), the conditions were not suitable for doing those rituals. Nonetheless, rituals performed before death by Hindu respondents do not correspond to the prescribed ones.

Sikhism and Buddhism

Sikh texts, particularly *Rehat Maryada*, do not prescribe any specific rituals to be performed for the deceased in anticipation of death. In all situations, Sikhism preaches chanting the name of God and accepting everything as God's will. *Rehat Maryada* particularly proscribes Hindu practices of giving donations and laying the deceased on the floor. Sikh respondents were asked whether they performed any practices for their dying kin or not. 78% said nothing was done. 22% of respondents confirmed reciting a *path* for the deceased when death was anticipated. They said, 'We used to sit beside him and recite *path*'; '*Unke kamre mein Gurbani laga dete the*' (We play *Gurbani* in the room); 'In the last moments, we made him chant *Waheguru!*'; and '*Jihni der* papa ICU *ch rahe, assi baar naam japp de rahe. Path tan assi ik minute vi band nahi kitta*'

(While my father was in ICU, we were praying outside. We didn't stop praying even for a minute). So, it appears that before death, most of the Sikh respondents practised what is prescribed; either they didn't do anything or just recited God's name.

Buddhism, too, doesn't categorically prescribe any rituals in particular for the moment of death. All schools of thought preach that contemplation on death while alive is the only way to secure rebirth in spiritually higher realms. However, in Tibetan Buddhism, for the smooth release of consciousness, it is essential that the corpse is not touched till the lamas reach and offer prayers for the well-being of the consciousness. Also, in Buddhist tradition, with the idea of merit transference, practices like releasing animals, doing prayers, and giving alms (food, clothes, etc.) to the poor, are prevalent for the deceased before death.[1] So, Buddhist respondents were asked whether they practised any rituals for the deceased on the anticipation of death. 46% confirmed that lamas were invited for prayers, and they also offered alms to them. However, a larger proportion (54%) revealed that death occurred in hospitals and in some cases, it was so sudden that it wasn't possible to invite the lamas before death, but they did arrive after death.

Christianity

In most of the Christian denominations, sacraments of penance, anointment of the sick and Eucharist are prescribed for the

1. Merit transference: According to Mahayana Sutra of The Great Vows of Ksitigarbha *Bodhisattva*, one can transfer one-seventh of the merit of an act they have performed to a deceased. It is believed that the highest gift to the departed is the transferring of merit. The doctrine is said to be influenced by Hinduism's belief in benefiting the *pretas* (departed souls) by rituals and material things. The idea became very popular in China, and many funeral rituals were established to transfer the merits to the departed for their better rebirth. These include practices like giving alms to monks in the name of the deceased and releasing animals/birds with the thought of benefiting the departed. Gradually, these practices became an important part of death rituals, particularly in *Mahayana Buddhism*. See: Becker, 1993.

deceased on the anticipation of death.[2] A larger number of the Christian respondents (77%) said that the sacraments were not performed. However, in most cases, the parish priest visited to bless the deceased, and they collectively prayed for the deceased. Since the majority of the deaths happened in the hospital, performing the sacrament of penance and Eucharist wasn't possible. A few Protestant respondents stated that the anointing of the sick is just a symbolic ritual, and actually, only reciting prayers is important, so only the prayers were said.

However, in seven cases (23%) where the deceased was at home in his/her last stage, all the prescribed sacraments were performed. Thus, from the responses, it appears that either the practice could not happen because of the hospitalisation of the deceased or Protestants did not do it because Protestantism doesn't emphasise rituals. In some cases, respondents were regretful about not being able to perform these sacraments.

Thus, in the era of modernisation, medical interventions and prolonged treatments often result in individuals dying in isolation. This, in turn, leaves the bereaved with a sense of loss not only due to the death itself but also because they are unable to perform traditional comforting sacraments for their loved ones. Accordingly, it appears that our Christian respondents, though they had the intention to carry out these sacraments, were unable to do so due to various circumstances.

Islam

Laying the deceased in the direction of *Qiblah* and reciting *ayats* from the Quran are the rituals (*Ehtezar*)[3] prescribed in Islam on the anticipation of death. In most cases, especially where death

---

2. Webster, W. (n.d.). *Christian Resources.* Retrieved 2 June 2020, from www.christiantruth.com: https://christiantruth.com/articles/articles-roman-catholicism/penancehistory/

3. Kermaili, H. Muhammad (n.d.), 'Burial Rituals', https://www.al-islam.org/pt/node/17907

occurred at home, both of these practices were performed for the deceased in his/her last phase of life.

Respondents informed that the face of the dying was turned towards *Qiblah* and efforts were made to make him/her recite verses from the Quran. Also, *ayats* (verses from the Quran) were recited, and *dua* (prayer) was done for the dying by the family members with the belief that it reduces the pain of the deceased.

One respondent who lost his grandmother mentioned that at the time of death, holy water called '*Aab-e-ZamZam*' (water collected from the well in Mecca) was put in her mouth. For those who died in the hospital, respondents said that they could not help the deceased face the desired direction, but recited *ayats* for the deceased. In the accident cases, respondents regretfully said that both could not happen.

Thus, Hindu respondents largely did not follow prescribed end-of-life practices, mainly due to a lack of awareness and reliance on familiar or convenient rituals. Sikh participants adhered to their tradition by avoiding rituals for the dying. Buddhist and Christian respondents also did not engage in anticipatory rites, often because death was either unexpected or occurred in hospitals. Muslim respondents, by contrast, mostly followed prescribed practices, with exceptions primarily in cases of sudden or hospital deaths.

How Families Prepared Their Loved Ones for the Final Journey

As elaborated in the third chapter, religions prescribe their own course to prepare the body for the final disposal. Hence, the respondents following different religious faiths were asked whether they adhered to the practices prescribed in their respective faiths for the preparation of the body disposal.

Hinduism

Most Hindu respondents reported following religious guidelines when preparing the body. Yet, there was no single, unanimous way of doing things—especially when it came to positioning the body. About 70% agreed that the deceased was laid in a specific direction, but those directions varied. Some said the head should face north, others east. A few placed the feet towards the main door, and some simply followed the guidance of family elders. An overwhelming 95% of families lit a lamp near the body—a symbol of light in darkness. But here, too, practices differed. While sesame and mustard oil were the most common choices, a few used *desi ghee*. Regardless of the substance, the intention was clear: to uphold tradition and bring peace to the soul. In every case, the body was bathed and dressed by close relatives of the same gender as the deceased—a ritual deeply rooted in intimacy and respect. New clothes were used in nearly all instances (95%), and their colour carried significant meaning.

For deceased men, plain white was the norm. For married women whose husbands were alive, the scene was strikingly different—they were adorned in bright clothes, usually a salwar kameez, complete with makeup and jewellery. One common phrase echoed in the responses: '*Dulhan ki tarah tyaar kiya tha*' (She was dressed like a bride). In contrast, elderly women, particularly widows, were dressed in simpler, lighter tones. The practice of closing the body's natural openings with cotton—especially the nose and ears—was followed by 78% of respondents, with some specifically mentioning the use of camphor in the nose. A similar attention to ritual detail was seen in the shaving of the chief mourner's head, typically a male relative. While 68% confirmed this was done, in a few cases, the ritual was modified—two women served as chief mourners, and some men trimmed hair instead of shaving it completely.

Amidst these age-old customs, a glimmer of modern consciousness emerged. In five cases, the deceased's eyes were donated—three by their own pledge and two by the family's decision. Interestingly, while 87% of respondents expressed willingness to donate organs, only these five families acted on it, showing a gap between intent and action.

This glimpse into how Hindu families prepare the body after death shows that while traditional rituals remain deeply respected, they are not rigid. Families interpret and adapt customs based on beliefs, guidance from elders, or even logistical realities. The acceptance of eye donation, though limited, hints at a quiet shift—a blending of ancient ritual with modern altruism.

Sikhism

As already discussed, for Sikhs, the *Rehat Maryada* (the Sikh code of conduct) outlines specific practices and prohibitions related to death and the preparation of the body. While most Sikh respondents reported traditional methods in preparing the body, some of the practices they observed are categorically discouraged in the *Rehat Maryada.* The practice of laying the body on the floor was done by all except one. When asked why, many simply responded, 'That's how it's done.' This suggests that for some, this practice may have been inherited from Hindu traditions or simply followed out of habit, without awareness of what the religious code actually prescribes. In the one exceptional case, the body was taken directly from the hospital to the cremation grounds, so there was no opportunity to lay it down at home, not a religious choice, but a matter of circumstance. Most families (73%) did not lay the body in any specific direction, which aligns with Sikh teachings. However, a notable minority (27%) did, choosing directions like the head facing east or north, or feet pointing toward the door—again reflecting influences from Hindu customs or elder-led traditions, rather than the *Rehat Maryada*.

As mentioned in the *Rehat Maryada*, in all cases, the lamp was not lit near the deceased. However, some families did light incense or *dhoop*, not as part of any ritual, but to mask odour. Sikhism doesn't prescribe the use of holy water after death. And in most cases (89%), families did not offer any. Still, five respondents mentioned giving *Ganga jal* (from the Ganges) or *Amrit* (from the gurdwara)—a clear sign that, even among Sikhs, some Hindu practices have been quietly integrated, often without questioning their origins. A deeply personal and respectful act, washing and dressing the body, was usually carried out by family members—something the *Rehat Maryada* also prescribes. Only in one case did hospital staff handle this due to logistical reasons.

Most deceased were dressed in new clothes (82%), with colour choices often reflecting gender, marital status, and family sentiment. Men were typically dressed in white *kurta-pyjamas* with turbans, while married women were dressed in bright, festive attire—sometimes described as being 'prepared like a bride'. Widows were usually dressed in lighter tones. In a few cases, rather than following tradition, families chose to dress their loved ones in clothes they liked in life, honouring the person more than the protocol. Interestingly, in 18% of the cases, the deceased were *Amrit Dhari* (baptised Sikhs) and wore their religious symbols, such as the *kirpan* (steel sword), even in death. However, some families reported removing the *kirpan*, showing the variation in how this rule is interpreted or applied. In every single case, the Sikh prayer (*ardas*) was recited before cremation, either at home or at the cremation grounds. Families also reported reciting or playing Sikh scriptures, such as *Chaupai Sahib* and *Sukhmani Sahib*, immediately after death. Some invited *bhai jis* (priests) from the gurdwara to lead the prayers. This widespread spiritual engagement shows strong alignment with Sikh traditions, either at home or at the cremation grounds.

One of the most intriguing insights emerged around organ donation. While the majority of the respondents expressed willingness to donate organs, only one family actually did so. When asked, they cited reasons like: 'We didn't think of it at the time'; 'The deceased was very old'; 'We weren't sure if the organs were usable'; 'We were in a hurry for cremation'. It is clear that while the spirit of giving is present, the practical barriers, emotional overwhelm, or lack of planning often prevent families from following through.

Buddhism

The ***Tibetan Book of the Dead*** (*Bardo Thodol*) offers a comprehensive guide to the rituals and practices that should be followed when preparing the body for disposal. This sacred text outlines specific practices for how the body should be handled, but like with many traditions, the actual customs followed by people can sometimes differ—especially when influenced by local customs or practical considerations.

In this case, Buddhist respondents mostly followed the traditional customs when preparing the deceased for their final journey. However, some of their practices, especially around the handling of the body, reflect an influence from Hindu traditions. According to Buddhist teachings, the body should not be touched until the lamas (monks) direct the family to do so. However, every Buddhist respondent in the study reported placing the body on the floor immediately after death, something that is not specifically prescribed in Buddhist texts. In cases where death occurred in the hospital, the body was transported home, placed on the floor, and covered with a sheet. However, in all the cases, lamas were invited after death. And as prescribed in *The Tibetan Book of the Dead*, prayers were offered for the deceased.

While not specifically mentioned in Buddhist texts, lighting lamps was a common practice among the respondents. In 73% of the cases, earthen lamps were lit near the deceased. One respondent, who followed the Vajrayana school of Buddhism, even shared that 108 lamps were lit—a practice popular in her village. While **lamas** and respondents alike explained that lighting lamps is part of their usual prayer rituals, it's not something formally prescribed in the scriptures. In every case, the body was washed and cleaned—a practice aligned with Buddhist tradition. However, when it came to dressing the body, responses were divided. About 50% of respondents said the body was dressed in new clothes, while the other half mentioned that the body was dressed in old but fresh clothes, only after the lamas completed their prayers and gave them permission to do so.

According to Buddhist tradition, the calculation of the auspicious time for the disposal of the body should be at least two to three days after death, but this was only followed in three instances. In the remaining 86% of cases, the body was disposed of on the same day as death. Most respondents explained that while the auspicious time is important, it was simply too inconvenient to keep the body for several days. One respondent even mentioned, 'If we were back in our village, we would have followed tradition,' suggesting that practical considerations—like the difficulties of storing a body for an extended period away from home—took precedence over strict adherence to the traditional timing. Additionally, one respondent mentioned a practice where, in their village, the deceased's body would be made to sit up before being removed from the home, but they couldn't carry this out due to the challenges of living away from their native place.

Buddhist death practices in Chandigarh are a blend of their traditional practices and local Hindu rituals.

Christianity

Most respondents adhered to the methods prescribed in their religion. In all cases, the body was cleansed by members of the parish collectively, rather than solely by close kin. In instances of hospital deaths, some respondents reported that hospital staff were directed and paid to perform the cleansing—a development that suggests the emergence of a new practice among Christian respondents. With regard to dressing the deceased, 63% stated that the body was dressed in new clothes, while the remaining 37%, largely Protestants, preferred dressing the deceased in their favourite attire so that the soul might feel comforted. A majority (86%) confirmed that perfumes or fragrances were used during the dressing, and in all the cases, Holy Water from the church was sprinkled on the body by the priest, sometimes at the graveside as well, before burial. Respondents also noted that the deceased's face was generally left uncovered until the coffin was lowered into the grave. A few emphasised that while most other rites are performed collectively by the community, covering the face is a ritual reserved for the son and close kin.

In Christian tradition, coffin colours—typically white or black—are allocated according to the age of the deceased. 43% affirmed this practice, while five (17%) admitted to ignoring the colour convention, and twelve (40%) were uncertain. Nonetheless, nearly all confirmed that coffins were decorated with flowers and garlands, particularly wreaths, which a few respondents explained are symbolic of resurrection.

Although almost all Christian respondents were aware of organ donation and many expressed willingness, none reported it being practised in their cases. Other prescribed practices—such as vigil and Mass before burial, the recitation of prayers, and blessing of the grave—were consistently observed. All respondents confirmed that the deceased was taken to the church for final blessings. The vigil and Mass were held before the burial, and prayers were offered at the graveside. Respondents explained that the Mass for the dead resembles a routine service, with additional prayers for the departed, and at times, members of the congregation shared words of remembrance. Some also mentioned that carols were sung before the Mass at the church.

In sum, respondents largely adhered to the traditional Christian practices surrounding preparation of the body and burial. Particularly, taking the deceased to church and reciting prayers at the graveside remained common across denominations.

Islam

Islam prescribes *ghusl* (washing), *kafan* (shrouding) and *namaz-e-janaza* (Funeral Prayer) as *wajib* (compulsory practices) before the disposal of the body. Respondents were asked whether they adhered to all these practices.

All respondents adhered to all the practices prescribed in their texts for body preparation before disposal. In 67% cases where death occurred at home, respondents confirmed that, as prescribed, they immediately closed the eyes and mouth, tied the toes, and started reciting *ayats*. The remaining 33% said that since the death occurred in the hospital, these practices were done only when the body reached home. All respondents agreed that the *Ghusl-e-Mayyit* (bathing of the dead body) was performed. Most of them shared that this is an act of utmost importance done for the deceased. One of the respondents, while explaining the importance of this ritual, said, '*Insaan do hi baar nahata hai, jab woh is duniya mein aata hai aur jab duniya se jaata hai*' (A human being bathes only twice in a lifetime—once upon entering this world and once upon leaving it).

They explained that there are multiple steps involved in *Ghusl-e-Mayyit*. While a few respondents mentioned using camphor and berry leaves, as prescribed, most reported using perfume during the bathing ritual. One respondent emphasised the thoroughness of this act, stating: '*Hamare mein kehte hain, ki* body *ko aise nehlana hai ki baal barabar bhi jagah nahi hoti jahan se pani na jaaye*' (In Islam, it is believed that the body should be washed so thoroughly that not even a space as thin as a strand of hair remains untouched by water). Some respondents, particularly close kin, shared that they did not personally perform the washing, noting that it is usually carried out by learned members of the community who are trained in the precise details of the ritual.

Regarding *Kafan-e-Mayyit* (shrouding), all respondents confirmed its performance. For a female deceased, women kin undertook the shrouding, covering the private parts and removing ornaments worn by the deceased. One respondent explained, '*Yahan se sirf kafan jaata hai aur kuch nahi*' (Only the shroud goes from here, nothing else). The *kafan* was described as being white in colour and consisting of five pieces. After bathing, the body was placed on a wooden bier brought from the mosque, the shroud was tied at both ends, and provision was made to view the face. However, restrictions were observed—'*shakal sirf woh dekh sakta hai jiske saath niqah jayaz nah ho*' (The face may be seen only by those with whom marriage would not have been permissible). Respondents elaborated that since the deceased is considered to be in the purest state, ready to return to God, access to the face is restricted to prevent the intrusion of impure thoughts. Some also remarked that even the husband is not permitted to touch his wife at this stage. For the male deceased, respondents reported that the body was wrapped in three layers of shroud. Most did not mention restrictions on viewing the face, though a few noted that only women who were ineligible to marry the deceased were permitted to do so. In all the cases, verses from the Quran were recited while the shrouding was performed.

With respect to the **funeral procession**, male respondents stated that they participated in carrying the bier, often considering it a noble deed: '*Janaze ko kandha dena nek kaam hota hai*' (Carrying a dead body on one's shoulder is a virtuous act). In some cases, due to distance, the body was transported in a funeral van. Female respondents noted that they did not join the procession, explaining that it is not permitted in Islam, though they visited the grave days after the burial.

All respondents confirmed the performance of *Salatul-Mayyit* (*Namaz-e-Janaza*). Male respondents explained that in the graveyard (*kabristan*), the body is placed in the mosque before burial. After performing *wudhu* (ritual cleansing), the imam leads the prayer, with the male congregation repeating after him. One respondent explained: '*Teen baar takbir padhte hain; yeh namaz alag hoti hai, khade hoke karte hain*' (*Allah hu Akbar* is recited three times; this prayer is distinct as it is performed while standing). Others added: '*Iss mein sajdah nahi hota kyunki hum sirf Allah ke samne sajdah karte hain. Yeh toh banda hai*' (There is no prostration in this prayer, as prostration is reserved for *Allah* alone; the deceased is but a human being). Women respondents reiterated that they did not participate in this ritual but offered prayers for the deceased at home. It is therefore evident that respondents strictly adhered to the rituals prescribed in Islamic texts for preparing the body, often with careful attention to detail.

When compared across religious faiths, distinct patterns emerge. Hindu respondents appeared more conformist than religious, following prescribed practices largely to uphold tradition rather than spiritual conviction. Sikh respondents were found to be less dogmatic, sometimes practising rituals that are explicitly prohibited in the *Rehat Maryada*, suggesting a gap between belief and practice. Buddhist respondents tended to follow convenient practices, adapting rituals to suit their circumstances, particularly as many lived away from their hometowns. By contrast, Christian and Muslim respondents displayed strong religious conformity, consistently adhering to the practices prescribed in their sacred texts. This suggests a greater alignment between what is prescribed, what is perceived, and what is practised in these two faiths. In the end, these practices are not just about death—they are acts of love, memory, and continuity. Even if these customs differ, the heart of the ritual remains the same: to honour the life that was.

Method of Body Disposal

In Hinduism, Sikhism, and Tibetan Buddhism, cremation is the prescribed method for disposing of the body, whereas Christianity and Islam recommend burial as the appropriate practice. As discussed in an earlier chapter, a considerable number of Hindu and Sikh respondents expressed preference for electric crematoriums over conventional cremation, viewing them as viable alternatives. In light of this, respondents were asked about the specific method they adopted for the disposal of the body.

Among Hindus, cremation on a conventional wooden pyre was used in 90% of cases, thus aligning with prescribed practice. One lower-caste respondent reported using a brick pyre in a corner of the cremation ground: '*Hamari* caste *ke liye alag bana rakhe hain, chotte hain aur kone mein*' (Our caste has been allotted a separate area in the cremation ground; smaller in size and placed in a corner). When cremation ground attendants were questioned about caste-wise allocation, they denied it, stating: '*Yeh shamshaan hai aur yahan sab samaan hain*' (This is the cremation ground and here all are equal). Further probing revealed that the municipal corporation had installed two brick-supported pyres to reduce wood consumption, with explanatory boards displayed at the site. Despite this, perceptions varied. Five respondents acknowledged using these pyres, citing reasons such as vacancy '*wahi khaali padi thi*' (That was the only empty one), location '*kone mein thi, alag se, toh humne wahan kar diya*' (It was in a corner, separately, so we did it there), - and lower cost - '*sasta tha woh*' (It was cheap). Others associated them with unclaimed bodies or were simply unaware of their existence, often deferring to the *pandas* or cremation attendants for guidance. This suggests that ignorance, financial considerations, and dependence on functionaries also shaped practice.

10% Hindu respondents reported using electric crematoriums. Although nearly a quarter had earlier expressed a preference for this option, many did not opt for it in practice. Reasons included lack of awareness at the time of death, emotional turmoil, family elders' insistence on tradition, or logistical hurdles such as long waiting times. Thus, while cremation on wooden pyres remained dominant, factors beyond religious prescription—ignorance, practicality, and authority of ritual specialists—played a role in decision-making.

Among Sikhs, the *Rehat Maryada* prescribes cremation as the appropriate method for all age groups, with alternatives permitted only in exceptional circumstances. In practice, 91% respondents reported cremation on wooden pyres, aligning with the prescribed method. Although thirteen respondents had earlier expressed a preference for electric crematoriums, only four actually used them. Explanations echoed those of Hindu respondents: lack of awareness at the time, unavailability, or family resistance. Thus, while Sikh perceptions reflect some openness to alternatives, practice is largely aligned with the tradition.

In Tibetan Buddhism, cremation is emphasised as the proper method, ensuring no physical remains are left to confuse the consciousness of the departed. All respondents confirmed cremation on wooden pyres, often accompanied by offerings of food items to the fire. None reported elaborate funeral processions; instead, bodies were transported in hearse vans. This indicates both adherence to prescribed cremation and adaptation to contemporary practicalities.

In **Christianity**, burial in cemeteries, rooted in the doctrine of resurrection, has been the traditional and prescribed method. All respondents confirmed burial as the method followed. They described prayers and blessings by the priest before lowering the coffin, with the final rite of closing the coffin lid marking the moment of covering the face. Respondents noted uniformity in grave alignment: '*Saari kabren ek hi* direction *mein khodi jaati hain, sab ke sar ek hi line mein hote hai*' (All graves are dug in the same direction, with heads aligned in one line). A few mentioned the feet facing the cemetery gate. Some Protestant respondents expressed concerns about limited burial land, suggesting a need for alternatives in the future. Overall, the practice matched prescribed beliefs.

In Islam, too, burial is prescribed in line with the doctrine of resurrection, wherein the dead will rise on the Day of Judgment.

All respondents confirmed burial, laying the body so that the face was turned towards the *Qiblah*, though some noted variations, attributing guidance to the *imam*. Respondents elaborated on grave dimensions, explaining that depth allows space for the deceased to sit when questioned by angels. After placing the body, wooden planks were set to prevent soil from falling directly on it. In some cases, the clothes worn at the time of death were also buried separately within the graveyard. All respondents ruled out constructing tombs, citing the belief that countless souls will rise from each grave on Judgment Day ('*Ek-ek kabr mein se lakhon log nikale jayenge*'). Thus, practice strongly reflected belief in resurrection and conformity to prescribed burial rites.

Overall, across all religious groups, the method of body disposal largely conformed to prescribed practices. The only deviations were the limited use of electric crematoriums among Hindu and Sikh respondents, despite broader acceptance of the idea. Among Buddhists, Christians, and Muslims, practice, prescription, and belief are closely aligned, reflecting strong religious conformity.

Before and Mid-Cremation Practices

In Hinduism, rituals such as *kapalkriya*, *matka phodna*, and *pinda daan* are prescribed to be performed before and during cremation. Hindu respondents were therefore asked whether and how they observed these practices.

Hinduism

The majority of Hindu respondents reported adhering to the prescribed rituals performed just before and during cremation. In most cases (73%), attention was paid to the prescribed direction while laying the deceased on the pyre. A majority (75%) affirmed performing the *parikrama* of the body. An overwhelming (95%) confirmed observing the rite of *matka phodna*, while in 72% cases, *kapalkriya* was performed. Similarly, 57% reported offering *pindas* to the deceased, both at home and at the cremation site. However, most noted that these rituals were carried out as directed by the *pandit ji*.

Beyond these widely recognised rites, several additional practices were mentioned. These included: cracking a coconut before lighting the pyre and distributing it as *prasad*; placing a small golden ladder with three steps on the pyre, symbolising survival by children, grandchildren, and great-grandchildren; offering *panch dhatu* (five metals); decorating the hearse with flowers and coins; flying balloons (*gubbare udaye the*) in memory of elderly deceased; placing honey in the mouth; and offering *chaddars* and shawls, which were later removed and kept aside.

This suggests that Hindu cremation incorporates a wide range of rituals—some, such as *kapalkriya*, *pinda daan*, and directional placement of the body, have a scriptural basis, while others seem to have evolved through local traditions. Nevertheless, all reflect deeply religious practices, with little evidence of change or innovation in contemporary observance.

As noted earlier, Hinduism also regards death occurring during *panchak* (a specific five-day period) as inauspicious, prescribing additional rites in such cases. Four respondents (7%) reported deaths during this phase and described the practices followed: '*Panchakein chal rahi thi toh ghas ka putla banake saath daal diya tha*' (Since the quintet days were ongoing, an effigy of grass was burnt with the corpse); '*Kuch din galat tha us din toh Narayan Bali ki pooja karayi thi*' (As the days were considered inauspicious, a special prayer was performed); '*Panchak thi toh koi pooja karayi thi*' (A ritual was conducted due to the quintet phase); and 'Last day *tha panchak ka isliye ek putla jalaya tha*' (Since death occurred on the last day of the phase, an effigy was burnt). By contrast, one respondent narrated that death occurring during *shraddh* days is considered auspicious, and was told that the deceased had certainly attained heaven.

Thus, the findings suggest that taboos surrounding *panchak* remain prevalent among Hindu respondents, and when death occurs during this period, families comply with the associated ritual obligations.

Sikhism

The *Rehat Maryada* explicitly prohibits the widely practised Hindu rite of *kapalkriya*. However, a significant number of Sikh respondents reported that both *matka phodna* and *kapalkriya* were performed before and during cremation.

On probing further, it was found that most respondents performed these rituals simply because they were instructed by functionaries or family members. This suggests that Sikh respondents were largely unaware of the code laid down in the *Rehat Maryada*. It can therefore be inferred that although Sikhism originally evolved with the intent of shaping a religious philosophy free from dogmas and superstitious practices, in matters of death, its adherents seem to be gradually reverting to Hindu traditions. Their perceptions may appear less dogmatic, but in practice, they remain deeply ritualistic.

Post-Cremation/Burial Practices

Post-cremation/burial practices are meant for the afterlife journey of the deceased. These practices include memorialising the deceased, doing away with the pollution caused by death, concluding the mourning phase, and helping the bereaved get back to their routine life after death. Accordingly, respondents from different religions were asked whether they observed the post-cremation/burial practices prescribed in their respective faiths.

Hinduism

In Hinduism, death initiates a phase of *asaucha* (impurity), during which mourners are prescribed specific practices. Since the faith also teaches that the soul undergoes an afterlife journey, additional rituals are prescribed to ensure better prospects for the deceased. Respondents were therefore asked about the post-cremation rites they observed.

Most respondents conformed to the religiously prescribed post-cremation practices. All confirmed bathing after cremation, particularly the chief mourners, and in all cases, the ritual of bone collection was performed. In instances where electric crematoriums were used, ashes were handed over by the operator the next day, rather than bones being collected. On the timing of ash collection (*phool chugna*), however, responses varied: some performed it on the third day, others the very next day, and some on the fourth day. All confirmed immersion of remains in the Ganges at Haridwar and performing *pinda daan*, though the days chosen for immersion and *kiryakaram* differed. Practical considerations often guided these choices:

- 'Relatives from afar cannot visit again.'
- 'It is better to finish the duties as soon as possible.'

This reflects a shift from strict adherence to prescribed ideals towards convenience and pragmatism.

Scriptural Recitations

A large majority (92%) confirmed reciting the *Garuda Purana* for ten days after cremation. A few replaced this with readings from the *Valmiki Ramayan*, the *Akhand Path* at a gurdwara, or the *Gayatri Jap*.

Pinda Daan and Donations

All respondents affirmed performing *pinda daan* at the site of bone immersion, usually at Khusha Ghat in Haridwar. Yet most admitted they had little understanding of the ritual itself, often deferring entirely to the *pandit*. For example:

- 'We did as directed by the *pandit.*'
- 'The flour was made into many balls; some were larger, some smaller.'

Donations were also widely reported, though often in commercialised forms. Some respondents purchased symbolic items locally in Chandigarh to avoid inflated prices at Haridwar:

- 'They made us touch the cow and charged money for it—just a symbolic cow donation.'

This highlights the growing commodification of rituals, with many performed mechanically rather than out of conviction.

Alms, Memorials, and Novel Practices

Meals and cash were commonly given to *pandits* on prescribed days, and food was offered to cows and dogs for thirteen days. Monthly (*varina*) and annual memorials were also widely observed, often involving *Brahmbhoj*, temple visits, or donations.

At the same time, some respondents adopted modern ways of remembering the deceased. One woman distributed chocolates to children each month in memory of her father, while another planned to publish his diary of literary writings on the first annual memorial. These indicate subtle but meaningful innovations in commemorative practices.

Social Pressure and Emotional Strain

Several respondents admitted that social expectations, rather than personal conviction, compelled them to perform the rites. One remarked, 'If it were up to me, I wouldn't have done any of these rituals. But in society, if we don't, people say children didn't even honour their parents.'

Another, reflecting on his mother's death, stated, 'There were so many rituals to complete, I didn't even get time to weep. The grief felt lighter than the burden of performing everything correctly.'

Mourning Restrictions

The majority (88%) observed mourning restrictions, including:

- not cooking on the day of death;
- sleeping on the floor for thirteen days;
- abstaining from shaving or washing hair;
- eating *satvik* food without onion and garlic;
- avoiding festivals and new purchases for a year;
- postponing marriages or other *samskaras;*
- widows, in particular, reported avoiding ceremonies and community gatherings for an entire year.

Overall, while most Hindu respondents followed prescribed post-cremation practices, many did so out of social obligation or habit rather than belief. Increasingly, convenience, commercialisation, and societal expectations influence ritual observance. Yet alongside continuity, new and creative ways of memorialising the deceased—such as distributing chocolates or publishing a book—are also emerging, reflecting gradual shifts in practice.

Sikhism

Sikhism prescribes certain post-cremation practices such as immersion of bones and ashes in flowing water, commencement of the *path*, and the culmination of the mourning phase on the tenth day after death with *bhog*. Sikh respondents were asked about the rituals they observed.

Certain practices like *ardas* after cremation, bone collection, immersion of remains at Kiratpur Sahib, and the *path* followed by *bhog* were observed in all cases. However, there was variation in the timing of the *path* and *bhog*. The most common explanations were practical:

- 'It was done on an upcoming Sunday.'
- 'We did it on the seventh or tenth day.'

Interestingly, *pinda daan*, which is explicitly rejected in the *Rehat Maryada*, was also performed by eight respondents (18%) at Haridwar. When asked why, they gave reasons such as:

- 'It brings peace of mind.'
- 'Someone told us it was important.'
- 'It helps the soul attain liberation; otherwise, life faces obstacles.'

Similarly, 78% respondents observed restrictions during mourning that are not sanctioned in Sikh texts. These included: sleeping on the floor; avoiding elaborate meals; abstaining from shaving (among those who had already cut their beards); avoiding bright clothing or makeup (for women); not cooking on the day of cremation; and not celebrating festivals for a year.

Donations and Memorials

Although donations in the name of the deceased are explicitly rejected in Sikh doctrine, 80% admitted to practising them. Items donated ranged from clothes, footwear, bedding, and utensils to other household articles, often given to the gurdwara. Donations of utensils at Patalpuri in Kiratpur Sahib were particularly common. Those who refrained from making material donations explained that they instead contributed the standard charges to the gurdwara for conducting *path*, *bhog*, and *langar*. They also typically offered a *rumala* (cloth covering) to the Guru Granth Sahib. For memorialisation, most respondents conducted a *path* and *ardas* on the first death anniversary at the gurdwara. A few reported providing monthly meals to the poor in memory of the deceased.

Overall, the majority of Sikh respondents adhered to the practices formally prescribed in Sikhism. Yet, a noticeable proportion also engaged in rituals like *pinda daan*, donations of goods, and mourning restrictions that reflect Hindu influence. This suggests that while Sikh post-cremation practices remain anchored in religious prescription, elements of long-standing Hindu traditions continue to shape actual observance.

Buddhism

Unlike Sikhism and Hinduism, Buddhism—particularly the *Theravada* school—does not prescribe fixed post-cremation practices. In *Mahayana* and *Vajrayana* traditions, however, certain rituals related to the collection and disposal of ashes, memorial observances, and recitation of sacred texts continue to hold significance. Tibetan Buddhism, for instance, prescribes memorial prayers on specific days and the reading of the *Bardo Thodol* (*The Tibetan Book of the Dead*). Given the regional variations within Buddhism, respondents were asked what practices they followed after cremation.

Most respondents adhered to customs related to ash immersion. 72% immersed the ashes in flowing water, often in their native villages or at Haridwar. Adhering to their traditional way, a smaller proportion—six respondents (28%)—reported crushing the remains, mixing them with clay, and placing them on higher terrains for birds. Importantly, all respondents denied performing *pinda daan*.

Memorials were universally observed. Prayers were conducted for 49 days after death, with lamas invited on significant days such as the third, seventh, fourteenth, and forty-ninth. Some respondents mentioned that, in their villages, lamas conducted prayers daily throughout this period. These observances were accompanied by giving alms to lamas and offering meals to relatives and community members. 68% specifically noted that the *Bardo Thodol* was read by lamas during this period, typically in the room where the body of the deceased had been kept. However, the making and disposal of an effigy on the forty-ninth day, as prescribed in some texts, was not practiced. A significant number (68%) stated that from cremation until the culmination of funeral rites, a portion of each meal was set aside in the name of the deceased and later fed to birds and animals. Additionally, in all cases, alms in the form of food, clothing, or money were donated to monks and monasteries.

The findings indicate that Buddhist respondents largely adhered to practices associated with Tibetan Buddhism. While *pinda daan* was universally rejected, rituals such as ash immersion, forty-nine days of prayers, recitation of the *Bardo Thodol*, and giving alms remained widely observed. Overall, their responses highlight a strong continuity of post-cremation traditions rooted in *Vajrayana Buddhism*.

Christianity

Christianity teaches that death ensures eternal life with God, yet memorial services continue to hold an important place in Christian tradition. As noted earlier, many respondents expressed that they did not consider memorials essential. However, nearly all of them observed these practices. The timing of memorial services varied: most were held on the third, seventh, and fortieth day after death, while a few were scheduled according to the convenience of family members and relatives.

The memorial service typically included a Mass with special prayers for the departed, followed by a shared meal at the church or the deceased's home. In some cases, food and clothes were distributed to the poor in the name of the deceased, though all respondents denied giving donations directly to the church or priest. In 86% cases, the first death anniversary was marked with a Mass, a visit to the grave, and a collective meal. A few Catholic respondents also mentioned visiting graves on *All Souls' Day* to remember their dead and offer prayers for all souls in general.

The majority (63%) denied any symbolic observances to mourn death. In their words: 'We don't mourn death!' The remaining 37% mentioned that no cooking was done on the day of death, sometimes because the family was preoccupied, and at other times until the priest had blessed the home with holy water. Interestingly, one respondent shared that after her mother's death, the family chose to celebrate her memory by singing her favourite songs and preparing her favourite food.

Overall, the findings suggest that Christian respondents largely adhered to traditional post-burial practices, even when they personally considered them unimportant. This reflects a shift in perception—away from viewing memorials as religiously obligatory—yet continuity in practice, maintained as a way of honouring the deceased and sustaining communal remembrance.

Islam

Islamic texts do not prescribe stringent post-burial rituals, though tradition allows for a period of mourning. When Muslim respondents were asked about practices after burial, several patterns emerged.

All respondents shared that upon returning from the burial ground, family and community members recited the Quran collectively; in some cases, this was followed by a shared meal. 42% reported donating food to poor children in the name of the deceased, often at a *madrassa* (Islamic school). They clarified that these donations were not religiously mandated but were carried out at the wish of family members. While Islamic teachings do not emphasise an extended mourning period, most respondents (86%) observed three days of mourning. In cases where the deceased was male, widows observed a forty-day mourning period, during which they stayed indoors and refrained from meeting outsiders.

When asked about festivals and celebrations, many respondents said that while they continued to fast during Ramadan, they avoided feasting on Eid, limiting observances to prayers. Regarding memorials, most respondents said they remembered the deceased in their prayers, and a few mentioned visiting graves to recite *dua*. These findings suggest that although Islam does not mandate elaborate post-burial practices, Muslim respondents adopted certain traditional observances, largely as a way of honouring the deceased and sustaining community bonds.

Taken together, these responses reveal that post-cremation and post-burial practices serve multiple purposes: to affirm religious identity, maintain social cohesion, and provide psychological solace. While texts may not always mandate them, tradition, family expectations, and cultural continuity ensure that these practices remain integral to how communities deal with death.

Cost Incurred in Carrying Out Death-Related Practices

In contemporary times, particularly in the West, the funeral industry has emerged as a thriving sector. Service providers play a central role in assisting families with death-related arrangements, often turning these services into a highly profitable enterprise.[4] Jonathan Parry has also emphasized the commercialization of death rituals in Banaras—a city regarded as the most 'apt' place to die, believed to ensure salvation.[5] To gain insight into the extent of commercialisation in death-related rituals, respondents were asked about the expenses they incurred while dealing with death.

Among Hindu respondents, the largest proportion (73%) reported spending between ₹200,001 and ₹300,000. In eight cases (13%), expenses reached up to ₹400,000, and in one case, exceeded ₹400,000. Seven respondents spent ₹100,001 to ₹200,000. Even low-income families often had to shell out substantial amounts. Major expenses included performing rituals at Haridwar, donations (cash and kind) to *pandits,* and meals during memorials. Common donations included cash equivalent to the cost of a cow, clothing, bedding, utensils, and food. Some respondents also purchased tickets and food for the deceased during travel. Interestingly, in certain cases, the consanguineal kin of female family members bore part of the costs, a practice with no textual reference but likely evolved as a support mechanism. Overall, Hindu death rituals are expensive, reflecting commercialisation as noted by Jonathan Parry in Banaras.

Among Sikh respondents, although rituals prescribed by Sikhism are less elaborate, 60% reported expenses between ₹100,001 and ₹200,000, 36% up to ₹300,000, and in a few cases, exceeding ₹400,000. Costs were incurred for body preparation, cremation, post-cremation rituals, obituaries, donations, and meals. Some practices, such as *pinda daan,* increased the costs. Similar to Hindus, expenses for certain ceremonies were sometimes

4. Metcalf, P., Huntington, R. Frontmatter. (1991). *Celebrations of Death: The Anthropology of Mortuary Ritual.* Cambridge University Press.

5. Parry, Jonathan. (1994), *Death in Banaras,* New York. Cambridge University Press.

borne by female kin, reflecting either traditional support or influence from Hindu practices. Sikh funerals, therefore, also reflect significant commercialisation.

For Buddhist respondents, expenses were comparatively lower. While four of 22 respondents spent ₹50,000–₹100,000, most (81%) spent ₹100,000–₹200,000, primarily on lamas' fees, donations, and meals during memorials. Fees for lamas varied, depending on the number of monks and the duration of prayers, and donations were voluntary. Although lower than Hindu and Sikh expenses, a commercial element was still present in Buddhist funerals due to reliance on paid services of lamas.

In their words: '*Ek* lama *ek din ka 3–4 ghanta* prayer *karne ka ₹350 tak leta hai. Jitne zaada* lama *honge utna acha maante hain. Jo log zaada ameer hai, poora 49 din pooja karata hai; unka kharcha toh bahut hota hai*' (One lama charges about ₹ 350 for one day's service, it is believed that having more of them in number is good for the deceased. For rich folks who prefer to have prayers for all 49 days, it becomes a very expensive affair); '*Marne waale ki grahdisha ke hisaab se, patre dekh ke kitne din ki pooja hogi or kitne* lama *langenge, yeh bhi* lama *log hi batate hain. Toh utna toh kharcha dena padta hai*' (Considering the cosmic condition of the deceased, the monks decide about the prayers and rituals that have to be done as well as the number of monks required. So, that much expense has to be borne). However, a few respondents also said that lamas do not charge any fixed amount as their fees, but they are given money as donations.

Christian respondents reported much lower expenses. In most cases (66%), costs ranged from ₹50,000 to ₹100,000, and in 27% of cases, less than ₹50,000. Minimal expenses included coffin, shrouding, decorations, wreaths, candles, and cemetery labour charges. Larger expenses (up to ₹1.5 lakh) involved meals and donations to the poor. Church priests do not charge fees for funeral services, and the community often assists families in need. Tombstone construction, although costly, was avoided due to limited cemetery space. Thus, the commercialisation of death rituals is negligible among Christians.

Among Muslim respondents, funeral expenses were very low. Costs rarely exceeded ₹50,000, and in more than half of the cases, only ₹5,000 was spent on the shroud, grave digging, and wooden planks. Donations were voluntary, and funeral assistance from the *imam* or community members incurred no fees. In their words: '*Mayyit ke liye toh dua karna unka farz hai, iska kya paise?*' (It is their duty to pray for the deceased; there is no money required for it); 'It is the right of every Muslim to receive these rituals for his/her final journey from his/her brethren'. Thus, the community collectively ensures that financial constraints do not prevent proper funerals.

Overall, the commercialisation of death-related rituals is evident in Hinduism, Sikhism, and Buddhism, with substantial expenses borne by families and service providers profiting from assistance in rituals. In contrast, death practices among Christians and Muslims remain relatively frugal, with community support and religious institutions minimising costs.

Women's Participation in Death-Related Practices

In Hinduism, gender-based dichotomies have existed since the **Smriti** phase, with clearly defined roles in both public and private spheres. Ritual responsibilities, especially those related to death, were traditionally designated as male prerogatives. The role of the *karta*—the chief mourner who performs the last rites and lights the funeral pyre—has historically been reserved for men. Therefore, when women take on this role, it signifies a noteworthy shift from tradition and suggests the emergence of new cultural patterns.

To examine whether such a change is occurring, Hindu respondents were asked whether women had taken on the role of chief mourner and lit the funeral pyre. In 97% cases, the last rites were performed by male family members—typically sons, or other male kin if there are no sons of the deceased. Only in two cases women assumed the role of *karta* and performed the final rites themselves.

One such instance was narrated by a woman who, being the only child, performed the last rites at her mother's funeral. She recounted: '*Mere* in-laws *ne bahut mana kiya tha aur wahan pe bhi* scene create *kiya tha, lekin meri chachiyon ne unhe chup karwaya* (My in-laws strongly opposed it and created a scene at the funeral, but my aunts intervened and silenced them). My children (son and daughter) and husband were not allowed to participate in the *Shanti Puja* I conducted at home, because my in-laws were upset that I had performed the rites myself. My in-laws are highly educated, liberal, and modern—my mother-in-law wears short skirts, attends parties, and has no issues with drinking. She's even accepted live-in relationships within the family. We had a love marriage, and she never imposed traditional norms like wearing bangles or a *bindi*. I've always had the freedom to wear what I want, go to parties, and live life on my own terms. But when she objected to me performing the last rites, it felt like the ground had slipped from under my feet. I was deeply shocked. I could never have imagined she would oppose me on this. Ironically, it was my aunts—who are illiterate—who stood by me and supported my decision.'

This narrative powerfully illustrates the deep-rootedness of ritual conservatism, even among families that otherwise identify as progressive or liberal in lifestyle. It reveals the layered and often contradictory nature of modernity in Indian families, where outward liberalism may coexist with entrenched traditionalism in matters of ritual and religion.

On the other hand, another woman respondent—also an only child who performed the last rites for her mother—shared a different experience. In her case, there was no familial objection, as her mother had been living with her for many years and passed away in her home. However, she recounted facing resistance and scepticism at every ritual stage—from cremation and bone collection to the immersion of ashes in Haridwar. In her words: '*Mujhe har jagah* explain *karna padhta tha, pandit ji maine hi karna hai sab kuch. Phir bhi kehte the, "koi* cousin, *koi* uncle *se karwa lete"*.' (At every place, I had to explain that I was the one performing the rites. Yet, the priest would insist, 'Why not have a cousin or uncle do it instead?')

This account highlights the institutional and priestly gatekeeping that continues to restrict women's full participation in death rituals, regardless of familial acceptance.

In all other cases, the majority of women respondents shared that while they did visit the cremation grounds, they remained on the periphery—often standing at a distance without directly witnessing or participating in the rites. One respondent, whose father had passed away, explained that she and her sister (with no brother in the family) were given the opportunity by their uncle to light the pyre. However, engulfed in grief and fear, they did not feel emotionally or mentally prepared to perform the act themselves. Despite this, they chose to remain present and observed the proceedings closely.

In Sikhism, the *Rehat Maryada* notes, 'The dead body should then be placed on the pyre and the son or any other relation or friend of the deceased should set fire to it.' Though the term 'son' is mentioned, at the same time, terms 'other relation' and 'friend' are also included; therefore, Sikhism doesn't categorically prohibit women from performing last rites.

However, among Sikh respondents as well, women lighting the funeral pyre remained a rare occurrence. In only two cases did women perform this role, while in all other (96%) cases, the last rites were conducted by male family members. In these instances, the sons were given first preference; in their absence, sons-in-law or other male relatives assumed the responsibility.

In one case, where all the siblings were daughters, the youngest daughter took the initiative to perform all the last rites. Recalling her experience, she said: *'Maine kaha ki mere* papa *hain, main hi karungi. Nahin toh bade behanon ke husbands ko bol rahe the, par meri sisters ne support kiya mujhe.'* (I said, he is my father, so I will do it. Otherwise, they were suggesting that the husbands of my elder sisters should perform the rites, but my sisters supported me.)

This instance reflects both the resistance women may face and the solidarity that can enable them to assert their right to perform such rituals, especially in the absence of male siblings.

There was only one case where, despite the son being alive, the daughter—along with her husband—performed the last rites for her mother. The decision was based on the fact that the mother had been living with her daughter for several years and passed away at her residence. Recounting the experience, the daughter shared: 'Mummy *hamare saath hi reh rahe the kaafi saalon se, bhai toh bahar tha. Us samay unhone kaha, tum karo. Waise toh hum sab saath mein hi the, lekin aag maine aur mere husband ne di. Lekin baad mein bhog bhai ne hi karwaya.'* (My mother had been staying with us for many years, while my brother was living away. At that time, he told me to go ahead. Though we were all present together, it was my husband and I who lit the pyre. However, the bhog ceremony was conducted by my brother.)

This case highlights a rare deviation from normative practice, where practical circumstances and mutual family consent allowed the daughter to assume ritual responsibility, even though the son was alive and ultimately resumed the traditional role in the post-cremation ceremonies.

Although the Buddhist texts (referred to in the present study) do not contain explicit gender-based prescriptions regarding participation in funeral rituals, however, in practice, women are traditionally assigned a very passive role in death-related rites. Respondents explained that women's involvement was generally limited to washing or preparing the body in the case of a deceased woman and assisting in meal preparations for memorial events. In the majority of cases, the pyre was lit by male members of the community, often alongside lamas. In fact, women did not visit the cremation grounds at all in any of the Buddhist cases studied. Some respondents clarified that this exclusion was not merely based on gender norms but stemmed from specific spiritual beliefs. According to them, in Tibetan Buddhist traditions, based on the exact moment of death and what is believed to be best for the soul's transition, the decision regarding who participates in the funeral rituals and who goes to the cremation site is made by the lamas, In one particular case, the respondent noted that only lamas lit the pyre, stating: '*Humne haath bhi nahi lagana hota, sirf lama log karte hain.*' (We don't even touch the pyre; only the lamas perform the rites). They further added that even the ashes and remaining bones are collected solely by lamas.

These findings make it evident that women are not assigned an active role in death-related rituals within Buddhist communities. The likely reason lies in the metaphysical understanding of death in Tibetan Buddhism. Death is seen not as a sudden cessation but as a transitional phase where consciousness does not immediately leave the body. Instead, it undergoes a process—moving through dream-like states before rebirth. In this critical period, any disturbance is believed to hinder the soul's journey. Therefore, most death-related responsibilities are considered the domain of trained lamas rather than laypersons—irrespective of gender, though in effect, women remain largely excluded.

Christianity and Islam

Christianity doesn't subscribe to the idea of a chief mourner, and death-related practices are collectively performed by the members of the community. It was notable that in all cases, women participated in most of the funeral rituals held at home, in the church, and at the graveside. They mentioned that only the cleansing of the body is done by the members of the same gender and the last ritual of covering the face of the deceased is the prerogative of the son; in all other practices, women in the family are equally involved.

As discussed earlier, in Islam, women are traditionally barred from visiting mosques for certain religious functions, let alone graveyards for burial rites. In the present study, it was found that women's participation in death-related rituals was limited to practices conducted within the home, such as *ghusl* (ritual washing) and *kafan* (shrouding) in cases involving a female deceased. They are prohibited from participating in the funeral procession, the digging of the grave, and the *Namaz-e-Janaza* (funeral prayer) at the burial site. Despite this visibly minimal role, women respondents were still asked whether they participated in rituals performed at the graveyard; in none of the cases did women accompany the funeral procession to the burial ground.

Upon deeper probing, it was found that the majority of respondents believed these restrictions to be in accordance with religious prescriptions and therefore justified. Some explained that women are excluded because funeral processions and burials are considered *emotionally demanding and are thought to require mental and emotional fortitude—qualities often (problematically) not associated with women.* More strikingly, such justifications were echoed by many female respondents themselves, reflecting deep internalisation of the traditional gender norms.

Only two women expressed a desire to be part of the funeral procession and present at the burial site. As they put it: *'Saath jaa sakein procession mein toh achha hai'* (It would be good if we were allowed to go along in the funeral procession); *'Jitne log zyada honge utni dua milegi.'* (The more people there are, the more prayers will be offered).

These responses highlight not only the restricted roles of women in Islamic death rituals but also the overwhelmingly conventional outlook among Muslim respondents, with religious texts and traditions continuing without any change.

Consequently, in religious traditions such as Hinduism,

Sikhism, Buddhism, and Islam, women's participation in death-related rituals remains subdued and largely restricted to a limited set of practices. Their roles are often shaped by scriptural prescriptions, cultural norms, or institutional authority, leaving little room for active involvement in main rituals. Therefore, when women do assume the role of chief mourner and engage in rituals traditionally reserved for men, it marks a significant deviation from established norms and serves as a clear indicator of societal transformation.

Children's Participation in Funeral Rites

Death is often hidden and sequestrated from everyday life.[6] So it was tested on one more parameter; respondents were asked, if children in the family were allowed to participate in funeral rites.

In 65% of Hindu cases, children did not participate in funeral rituals. Only in twenty-one cases children were involved in some practices. Among those who excluded children, the most common responses included: 'They were taken away', 'Sent to a relative's place', and 'They were too young to comprehend'. Conversely, among respondents who allowed children to witness parts of the funeral process, the participation was generally limited to observing preparations at home. Common explanations included: '*Ghar pe sab dekha, par saath nahi leke gaye*' (They saw everything at home but were not taken to the cremation grounds); and '*Hum chahte the dekh len taaki pata ho ki kya hota hai*' (We wanted them to see it so they would understand what happens).

Furthermore, all respondents unanimously stated that children were not taken along for bone collection (*asthi sanchay*), immersion rituals, or *pinda daan*.

Among Sikh respondents, in 67 % cases, children participated—if not directly, then at least as observers—witnessing

6. Willmott, H. (2000). Death. So What? Sociology, Sequestration and Emancipation. *The Sociological Review,* 48 (4), 649–665.

the preparations and rituals performed for the deceased. Some respondents even mentioned that children accompanied the family to the cremation ground. However, a significant minority (33%), chose to withhold this experience from their children, either by sending them away or keeping them at home.

Among Buddhist respondents, in the majority of cases (86%) children did not participate in funeral practices. However, upon further probing, it became clear that this exclusion was not motivated by a desire to hide death from children. Rather, it stemmed from deeply held religious beliefs about the post-death journey of consciousness.

To facilitate a smooth transition, the body is kept undisturbed, and rituals are conducted in a highly controlled and sacred environment. As discussed earlier, it is the lamas—after performing cosmic calculations—who decide who may participate in the rituals, and this often excludes children. Respondents clarified that while children were not physically involved in the rites, they were made aware of what was happening.

Among 80% Christian respondents, children in the family participated in funeral rites. In the remaining six cases, respondents explained that there were no children in the immediate family or close circle of relatives. When further probed about children's exposure to death-related aspects, most respondents affirmed that the deceased's body is not hidden from children. Several also noted that children are familiar with the concepts of death and resurrection through regular exposure to the story of Jesus, which is shared during church services and routine prayers at home.

In the case of the majority of Muslim respondents (67%), children in the family participated in death-related practices; children were involved in funeral rites. Respondents specifically noted that young boys in the family often accompanied male relatives to the graveyard. Additionally, several respondents shared that children are regularly introduced to the concept of death from an early age. They explained that discussions around the meaning of death, the soul's journey after death, and the Day of Judgment are integral parts of religious education, beginning as soon as children start reading the Quran.

Therefore, this clearly indicates that, among Hindu respondents, death is intentionally concealed from children. While death is frequently visible to children through television, video games, and cartoons—often in dramatised or fictionalised forms—real-life encounters with death are deliberately avoided. Families make a conscious effort to shield children from the emotional and ritual dimensions of death by excluding them from participating in funeral rites. Among Sikh families, it appears that death is not treated as a taboo subject and is generally not hidden from children. Instead, there seems to be a greater openness in allowing children to witness and, in some cases, engage with death-related practices. Amongst Buddhists, minimal or no-participation of children in death practices is not an attempt to sequestrate death but rather as a religiously motivated effort to protect the spiritual integrity of the deceased's consciousness during its journey toward rebirth. Amongst Christian and Muslim families, death is not sequestered from children. Rather, it is integrated into religious narratives and everyday spiritual life, offering children both direct and symbolic exposure to the concept of death from an early age. Notably, in the case of Christians, this stands in contrast to the widely discussed Western model of the sequestration of death—a cultural shift that ironically evolved within Christian-dominated societies themselves.

Unique Death-Related Practices

During fieldwork in the research area, three noteworthy cases emerged in which unconventional practices were followed at the time of death. These cases deviated from the traditionally prescribed religious norms and offer valuable insight into the evolving landscape of death-related rituals. As this book aims to capture the **diversity and dynamism** in contemporary death-related practices, these cases are important to document. They highlight not only the influence of modern institutions and personal agency but also the **emerging shifts** in how death is understood, ritualised, and commemorated beyond rigid religious frameworks.

A Lasting Gift: Body Pledged to Science

Case 1

In two cases among Hindu respondents, the deceased bodies were **donated to medical institutions** rather than being cremated according to customary rites. This practice, though still relatively rare, is gaining visibility through **awareness campaigns and motivational drives led by hospitals and medical colleges,** which emphasise the societal value of body donation for scientific and educational purposes.

Mrs Santosh is a 41-year-old graduate, living with her two daughters and son, and working in a government organisation with an approximate annual income of ₹4 lakh. She is a Hindu *brahmin* who prays twice daily and visits the temple at least once a week. Her father passed away at the age of eighty due to a brain stroke at P.G.I. Hospital, Chandigarh. With the approval of other family members, Mrs Santosh and her brother chose to donate the body to P.G.I. for medical purposes, instead of bringing it home for cremation as per religious customs. In her own words: 'What we did was a very bold decision for our entire family; no one else in the extended family would have had the courage to do this.' When asked what motivated this decision, Mrs Santosh replied, 'It was my father's wish.' She explained that her father had worked as a Block Extension Educator for the Department of Health, Punjab, and likely learned about body donation through his job. Although she was unsure what specifically inspired him, he was adamant about donating his body, even pledging it against the wishes of other family members.

She recalled, ‘He used to carry the donation cards with him. When my niece passed away unexpectedly, at her memorial ceremony, he stood up in front of everyone and said that his body must not be cremated but given to the hospital to help children learn.’ For their middle-class relatives, this was a shocking declaration. Her in-laws remarked, ‘It doesn’t seem right; what is he talking about at someone else’s death?’ She also mentioned that her brother had strained relations with her father, leading some to believe that her father took this decision out of resentment, to prevent his son from performing the last rites.

On the day of his death at P.G.I., doctors from the eye donation department came to collect his eyes. Afterwards, the hospital staff were informed of his wish to donate the body. Relatives were called to the hospital for the *antim darshan* (final homage). The Anatomy Department staff arrived, a collective prayer was offered, and the body was taken away. Mrs Santosh said, ‘We didn’t ask what they would do or if anything would be returned. The doctors explained that the body would be preserved with chemicals and then used for teaching students.’

Regarding post-cremation rituals, she said that all other religious practices were observed according to tradition. On the third day, her brother, as chief mourner, went to Haridwar and performed *pinda daan* despite the absence of ashes. At home, the *Garuda Purana* was recited for ten days, and donations were made at Haridwar and to *brahmins* as directed by family elders. On the eleventh day, *kriyakaram* was performed, followed by a visit to *Pheowa* for further *pinda daan*. Monthly rituals continued for a year, culminating in the annual *barsi* ceremony. She estimated that these rites cost approximately ₹3.75 lakh.

When questioned about why they followed these rituals despite not cremating the body, she said, ‘The traditional rites meant for the peaceful journey of ancestors must be performed.’

Reflecting on the experience, Mrs Santosh admitted that initially the family felt uneasy and faced criticism from relatives who voiced various fears. However, over time, many began to appreciate their decision. Doctors at P.G.I. even acknowledged their gesture in a newspaper article. She added that her brother has also pledged his organs and body, and she herself has pledged her organs and is considering body donation as well. She concluded with confidence, 'Death seems less fearsome now!'

This case illustrates a significant shift—choosing a secular mode of body disposal due to the deceased's prior commitment. For a middle-class Hindu *brahmin* family, this was a bold step. Despite social pressures, they adhered to all other traditional rituals to ensure the smooth transition of the soul, demonstrating that while their actions deviated in practice, their underlying beliefs remain rooted in Hindu death customs. Ultimately, they fulfilled the deceased's wish while maintaining faith in ancestral rites.

Case 2

A similar case is that of Mr Neeraj, a 52-year-old post-graduate (MBA) entrepreneur, with an annual household income of approximately ₹5–6 lakh. He lives with his wife and two daughters. A Hindu Khatri by caste, Mr Neeraj follows the Arya Samaj sect. He performs *havan* (Vedic fire ritual) every morning but does not follow any other prayer routine. Within the span of six months, he lost both his parents. His mother, a retired school teacher, passed away at the age of 75, followed by his father, a retired government officer from Chandigarh, at the age of 85. Both had suffered from cancer. Mr Neeraj stated that his parents were also followers of the Arya Samaj doctrine—'*Dono havan karte the aur Arya Samaj mandir jaate the*' (Both performed *havan* and regularly visited the Arya Samaj temple). After their deaths, he donated their bodies to the Department of Anatomy at GMCH, Sector 32, Chandigarh. When asked what inspired him to do so, he shared that a friend had introduced him to the option of body donation. In his words:

'A friend had donated his father's body at a time when hospitals in Chandigarh did not even accept dead bodies. He had to put in a lot of effort to get the body accepted at PGI.'

He added, 'Since then, I was inspired by him. Though my parents hadn't pledged, when my mother died, I discussed with my father not to cremate her, and he agreed. So we decided to send her body to the hospital. When my father passed away a few months later, we did the same for him.'

Both deaths occurred at home—his mother, late at night, and his father, early in the morning. In each case, the bodies were cleaned and dressed, and relatives were invited for *antim darshan* (final homage). A *havan* was performed by a *pandit ji* from the Arya Samaj temple, along with Mr Neeraj himself. After keeping the bodies at home for about three hours, the anatomy department was contacted, and a vehicle was sent to receive them.

Regarding other post-death rituals, he stated that they did not perform any traditional rites such as visiting Haridwar, *pinda daan*, *uthala*, or *brahm bhoj*. Instead, he continues to offer oblations for his parents during his routine morning *havan*. He expressed belief in the doctrine of reincarnation but rejected the ideas of afterlife realms like heaven or hell, and therefore, sees no importance in post-death rituals. In his words, '*pakhand hain sab*' (All these rituals are superstitions). When asked if this experience affected his and his family's understanding of death, Mr Neeraj revealed that his wife and children are comfortable with the decision. While they were initially fearful during his mother's donation, by the time of his father's death, they were more accepting. He said, 'After my mother's death, my father himself told us not to cremate his body. My wife and I have also pledged our bodies.'

This case clearly illustrates that Mr Neeraj's perceptions of death diverge from traditional prescribed beliefs. Consequently, he chose the secular option of whole body donation out of personal conviction rather than compulsion or social pressure. Moreover, he has successfully convinced his close family to follow the same path, indicating a conscious and deliberate adoption of non-religious death practices.

In the Embrace of the River: A Case of Water Burial in a Sikh Family

In the third case, a Sikh respondent and his family chose water burial for the deceased father in a flowing river, diverging both from normative Sikh practices and from broader Indian customs. While the motivation for this act was not deeply elaborated upon, it stands out as a symbolic return to nature and possibly reflects personal or ecological considerations.

Sardar Gurjit Singh, a 67-year-old resident of Chandigarh, lives in a joint family with his wife, son, daughter-in-law, and three grandchildren. A law graduate by education, he sustains his livelihood through agricultural land holdings in Punjab and Uttar Pradesh, which are managed by contracted caretakers. The household's annual income is estimated between ₹8 lakh and ₹10 lakh.

Belonging to the Jatt Sikh community, Sardar Gurjit Singh is a disciple of Sant Baba Dharna Singh. The family does not adhere to a strict daily prayer routine; however, members recite *path* individually whenever they feel inclined, and they visit the gurdwara occasionally. His father passed away at the age of 95, due to a brain haemorrhage.

Upon his father's passing, Sardar Gurjit Singh chose to fulfil his father's long-standing wish by immersing his body in the waters of the Sutlej River, near Gurdwara Bhabour Sahib, located in Nangal, Punjab. This gurdwara holds historical significance, as it is believed that Guru Gobind Singh, the tenth Sikh Guru, once halted there for several months.

When asked what motivated the family to opt for this unconventional practice, Sardar Gurjit Singh responded: *'Unki hi ichchha thi. Woh hamesha kehte the jab main jaaun toh mera antim sanskar jal pravah ke roop mein ho. Pandrah-bees sal se keh rahe the. Chahte the ki deh kisi kam aaye—paani ke jeev-jantu kha lenge.'* (It was his wish. For nearly fifteen to twenty years, he had been expressing that after his death, his final rites should be performed by immersing his body in water. He believed that his body should serve a purpose—even in death—and that aquatic life would benefit from it.)

The family honoured this deeply personal and ecologically inspired request, bypassing the traditional practice of cremation. The decision, while rare and non-normative within the Sikh tradition, was rooted in the deceased's personal philosophy and long-expressed desire.

Sardar Gurjit Singh shared that this was not a standard or commonly accepted method of body disposal; to carry out the immersion special permission had to be obtained from the local city administration and Takht Shri Keshgarh Sahib.[7] He recounted the sequence of events with clarity and reverence. He said: *'Pehle unhe unke* bathroom *mein hi nehlaya, safed rang ke kapde aur safed pagri mein tiyaar kiya. Amrit shakha huya tha unhone. Lakkadi ka box banwaya, usme jagah–jagah ched karwaye, fir andar unhe rakha, band karwane se pehle andar bade-bade patthar dale tanki neeche chala jaye.* Bus *karke gaye yahan se. Pehle gurdware mein* ardaas *karwayi, fir do boats mein gaye, ek mein* body *aur hum sab aur doosri mein aur log jo aana chahte the. Beech mein gaye pani ke, wahan utaara unhe.'* (First, he was bathed in his own bathroom and dressed in white clothes and a white turban. He was a baptised Sikh. A wooden box was specially made, with multiple holes drilled into it. He was placed inside, and before sealing it, heavy stones were added to ensure the box would sink. We hired a bus to go to the gurdwara, where an *ardas* (prayer) was offered. Then, in two boats—one carrying the body and close family, and the other for additional attendees—we reached the centre of the river and immersed the box.)

7. Keshgarh Sahib is a prime gurudwara in this region, located at Anandpur Sahib.

He shared that all members of the family, including women and even children, accompanied the body on the boat journey—marking a deeply inclusive farewell. However, the physical act of immersion was carried out only by the men. Following the immersion, a recitation of *path* and *kirtan* (devotional singing) was held at Gurdwara Bhabour Sahib, concluding with *langar* (the sacred community meal). Upon returning home, the family organised an *Akhand Path* (a continuous 48-hour recitation of the Guru Granth Sahib), and later, another *Akhand Path* was held in their ancestral village in Uttar Pradesh, where the deceased was highly respected. On his *varina* (death anniversary), the deceased was commemorated at both places again. The family also intends to continue this commemoration for five annual anniversaries.

The total expenditure involved in these rituals and arrangements amounted to approximately ₹4.5 lakh to ₹5 lakh. While the act of water immersion was a deeply personal and spiritual choice—carried out to honour the deceased's long-held wish—it was also clear that the death rituals became a significant social event. The scale of the arrangements and expenses suggests that, beyond personal grief and religious obligation, the event of death also functioned as a means for expressing social identity.

Thus, this case reflects a unique deviation from traditional cremation, shaped by the deceased's ecological and spiritual outlook. It also illustrates how death can be both a site of personal meaning and public display, where ritual performance intertwines with identity, belief, and social affirmation. The *Rehat Maryada*, the Sikh code of conduct, also permits the immersion of the dead body in flowing water in situations where cremation is not feasible. This case was therefore considered important to document, as it represents an unconventional yet religiously sanctioned method of body disposal.

Perceptions and Practices: The Paradox

Hinduism offers a broad spectrum of beliefs and rituals surrounding death. Among Hindu respondents, many expressed doubts or non-belief in certain doctrinal elements such as the existence of hell, heaven, or the idea of post-death punishment. Yet, when faced with an actual death in the family, most of them strictly followed the prescribed rituals—sometimes to great financial expense. The only exception seemed to be practices performed in anticipation of death, which were less commonly followed. This paradox suggests that social norms and fear often compel individuals to perform rituals they may not entirely believe in. Furthermore, the high service charges paid to priests and ritual specialists highlight the commercialisation of death in many cases.

Sikhism promotes a relatively minimalist approach to death, viewing it as the divine will and emphasising acceptance over ritual. However, Sikh respondents often followed not only the rituals prescribed in Sikh scriptures but also borrowed elements from Hindu traditions—many of which are explicitly discouraged by the *Rehat Maryada* (Sikh code of conduct). This contradiction reflects a duality: while ideologically they aligned with the Sikh view of simplicity and rebirth, in practice, extensive rituals and high expenditures were observed. Social expectations and cultural overlap with Hindu customs likely drive this dual adherence.

In Buddhist traditions, death is understood as a transitional moment in the journey of consciousness toward rebirth. The focus is on rituals that support a peaceful transition of consciousness rather than public mourning or elaborate rites. Buddhist respondents' perceptions closely aligned with their religious teachings. However, when performing rituals, many faced practical constraints—such as distance from monastic institutions or lack of access to lamas—limiting their ability to follow every tradition as prescribed in their texts. Despite this, they made significant efforts to conform to religious practices, often at considerable cost, reflecting a desire to conform to the tradition even when logistically challenged.

Christianity conceptualises death as the beginning of eternal life with Christ. Christian respondents demonstrated strong alignment between their beliefs and practices. Unlike in Hindu and Sikh communities, the rituals were relatively modest and did not reflect any commercialisation. The church plays a central role in assisting bereaved families, and most services are provided without charge. Interestingly, some respondents reported incorporating modern practices like personalised memorials, reflecting a blending of tradition with contemporary forms of remembrance. However, these changes were not driven by disbelief but rather by evolving cultural preferences.

Islamic teachings present death as a gateway to eternal life, with the soul's fate determined by earthly deeds. Muslim respondents showed an exceptional level of conformity, both in belief and practice. They were well-versed in religious doctrines across ages and educational backgrounds. Rituals were performed uniformly and with deep conviction. Further, the financial frugality of Islamic funeral practices stood out. Unlike in other traditions, there was no indication of ritual commercialisation. The emphasis remained on strict religious adherence.

Cultural Lag

The persistence of traditional rituals despite modernity and individual disbelief points to what sociologist William F. Ogburn termed 'cultural lag'.[8] While material culture—technology, medical advancements, and mobility—has evolved rapidly, non-material aspects such as beliefs, values, and customs continue to lag behind. Respondents adapted to modern tools (e.g., hospital

8. Ogburn, W., & F. (1922). *Social Change with Respect to Nature and Original Culture.* New York: Viking.

deaths, organ donations (in a few cases), hearse vans, etc. Yet when it came to symbolic aspects of death—rituals and prayers—they overwhelmingly conformed to longstanding traditions. This pattern illustrates that the ritualistic dimensions of death remain deeply traditional, even as other aspects of life modernise.

CHAPTER 6

The 'Three Cs': Conformity, Conviction, and Change

The mysterious reality of death has intrigued humanity for as long as we can remember. Anthropologists suggest that early humans, particularly aborigines, sought to understand death by considering the separation of blood and flesh. In their attempts to grasp its mystery, they developed unique methods to recognise the moment of death and established rituals to manage it. Over time, the concept of religion emerged as a structured institution, providing more systematic explanations for the phenomenon of death. Religions introduced concepts such as the soul or spirit, the continuity of life after death, resurrection, different realms of existence, and the means to connect with the deceased through specific rites and memorials. Scholars like Edward Burnett Tylor and Bronislaw Malinowski even argue that death itself was the catalyst for the birth of religious beliefs—without the concept of death, they claim, religion would not have originated.[1] For a long

1. Ebersole, L.G. (2005). Death. In L. Jones, *Encyclopedia of Religion, Second Edition* (pp. 2235–2245). USA: Mcmillan.

span of time, religion was the only institution that monopolised all speculations on death and produced all knowledge about understanding and dealing with it. Scholars also believe that the religious orientation plays an important role in forming individuals' perceptions of death.

As Auguste Comte argued, with the evolution of human civilisations from the theological stage to the metaphysical and scientific stages, there was a shift toward questioning, critical thinking, rationality, and logic as the guiding principles for understanding all human phenomena. In this context, death, once firmly held within the realm of religion, gradually transitioned into the domain of science. The late nineteenth and early twentieth centuries marked a period of modernisation, during which scholars observe significant social transformations driven by scientific and technological advancements, secularisation, commercialisation, individualism, and the commodification of human experiences. This era heralded a new approach to understanding the world; the transition to the modern era is evident when societies began to organise themselves more along secular rather than religious lines. Life and its various dimensions are increasingly understood and addressed through the lenses of science and reason, rather than through the influence of supernatural forces, divine will, or fate. As societies moved from traditional to modern structures, these shifts in social organisation deeply affected how individuals conceptualised death and how they chose to confront it, with death increasingly viewed through the lens of science rather than spirituality. This period of change not only reshaped the social fabric but also fundamentally altered the ways in which death was perceived and handled. In contrast to religion, medical science introduced the ability to delay death to some extent, offering more precise and reliable criteria for determining the moment of death. With advancements in healthcare, indicators such as longer life expectancy, lower mortality rates across various age groups, and the development of sophisticated medical technologies have become key markers of societal progress. As a result, these ideals contributed to a new framework for understanding death and its many facets, fostering a more clinical, objective approach.

What was once regarded by religions as a natural reality to be met with acceptance and resignation gradually transformed into something to be feared—an event to be conquered or even outwitted. As medical science advanced, death came to be seen less as a passive inevitability and more as a challenge to be managed or postponed. Furthermore, studies suggest that death itself became commodified, first by medical practitioners, who offered ways to delay or intervene in the process, and later by funeral service providers, who capitalised on the rituals and services surrounding the end of life. In this way, death evolved from a spiritual or philosophical reality to a transaction within a broader market of health care, services, and societal expectations. In contemporary times, death is commonly characterised by the following features:

a. **Medicalisation and Shift in Attitudes Toward Death:** With the advancement of medical technology, people's attitudes toward death have become increasingly non-receptive. Death is often viewed as a morbid reality to be avoided, postponed, or fought against rather than a natural part of life.

b. **Commodification of Death-Related Rituals:** The booming funeral industry in the West exemplifies how death-related rituals have been commercialised. Service providers and funeral specialists capitalise on these rites, turning them into profitable enterprises, and often distancing the process from its spiritual or communal roots.

c. **Secularisation of Death Practices:** Practices like organ donation or donating one's body to medical institutions reflect the growing secularisation of death. These acts, which focus more on utility than religious or spiritual considerations, signify a shift in how we relate to death and its aftermath.

d. **Use of Technology:** Technology plays an increasing role in death-related practices. Electric crematoriums are now commonplace, and the rise of online platforms and websites has made it easier for the bereaved to navigate the rituals and logistics of death, providing a digital dimension to grief and remembrance.

e. **Liberal Opinions on Suicide and Euthanasia:** Society's growing acceptance of discussions around suicide and euthanasia reflects a more liberal, individualised approach to death. Ethical debates now centre around personal autonomy and the right to choose one's end, further distancing death from traditional religious frameworks.

f. **Planning for Death (Wills, Life Insurance, etc.):** The planning of death, through practices like drafting wills or securing death insurance, has become an integral part of modern life. Death is increasingly treated as a matter of personal responsibility, rather than a fate or event to be accepted passively.

Overall, it can be observed that in contemporary society, religion has significantly diminished its influence over matters of death and dying. Instead, new trends have emerged, shaped by secular, medical, and technological advancements, offering alternative ways of understanding and managing death. This book explores these shifts through both theological inquiry and empirical research, examining how followers of various faiths perceive death and the rituals they undertake when a close relative passes away. By analysing the responses of individuals from these religious communities, it reveals the intersection of tradition and modernity in contemporary attitudes toward death, shedding light on how death is understood and addressed across different religious contexts. Ultimately, this work establishes the evolving relationship between death and religion in the modern world.

Relationship Between Death and Religion: The Three Cs

From this study of the relationship between death and religion, three crucial aspects emerge: conformity, conviction, and change. Cecilia L. Ridgeway defines conformity as the process of aligning one's beliefs and attitudes with the norms of a group.[2] The primary motive behind conformity, she argues, is the desire for social acceptance and belonging. Through conformity, members of a group or a society at large can share standards of behaviour. Conformity to the established norms may result from subtle unconscious influences or direct social pressure.

Conviction in religious terms refers to a firmly held belief. Conviction means the act or process of convincing; the state of being convinced; a fixed or strong belief.

> *'By conviction we mean convictions or beliefs derived from and based on a commitment to Scripture, the Bible. As God's Holy Word, it is the absolute index for the whole of our lives—faith and practice.'*
> *(Rom. 4:16)*[3]

There is an interesting relation between conformity and conviction. Usually, both things tend to go together; if there is conviction, it usually leads to conformity. This study reveals that Muslim and, to a large extent, Christian respondents consciously conformed to

---

2. Ridgeway, C.L. (31 May 2020). *Compliance And Conformity*. Retrieved 6 June 2020, from https://www.encyclopedia.com/social-sciences/encyclopedias-almanacs-transcripts-and-maps/compliance-and-conformity

3. https://bible.org/seriespage/mark-6-biblical-conviction

the death beliefs and practices prescribed by their religions, driven by deep conviction.

However, there are instances where conformity occurs without conviction, with individuals following religious death rituals and beliefs more out of societal pressure or habit than genuine belief. '*In conformity, convictions may or may not be present. When members are convinced about the desirability of an action, they comply with it. But there is a great deal of overt conformity without convictions. Conformity without conviction occurs when the individual cannot withdraw from the group or values his membership in the group and does not wish to offend or is afraid of the consequences of non-conformity.*'[4]

This study finds that respondents from Hindu and Sikh faiths often practised conformity without conviction, adhering to traditional death rituals more out of habit and social pressure than from genuine belief or true conviction.

Contrarily, there are also instances where, despite conviction, conformity to the tradition has not been possible. Buddhist respondents intended to perform certain rituals, but they could not follow. For instance, keeping the corpse for a few days before disposal, reading *Bardo Thodol* for 49 days, inviting more lamas, etc., are the practices they believed to be important, but could not adhere to because they found it inconvenient to perform them.

The third dimension is that of change. Auguste Comte explains that there are two processes occurring simultaneously in every social reality, namely, social statics and social dynamics. The first sustains the social system, and the second transforms it. The former is seen in terms of status quo and continuity, and the latter is about novelty/newness in the existing patterns. The above-discussed two features, namely conformity and conviction, reflect the continuity of religious tradition in comprehending and

4. Abraham, C. (1999). *Sociology for Nurses: A Textbook for Nurses and Other Medical Practitioners.* Chennai: B.I. Publications.

dealing with death. Nevertheless, there is also a glimpse of change in the phenomenon of death. In the present study, the change is evident in the following areas:

a. **Perceptions of Respondents on the Idea of Good Death and Preferred Place of Death:** Respondents from across the religious faiths tend to perceive a 'good death' as one that is comfort-oriented, painless, and occurs after the fulfilment of all material goals in life. Mostly, their perceptions of a good death did not align with the ideals of a 'good death' as prescribed by their respective religious teachings. This divergence highlights change.

b. **Liberal Attitudes Toward the Practice of Euthanasia:** A significant number of Hindu and all Sikh respondents expressed their belief that euthanasia should be permitted in cases where an individual is suffering from an irreversible and severe health crisis. While both Hinduism and Sikhism traditionally consider euthanasia a sinful act, the respondents' views reflect a shift toward a more liberal stance.

c. **Support for the Practice of Organ Donation:** While traditional religious beliefs generally prohibit any interference with the body after death, the findings of this study reveal that Hindu, Sikh, Buddhist, and Christian respondents largely support the practice of organ donation. In fact, a small number of Hindu and Sikh respondents have even practised it themselves. This shift reflects a subtle but significant change in perceptions surrounding death, indicating a growing openness to reconciling traditional religious views with contemporary ethical considerations and medical advancements.

d. **Commercialisation of Death-Related Practices:** For Hindu, Sikh, and Buddhist respondents, it was evident that dealing with death has become a costly affair. A significant portion of the expense was allocated to the fees charged by service providers of these faiths, who assisted the bereaved in carrying out death-related rituals. This trend highlights the commercialisation and commodification of death practices in contemporary society, where service providers increasingly view death as an opportunity for profit, rather than solely as a religious or cultural obligation.

Therefore, the relationship between death and religion is established on the three Cs: conformity, conviction, and change.

Comprehension of Death in Pre-Modern, Modern, and Post-Modern Eras

From the perusal of literature and the results of this study, it is found that, in a nutshell, there are different ways of comprehending and dealing with the mystifying reality of death. In pre-modern times, death was looked at in a positive manner. Life and death were not seen as two different realities, but death was a part of life to be embraced with submission. Religion was supreme, and religious faiths largely portrayed it as not an end but as a transitional moment for a new beginning. Explaining the attitudes of Western people towards mortality, death prior to the seventeenth century was called 'tame'. In the last phase of life, people would accept that their end was near and the dying would prepare themselves for it, accompanied by religious rituals. It was accepted with normalcy, both by the dying person and the kin of that person. The dying person would be surrounded by the loved ones (family, friends, and children). There would be no attempt to hide it. '*Death was a ritual organised by the dying person himself, who presided over it and knew its protocol.*'[5]

5. Ariès, P. (1975). *Western Attitudes Toward Death: From the Middle Ages to the Present (The Johns Hopkins Symposia in Comparative History).* (P. Ranum, Trans.) London: Johns Hopkins University Press.

The evolutionary and functionalist approaches that emerged in pre-modern times also emphasised the functions of death and death rituals. These rituals were seen as a means of fostering group solidarity and re-establishing social order; they served to regulate social bonds and reaffirm the collective identity of the community. Death rites provided a way to assign a new status to the deceased, marking their transition and ensuring their place within the social fabric. In this context, death was regarded as an inevitable reality to be accepted, an integral part of the life cycle rather than something to be feared or avoided.

As societies progressed toward the phase of modernisation, marked by the rise of scientific knowledge as the primary source of understanding, significant transformations took place in technology, economic prosperity, commercialisation, and individualism. Anything that lay outside the realm of rationality and logic was increasingly regarded as irrelevant and less significant. Secularisation gradually superseded religious dominance, and modern individuals began to perceive themselves as stronger and more secure against the forces of nature. In this new paradigm, death itself became a pathological reality, viewed not as a natural part of life but as a negative phenomenon to be denied. This denial is reflected in various contemporary attitudes—such as the avoidance of death, the fear associated with it, discomfort around death-related rituals, and the increasing isolation of the dying in hospitals or hospices. The concept of death, once framed within religious teachings, shifted to the realm of reason. While religion emphasised the acceptance of death as part of life's cycle, modern medicine and technology focused on the idea of conquering or postponing death. Foucault, in his very famous medicalisation critique, has stated that the use of Western medicine has led to the objectification of death, deeming it finite and measurable.[6]

---

6. Lupton, D. (2009). Foucault and Medicalisation Critique. In S. Earle, C. Kamaromy, & C. Batholomew (Eds.), *Death and Dying A Reader* (pp. 20–24). London: Sage.

Advanced medicalisation led to the removal of death and dying from the community and has relocated it to institutions like hospitals and hospices.[7]

Since death cannot truly be prevented, it came to be perceived as the ultimate defeat—both of life and of the medical profession. In the modern era, rather than being seen as an inevitable part of life, death was reframed as an enemy to be resisted. This shift in perspective marked death as a forbidden topic, with societies increasingly denying and avoiding its reality. The natural course of life, including its inevitable end, was obscured, and death was relegated to the margins of consciousness, treated as something to be feared, evaded, and, if possible, eradicated. The denial of death thesis emerged in this era. It argued that the fear of one's own mortality is so deeply rooted amongst people in modern times that they devise mechanisms to avoid it; else, death anxiety would not let them lead a peaceful life. Hence, one of the important functions of society is to provide ways to avoid death. As death shifted from homes to hospitals and hospices (in the Western world), dying in isolation became the ultimate form of alienation.[8]

Even the dead got ghettoised, segregating the dead in the graveyards, which become 'ghettos'[9] and have no role to play in the community of the living. There is a famous quote:

---

7. Littlewood, J. (1993). The Denial of Death and Rites of Passage in Contemporary Societies. In D. Clark, *The Sociology of Death: Theory, Culture, and Practice* (pp. 69–86). Oxford: Blackwell Publishers.

8. Elias, N. (2001). *The Loneliness of the Dying.* New York: Continuum.

9. Jean Baudrillard in his *Symbolic Exchange and Death* (1993) says that death can also be denied, or, in a sense, abolished, by segregating the dead in graveyards, which become 'ghettos', where they no longer have a role to play in the community of the living. To be dead is to be abnormal, whereas for the primitives, it was merely another state of being human. For these earlier societies, it was necessary to use their resources through ritual feasts and celebrations for the dead in order to avoid a disequilibrium where death would have a claim on them. In more evolved societies focused on the economy, death is simply the end of life—the dead can no longer produce or consume, and thus are no longer available for exchanges with the living.

> *'Presence of death turned modernity's feet of clay into dregs of uncertainty: death was an emphatic denial of everything that the brave new world of modernity stood for, and above all of its arrogant promise of the indivisible sovereignty of reason. The moment it ceased to be 'tame', death has become a guilty secret; literally, a skeleton in the cupboard left in the neat, orderly, functional, and pleasing home modernity promised to build.'* [10]

So, the reality of death shook the ever-progressing dreams of the modern world. Therefore, the studies on death in the modern phase were also described as sadistic, cruel, pathological, and traumatic. Instead of focusing on core death-related practices, the sociologists in these times also picked up sub-disciplinary subjects like hospice care, bereavement, the funeral industry, etc.[11] Additionally, sociological studies that emphasise strategies for coping with death also contribute towards the avoidance of death as they represent death as a negative and morbid phenomenon that must be coped with.

In modern times, death became an indicator of defeat and a threat to life but actually could not be countered, so it was better to keep it at bay by hiding it. Anthony Giddens believes that a distinguishing feature of modernity is purchasing of ontological security through institutions and routines that protect us from direct contact with madness, criminality, and death. By ontological security, he refers to the sense of order and continuity in relation to the events in which human beings participate, and the experiences they have, in their day-to-day lives. For instance, we are so deeply involved in our daily schedules at home and work that we never expect any uncertain incident to happen. This sense

---

10. Bauman, Z. (1992). *Mortality, Immortality, and Other Life Strategies.* Cambridge: Polity.

11. Mellor, P.A., & Shilling, C. (1993). Modernity, Self-Identity, and the Sequestration of Death. *Sociology,* 27 (3), 411–431.

of order develops meaningfulness in life. Through his concept of 'Sequestration of Experience', he associates modernity with an exclusion of social life from fundamental existential issues, primarily death, that raise central moral dilemmas for human beings. According to him, societies keep the awfulness at bay by bracketing the uneasy events that breach the smoothness of daily life.[12] Advanced medicine and scientific knowledge in modern times contribute to keeping death at a distance from modern people, as they prevent life-threatening accidents, diseases, and illnesses.

Therefore, in modern times, there emerged a duality between life and death, with the latter threatening the former. Hence, it was better to counter it, and since that was not possible, deny, ignore, and conceal it. This denial and ignorance were reflected in both the attitudes of people and in theory.

However, in post-modern times, there appears to be a paradigm shift. Death, which was a denied and ignored phenomenon and subject, in the later years of the twentieth century, has made a comeback. Explaining this revival, Tony Walter (1994), in his book *The Revival of Death*, emphasises that so much of the literature that focuses on death denial in itself is making it more popular. Walter, offering an interpretive approach, contests the modern thinkers' view that death is secreted within medical establishments. Though death has become a private affair, the involvement of the dying and deceased in their end-of-life decisions is much more than before. The dying person no longer ends up as a mere spectator and recipient of what others decide for him/her. Religion or hospital/doctor, per se, is not the deciding factor for one's end-of-life decision; rather, the dying is in the centre to decide for oneself. Individuals exercising their agency on whether they want to be in hospice or in the hospital, want medication or want to

12. Giddens, A. (1991). *Modernity and Self-identity: Self and Society in the Late Modern Age.* Standford: Standford University Press.

stop it, are not hiding from death. Rather, they are heralding its revival. The practices where the deceased is involved in arranging one's own funeral while alive, writing a will, pledging organs, etc., are not attempts to hide death but to make it more visible.

> *'The revival of death, or the "cult of dying my way" is not very much individually oriented, but these private feelings are the manifestations of the more public interactions that emphasise the authority of the individual—only individuals can and should determine how they want to die or grieve.'* [13]

In the late twentieth century, the approach to death began to shift, with individuals becoming more involved in decisions regarding their own treatment, medication, and the role of medical professionals such as doctors, pathologists, and social statisticians. This shift represents a form of revivalism, where death, previously a remote or isolated event, is now subject to active participation and documentation. This increasing visibility of death is also reflected in contemporary media, where death is portrayed more frequently and graphically. Portrayal of mass killings, deaths due to terrorism, accidents and other tragic events in the mainstream media has increased manyfolds. The twentieth century saw the mass production of corpses through wars, and in the new millennium, the world has witnessed an outbreak of global terrorism, mass killings, and widespread accidental deaths. As a result, death has become far more visible, entering the public consciousness in ways that were once unthinkable.[14] Hence, in recent times, death has taken on a new and more pervasive form.

Jacobsen (2016) offers a similar perspective, referring to this shift as 'spectacular death'.[15] Critiquing Philippe Aries's concept

---

13. Walter, T. (1994). *The Revival of Death.* London: Routledge.

14. Noys, B. (2005). *The Culture of Death.* London: Bloomsbury Academic.

15. Jacobsen, M.H. (2016). 'Spectacular Death'—Proposing a New Fifth Phase to

of 'forbidden death'—which describes death as a denied and hidden phenomenon—Jacobsen argues that in the late twentieth and twenty-first centuries, there has been a resurgence of interest in death, dying, and bereavement across various spheres: professionally, politically, publicly, and personally. In contemporary society, death is no longer concealed or forbidden; instead, it has transformed into a spectacle—something people witness from a safe distance. While still kept at arm's length, there is a strong desire to know about it, talk about it, and engage with it. Jacobsen also highlights the intensity with which the media portrays death in all its forms—mass killings, mutilated corpses, deaths resulting from terrorism, and more. These images, broadcast globally, elicit emotional reactions from audiences worldwide. Mass mourning, as well as the exaggerated focus on the deaths of celebrities, further exemplifies how death is experienced as a spectacle, witnessed but not directly encountered. In this way, while people today may not face death directly, as was common in traditional times, they are far more exposed to it through digital platforms such as television and the internet.

Thus, in the post-modern era, death—which was once a denied and sequestered phenomenon—has undergone a revival. There is now more active participation from the dying in decisions concerning their treatment and body disposal, as well as greater visibility of death through the media.

The Take-Home Lesson

In light of the pre-modern, modern, and post-modern approaches to death, three distinct ways of comprehending death emerge. First, as a natural event, an integral part of life, it is to be accepted with submission. Second, as a fearful phenomenon, it is to be denied, hidden, or sequestrated. And third, as a phenomenon

Philippe Ariès's Admirable History of Death. *Humanities, 5* (19), 1–20.

that exists somewhere in between—neither fully denied nor sequestrated, but rather approached from a safe distance, with greater involvement of the dying person in decisions related to their end-of-life process.

In my study, I observed reflections of all three approaches. Respondents, particularly Christians and Muslims, generally comprehend death with a sense of normalcy, accepting it as an inevitable part of life. However, I also found evidence of the sequestration and denial of death among Hindu respondents, and to some extent among Sikhs and Buddhists. At the same time, I observed elements of the third approach, where there was some participation by the deceased in decisions regarding their body disposal. In a few cases, individuals had pledged their organs, and in two instances, whole body was donated for medical use. These findings illustrate a complex and evolving relationship with death, where elements of all three perspectives coexist in contemporary society.

Thus, from a discursive perspective, there is no singular way to comprehend the phenomenon of death. It varies across religions, individuals, and contexts. It is evident that there are multiple ways of understanding death, and these discourses are not mutually exclusive—they coexist and interact. The analysis of death is not simply about defining or perceiving it in either a negative or positive light, nor is it limited to debates on its sequestration or revival. These so-called 'debates' or 'binary issues' are merely different lenses through which death is perceived and understood. They represent three distinct discourses, each offering its own perspective.

The real challenge lies not in accepting or rejecting death, nor in critiquing or glorifying it, but in recognising that all societies are undergoing transformation. As the economy, polity, and social structures evolve, new trends in death beliefs and practices will emerge. These shifts should not be dismissed or criticised outright. Instead, there must be an effort to comprehend these changes and, if necessary, integrate them into existing frameworks of understanding death. And that will be the true challenge.

ANNEXURE A

Profile of the Respondents

The sample comprised 193 respondents belonging to different religious faiths. The largest proportion of 60 respondents was of Hindus, followed by 45 Sikhs, 36 Muslims, 30 Christians, and 22 Buddhist respondents. The sample was inclusive in terms of age, educational qualification, income, and caste/sect/school of thought. People who adopted different ways of dealing with death (three cases discussed in chapter 5), identified during the course of fieldwork were also selected as respondents. Additionally, sacred specialists – Hindu *pandits*, Sikh *bhai jis*, Buddhist monks, Christian priests/pastors, Muslim *imams* and the functionaries at the cremation grounds of sector 25, Chandigarh were also interviewed. The socio-economic profile of respondents is as follows:

Hindu Respondents

The 60 Hindu respondents belonged to different age groups, sexes, educational qualification levels, income groups, and castes. The ages of the respondents varied from 20 to 60 years, but the largest proportion of 41 out of 60 respondents (nearly 70%) fell in the age group of 31–50 years. In Hinduism, it is prescribed that death-related practices are largely the prerogative of males, so most of the respondents (39 out of 60) were males. Amongst female respondents, most of them had lost their husbands or parents, and I was able to identify two of them who performed the funeral rites for their parents. In terms of educational qualifications, Hindu respondents belonged to various educational categories ranging from those six (10%) who were illiterate to the ones (15 out of 60) who had qualified upto senior secondary level. However, the largest proportion of 39 out of 60 respondents (65%) were graduates, and out of these, 13 had also completed their post-graduation. They belonged to the income groups ranging from ₹1,00,000 per annum to more than ₹10,00,000 per annum; however, the larger proportion (40%) of the Hindu sample consisted of the respondents belonging to the income group of ₹100,001–₹5,00,000 per annum. As the caste system forms an integral part of Hinduism, respondents' caste was also asked. They belonged to all four major caste groups, namely, *Brahmins, Kshatriyas, Vaishyas*, and *Shudras*, but the larger proportion of 24 out of 60 respondents (47%) was of *Kshatriyas*.

Sikh Respondents

The sample of Sikh respondents comprised 45 Sikhs. Their ages varied from 20 to 65 years, with the largest proportion of 30 respondents (66%) falling in the age group of 41–60 years. The *Rehat Maryada*, the book of the Sikh code of conduct notes, '*The dead body should then be placed on the pyre and the son or any other relation or friend of the deceased should set fire to it.*'[1] Possibly, this is the reason that amongst Sikhs also, I got the largest proportion (26 out of 45) of males only. Among the remaining fifteen female

1. Article XIX - Funeral Ceremonies, *Rehat Maryada*, P. 19.

respondents, I again identified two respondents who performed major last rites for their parents. Further, in terms of educational qualifications, it was observed that the largest proportion (25 of 45 (56%) of the Sikh respondents was graduates, and five out of 45 had also completed their post-graduation. While 12 (26%) of them were qualified upto senior secondary level, three were found to be illiterates. In terms of the annual income, the largest proportion of 20 out of 45 respondents (44%) earn from ₹5,00,000–₹10,00,000 annually. Guru Nanak and his successors did not follow the philosophy and practices prevalent amongst Hindus and Muslims of that time. This included rejection of the caste system popular in Hinduism, as well.[2] Intriguingly, respondents revealed different castes when asked whether they belonged to any caste group. Most of them (87%) specified their castes, namely, *Jatt Sikh* (27 out of 45), *Khatri Sikh* (12 respondents), *Ramdassiye* (three respondents). Three respondents, however, said that they do not know about their caste. From this, it emerged that Sikh respondents are oriented towards caste based divisions, which was rejected by Sikh Gurus as the founding philosophy of Sikhism.

Buddhist Respondents

Buddhists in Chandigarh form the minority population and are migrants from Ladakh, Spiti Valley, Manali and the surrounding Himalayan region. They have migrated to Chandigarh on official transfers, to pursue higher education and for medical treatment. The sample comprised 22 Buddhist respondents varying in age groups, sexes, educational qualification levels, schools of thought,

2. Not believing in caste or descent, untouchability, magic spells, incantation, omens, auspicious times, days, and occasions, Chapter X – Beliefs, Observances, Duties, Taboos, and Ceremonies, Article XVI – Living in Consonance with Guru's Tenets, *Rehat Maryada*, P.12.

and income groups. The largest proportion, ten out of 22 respondents, belonged to the age group of 31–40 years. Amongst Buddhist respondents, the largest number (16 out of 22) were males. I got six female respondents in the Buddhist sample. Seven respondents were qualified upto the senior secondary level, and 15 respondents were graduates. In terms of annual income, the largest proportion of 15 respondents belonged to the income group of ₹1,00,000–₹5,00,000 per annum. Since Buddhism is a diverse religious tradition with three major schools of thought, it was pertinent to ask the respondents which school of thought they revere. While none of them belonged to the *Theravada* and *Mahayana* schools, the largest proportion (18 respondents) belonged to Tibetan Buddhism (*Vajrayana* school) because this doctrine is popular in the Himalayan region, and our respondents are largely migrants from this area. However, four of them stated that they are Buddhist and like Hindus, they have their own gods but don't know about different schools.

Christian Respondents

The sample comprised 30 Christian respondents. Like our Hindu respondents, the ages of the respondents varied from 20 to 60 years, but the largest number (19 respondents) fell in the age group of 31–40 years. Our Christian sample consisted of both sexes. Interestingly, unlike other religious categories studied in this research, amongst Christians, I got almost equal numbers of male and female respondents. There were 16 males and 14 female respondents in the sample of Christians. In terms of educational qualifications, Christian respondents belonged to various educational categories, ranging from illiterates to post-graduates. However, the largest number of 16 out of 30 respondents were graduates, and six were post-graduates. The remaining eight respondents had qualifications upto the senior secondary level. Respondents belonged to various income groups ranging from ₹1,00,000 per annum to more than

₹10,00,000 per annum; however, the largest proportion of 21 out of 30 (70%) of our Christian respondents belonged to the income group of ₹1,00,000–₹5,00,000 per annum.

Christianity is popular worldwide with numerous denominations and sects, so an equal number of respondents were selected from the major denominations and sects in Chandigarh. Ten respondents followed Roman Catholicism, ten followed Protestantism, and the remaining ten belonged to smaller sects, namely, the Seventh-Day Adventist church, the Baptist church, the Light House church, etc. However, they informed that their churches are offshoots of Protestantism and they largely adhere to the Protestant beliefs only. So, it can be said that most of the Christian respondents follow Protestantism.

Christians in Chandigarh are the minority population, but within this minority, they also follow different sects and denominations. Hence, churches of various denominations and sects exist in Chandigarh. During interaction with the church personnel and Christian respondents, it was found that the church is not merely a place of worship for Christians, but it works like a community organisation. One denomination functions by dividing the geographical territory into different parishes, and the church of the parish takes care of its members. The followers in the parish pay a fixed membership fee to the church and donate voluntarily. For instance, the Roman Catholic denomination in Chandigarh has divided the city into mainly two parishes. Each parish has its own church. Likewise, there are numerous such church organisations like the Seventh-Day Adventist church, the churches of Eastern Orthodoxy, the church of North India (preaching Protestantism), etc. Also, there are church organisations with registered members that do not have any buildings of their own, so they outsource other churches' buildings for weekly ceremonies on rent. Being registered with the parish's church, members are given assistance on occasions like birth, marriage, death, etc.

The priests who were interviewed stated that they share an intimate and close relationship with the members, and they often visit their homes and intervene as and when required. Even if any of the members misses the weekly Mass for quite some time, someone from the church is sent to their home to find out if everything is fine. This was cross-checked with the respondents, and they said, 'Blessing *ke liye* Father *ghar pe aate hain*' (Father visits home to bless); '*Kuch bhi zarurat ho toh aate hain*' (If I need any help, Father comes); another respondent said that once when he needed financial assistance, the church helped. Despite the existence of so many churches and their parishes, the striking commonality is that the cemetery used largely by Christians is one, i.e. in Sector 25 cremation grounds (which was selected as the universe for this study), Chandigarh. The pastors affirmed that it is the prerogative of the church to which the deceased was registered to assist in his/her committal and minister the last rites. There is an association of members of different denominations that takes care of the functioning and maintenance of the cemetery. In the event of death, the staff at the parish church communicates with the caretaker in the cemetery, who then makes the necessary arrangements for the burial. Thus, the churches in Chandigarh are not just places of worship, but the members are extended support as and when required.

Muslim Respondents

The 36 Muslim respondents also belonged to different age groups, sexes, educational qualification levels, sects, and income groups. Like Hindus and Christians, they also belonged to the age groups ranging from 20 to 60 years, but the largest number (15 out of 36) belonged to the age group of 31–40 years. Ten respondents belonged to the age group of 20–30 years. The ages of the remaining 11 respondents fell between 41 and 60 years. Like the Hindu, Sikh, and Buddhist samples, the Muslim sample also had more male respondents. 29 out of 36 respondents were males, and the remaining seven respondents were females.

Further, in terms of their educational qualification, it was noted that while the largest number of 13 out of 36 respondents were graduates, there were an additional five who had qualified upto the post-graduation level. One post-graduate respondent shared that he had also attained education in Islamic religious studies, *'Alim-Fazil'*. Twelve respondents were qualified upto the senior secondary level, and six respondents were illiterates. In terms of annual income of the Muslim respondents, it was found that their income ranged from ₹1,00,000 to ₹10,00,000 per annum. The largest number of 17 out of 36 respondents have an annual income ranging from ₹100,000 to ₹5,00,000. 11 of them belonged to the income category of ₹500,001–₹10,000,00 per annum. Eight respondents' income was found to be less than ₹1,00,000 per annum. Though Islam doesn't prescribe any caste based divisions, in the Muslim tradition, various sects and sub-sects exist. So, it was pertinent to ask respondents about their sect. The largest number (22 out of 36) in the Muslim sample was of *Sunnis*. Five respondents were *Shiaites*. The remaining ones could not acquaint themselves with terms like caste or sect, but they called themselves *Pathans, Salmani Musalman*, and *Kasars*. When probed whether they revere any particular doctrine within Islam, most of them said that they follow all tenets of Islam.

Therefore, in my sample, each religious category was inclusive in terms of educational qualifications, income, and caste/sect/school of thought. Though Sikhism doesn't subscribe to the caste system, most of the Sikh respondents revealed their castes. The majority of the Buddhists follow the Tibetan school of thought, and largely, our Christian sample follows Protestantism.

ANNEXURE B

The Tabular Representation of the Responses Pertaining to Chapter 4

Religious Inclination

Table 4.1a: Distribution of Respondents on the Basis of Their Frequency of Visiting their Place of Worship

Response Categories	Frequency (Percentage)				
	Hindus	Sikhs	Buddhists	Christians	Muslims
Daily	8 (13)	9 (20)	5 (23)	10 (33)	Nil
More than once a day	Nil	Nil	Nil	Nil	13 (36)
Weekly	12 (20)	5 (11)	Nil	15 (50)	10 (28)
Occasionally	40 (67)	31 (69)	17 (77)	5 (17)	6 (17)
Never	Nil	Nil	Nil	Nil	7 (19)
Total	60 (100)	45 (100)	22 (100)	30 (100)	36 (100)

Table 4.1b: Distribution of Respondents on the Basis of Their Frequency of Praying Routine at Home

Response Categories	Frequency (Percentage)				
	Hindus	Sikhs	Buddhists	Christians	Muslims
Once a day	12 (20)	Nil	4 (18)	18 (60)	Nil
More than once a day	41 (68)	17 (38)	18 (82)	6 (20)	30 (83)
No specific routine	7 (12)	28 (62)	Nil	6 (20)	6 (17)
Never	Nil	Nil	Nil	Nil	Nil
Total	60 (100)	45 (100)	22 (100)	30 (100)	36 (100)

Fear of Death

The questions asked:

- whether they fear their own death (coded as 1);
- whether they fear the death of a loved one (coded as 2);
- and whether they participate in the activities where risk to life is involved (coded as 3).

Table 4.2: Distribution of Respondents on the Basis of Their Responses on Fear of Death

Responses	Hindus			Sikhs			Buddhists			Christians			Muslims		
	1	2	3	1	2	3	1	2	3	1	2	3	1	2	3
Yes	22 (37)	46 (77)	24 (40)	7 (16)	7 (16)	29 (64)	13 (60)	14 (63)	17 (77)	6 (20)	9 (30)	18 (60)	-	9 (25)	10 (28)
No	34 (57)	14 (23)	36 (60)	35 (78)	34 (76)	16 (36)	9 (40)	8 (37)	5 (23)	22 (74)	21 (70)	12 (40)	36 (100)	27 (75)	26 (72)
Can't Say	4 (6)	-	-	3 (6)	4 (8)	-	-	-	-	2 (6)	-	-	-	-	-
Total	60 (100)			45 (100)			22 (100)			30 (100)			36 (100)		

Death as a Theme of Discussion

Table 4.3: Distribution of Respondents on the Basis of How Often They Talked About Death

Response Categories	Frequency (Percentage)				
	Hindus	Sikhs	Buddhists	Christians	Muslims
Quite often	3 (5)	7 (16)	6 (28)	24 (80)	20 (56)
Rarely	20 (33)	5 (11)	Nil	2 (7)	3 (8)
Never	8 (13)	Nil	8 (36)	Nil	Nil
On the occasion of someone's death	29 (49)	33 (73)	8 (36)	4 (13)	13 (36)
Total	60 (100)	45 (100)	22 (100)	30 (100)	36 (100)

Good Death and Preferred Place for Death

Table 4.4: Distribution of Respondents on the Basis of Their Preferred Place for Death

Response Categories	Frequency (Percentage)				
	Hindus	Sikhs	Buddhists	Christians	Muslims
Home	52 (87)	38 (85)	17 (77)	27 (90)	27 (75)
Hospital	7 (12)	6 (13)	3 (13)	Nil	2 (6)
Some other place	1 (1)	1 (2)	1 (5)	1 (3)	7 (19)
Can't say	Nil	Nil	1 (5)	2 (7)	Nil
Total	60 (100)	45 (100)	22 (100)	30 (100)	36 (100)

Perceptions on Doctrine of the Afterlife Journey and the Existence of Other Realms

Table 4.5: Distribution of Respondents on the Basis of their Belief in the Afterlife Journey and the Existence of Other Realms as Prescribed in their Religious Faiths

Response Categories	Frequency (Percentage)				
	Hindus	Sikhs	Buddhists	Christians	Muslims
Yes	18 (30)	4 (9)	22 (100)	30 (100)	36 (100)
No	42 (70)	41 (91)	Nil	Nil	Nil
Total	60 (100)	45 (100)	22 (100)	30 (100)	36 (100)

Perceptions on Reincarnation/Transmigration and Resurrection

Table 4.6: Distribution of Respondents on the Basis of Their Belief in the Doctrine of Reincarnation/Transmigration or Resurrection

Response Categories	Frequency (Percentage)				
	Hindus	Sikhs	Buddhists	Christians	Muslims
Yes	46 (77)	12 (27)	22 (100)	30 (100)	36 (100)
No	14 (23)	33 (73)	Nil	Nil	Nil
Total	60 (100)	45 (100)	22 (100)	30 (100)	36 (100)

Perceptions on the Role of Deeds in Deciding Fate After Death

Table 4.7: Distribution of Respondents on the Basis of Their Belief in the Role of Karmas in Deciding One's Fate after Death

Response Categories	Frequency (Percentage)				
	Hindus	Sikhs	Buddhists	Christians	Muslims
Yes	22 (37)	8 (18)	20 (91)	11 (37)	36 (100)
No	38 (63)	37 (82)	2 (9)	19 (63)	Nil
Total	60 (100)	45 (100)	22 (100)	30 (100)	36 (100)

Perceptions on Organ Donation and Whole Body Donation

Table 4.9a: Distribution of Hindu Respondents on the Basis of Their Perceptions on Organ Donation and Whole Body Donation

Response Categories	Yes (%)	No (%)	Not Decided Yet (%)	Total (%)
Are you aware of organ donation after death?	56 (93)	4 (7)	Nil	60 (100)
Are you willing to donate organs?	52 (87)	6 (10)	2 (3)	60 (100)
Are you aware of the option of whole body donation to a medical institution?	41 (68)	19 (32)	Nil	60 (100)
Are you willing to donate the body instead of disposing of it in a religious way?	2 (3)	58 (97)	Nil	60 (100)

Table 4.9b: Distribution of Sikh Respondents on the Basis of Their Perceptions on Organ Donation and Whole Body Donation

Response Categories	Yes (%)	No (%)	Not Decided Yet (%)	Total (%)
Are you aware of organ donation after death?	43 (96)	2 (4)	Nil	45 (100)
Are you willing to donate organs?	43 (96)	Nil	2 (4)	45 (100)
Are you aware of the option of whole body donation to a medical institution?	29 (65)	16 (35)	Nil	45 (100)
Are you willing to donate the body instead of disposing of it in a religious way?	3 (7)	41 (91)	1 (2)	45 (100)

Table 4.9c: Distribution of Buddhist Respondents on the Basis of Their Perceptions on Organ Donation and Whole Body Donation

Response Categories	Yes (%)	No (%)	Total (%)
Are you aware of organ donation after death?	21 (95)	1 (5)	22 (100)
Are you willing to donate organs?	18 (82)	4 (18)	22 (100)
Are you aware of the option of whole body donation to a medical institution?	5 (23)	17 (77)	22 (100)
Are you willing to donate the body instead of disposing of it in a religious way?	2 (9)	20 (91)	22 (100)

Table 4.9d: Distribution of Christian Respondents on the Basis of Their Perceptions on Organ Donation and Whole Body Donation

Response Categories	Yes (%)	No (%)	Not Decided Yet (%)	Total (%)
Are you aware of organ donation after death?	30 (100)	Nil	Nil	30 (100)
Are you willing to donate organs?	20 (67)	7 (23)	3 (10)	30 (100)
Are you aware of the option of whole body donation to a medical institution?	16 (54)	14 (46)	Nil	30 (100)
Are you willing to donate the body instead of disposing of it in a religious way?	2 (7)	28 (93)	Nil	30 (100)

Table 4.9e: Distribution of Muslim Respondents on the Basis of Their Perceptions on Organ Donation and Whole Body Donation

Response Categories	Yes (%)	No (%)	Total (%)
Are you aware of organ donation after death?	32 (87)	4 (13)	36 (100)
Are you willing to donate organs?	2 (6)	34 (94)	36 (100)
Are you aware of the option of whole body donation to a medical institution?	22 (62)	14 (38)	36 (100)
Are you willing to donate the body instead of disposing of it in a religious way?	Nil	36 (100)	36 (100)

Preference for Any Alternate Method for Body Disposal Other than the One Prescribed by Religion

Table 4.10: Distribution of Respondents on the Basis of Their Preference for Any Alternate Method of Body Disposal

Response Categories	Frequency (Percentage)				
	Hindus	Sikhs	Buddhists	Christians	Muslims
Religiously Prescribed Method	45 (75)	32 (71)	17 (77)	28 (93)	36 (100)
Any Alternate Method	15 (25)	13 (29)	5 (23)	2 (7)	Nil
Total	60 (100)	45 (100)	22 (100)	30 (100)	36 (100)

Preference for Post-Cremation/Burial Rituals and Religiously Prescribed Ways of Mourning

Table 4.11a: Distribution of Hindu Respondents on the Basis of Their Preference for Post-Cremation Rituals and Religiously Prescribed Ways of Mourning in Hinduism

Response Categories	Yes (%)	No (%)	Total (%)
Asthi-Sanchayana (bone collection)	57 (95)	3 (5)	60
Immersion of bones as prescribed	56 (93)	4 (7)	60
Pindadaan and *Sraddha* rites	56 (93)	4 (7)	60
Other rituals and memorials (4th day, 13th day and annual)	51 (85)	9 (15)	60

Table 4.11b: Distribution of Sikh Respondents on the Basis of Their Preference for Traditionally Prevalent Post-Cremation Rituals and Ways of Mourning

Response Categories	Frequency (percentage)		
	Yes (%)	No (%)	Total (%)
Immersing of ashes in *Patalpuri* at Kiratpur Sahib	39 (87)	6 (13)	45 (100)
Donations in the name of the deceased	35 (78)	10 (22)	45 (100)
Holding *path* after death	43 (96)	2 (4)	45 (100)
***Bhog* ceremony**	42 (94)	3 (6)	45 (100)

Table 4.11c: Distribution of Buddhist, Christian, and Muslim Respondents on the Basis of Their Preference for Traditionally Prevalent Post-Cremation/ Burial Practices

Response Categories	Frequency (Percentage)		
	Buddhists	Christians	Muslims
Yes	20 (90)	8 (27)	30 (83)
No	2 (10)	22 (73)	6 (17)
Total	22 (100)	30 (100)	36 (100)

Views on Suicide and Euthanasia

Table 4.12a: Distribution of Respondents on the Basis of Their Views on Suicide

Statements	Frequency (Percentage)				
	Hindus	Sikhs	Buddhists	Christians	Muslims
It is a sin	59 (98)	39 (87)	22 (100)	30 (100)	36 (100)
Suicide is acceptable in certain circumstances	1 (2)	6 (13)	Nil	Nil	Nil
Total	60 (100)	45 (100)	22 (100)	30 (100)	36 (100)

Table 4.12b: Distribution of Respondents on the Basis of Their Views on Euthanasia

Statements	Frequency (Percentage)				
	Hindus	Sikhs	Buddhists	Christians	Muslims
It is a sin and an anti-religious practice	16 (26)	Nil	22 (100)	27 (90)	35 (97)
Should be allowed if the deceased is in an extreme health crisis and doctors assure no chance of recovery	43 (72)	36 (80)	Nil	3 (10)	1 (3)
Should be allowed as, at this stage, one's working organs can be used for others	1 (2)	9 (20)	Nil	Nil	Nil
Total	60 (100)	45 (100)	22 (100)	30 (100)	36 (100)

ANNEXURE C

The Tabular Representation of the Responses Pertaining to Chapter 5

Writing of Will by Respondents' Deceased Kin

Table 5.1a: Distribution of Respondents on the Basis of Whether the Deceased Left a Will

Response Categories	Frequency (Percentage)				
	Hindus	Sikhs	Buddhists	Christians	Muslims
Yes	7 (12)	5 (11)	2 (9)	5 (17)	4 (11)
No	45 (75)	38 (84)	20 (91)	25 (83)	27 (75)
Don't Know	8 (13)	2 (5)	Nil	Nil	5 (14)
Total:	60 (100)	45 (100)	22 (100)	30 (100)	36 (100)

Writing of Will by the Respondents

Table 5.1b: Distribution of Respondents on the Basis of Whether They Have Shared Their Wishes in the Form of a Will or Verbally

Response Categories	Hindus	Sikhs	Buddhists	Christians	Muslims
Yes	1 (2)	4 (9)	Nil	1 (3)	3 (8)
No	54 (90)	41 (91)	22 (100)	29 (97)	33 (92)
In the process of thinking	5 (8)	Nil	Nil	Nil	Nil
Total:	60 (100)	45 (100)	22 (100)	30 (100)	36 (100)

Practices Before Death

Table 5.2a: Distribution of Hindu Respondents on the Basis of Practices Done Before Death

Response Categories	Yes (%)	No (%)	Total (%)
Donations and alms given in the name of the deceased	9 (15)	51 (85)	60 (100)
Shifting the dying on the floor	Nil	60 (100)	60 (100)
Giving *Ganga jal* or *tulsi* leaves to the dying	24 (40)	36 (60)	60 (100)
Recitation of prayers/*mantras* for the dying	13 (22)	47 (78)	60 (100)

Table 5.2b: Distribution of Sikh and Buddhist Respondents on the Basis of Whether Some Practices Were Done Before Death or Not

Response Categories	Sikhs (%)	Buddhists (%)
Yes	11 (24)	10 (46)
No	34 (76)	12 (54)
Total:	45 (100)	22 (100)

Table 5.2c: Distribution of Christian Respondents on the Basis of Sacraments Practised Before Death

Response Categories	Frequency (%)
Sacraments of penance, anointment of the sick and the Eucharist	7 (23)
Only prayers, no sacrament	23 (77)
Total:	30 (100)

Table 5.2d: Distribution of Muslim Respondents on the Basis of Practices Performed Before Death

Response Categories	Frequency		
	Yes (%)	No (%)	Total (%)
Laying the deceased in the direction of the *Qiblah*	24 (67)	12 (33)	36 (100)
Recitation of *Ayats* from the Quran	31 (86)	5 (14)	36 (100)

Practices After Death for Body Preparation

Table 5.3a: Distribution of Hindu Respondents on the Basis of After-Death Practices for Body Preparation

Response Categories	Frequency (Percentage)			
	Yes (%)	No (%)	Don't know (%)	Total
Laying the deceased in a particular direction	42 (70)	10 (17)	8 (13)	60 (100)
Lighting a lamp near the deceased	57 (95)	3 (5)	Nil	60 (100)
Washing and cleaning of the body	60 (100)	Nil	Nil	60 (100)
Dressing in new clothes	57 (95)	3 (5)	Nil	60 (100)
Whether any colour consideration was kept in mind while dressing	57 (95)	3 (5)	Nil	60 (100)
Closing of openings like the nose and ears	47 (78)	Nil	13 (22)	60 (100)
Wrapping the body in a white sheet after the clothing	60 (100)	Nil	Nil	60 (100)
Donation of organs (eyes)	5 (8)	55 (92)	Nil	60 (100)
Shaving the head of the *karta*	41 (68)	19 (32)	Nil	60 (100)

Table 5.3b: Distribution of Sikh Respondents on the Basis of After-Death Practices for Body Preparation

Response Categories	Frequency (Percentage)		
	Yes (%)	No (%)	Total (%)
Laying the body on the floor after death	44 (98)	1 (2)	45 (100)
Laying in a particular direction	12 (27)	33 (73)	45 (100)
Lighting a lamp near the body	Nil	45 (100)	45 (100)
Putting holy water	5 (11)	40 (89)	45 (100)
Washing and cleansing the body	45 (100)	Nil	45 (100)
Dressing in new clothes	37 (82)	8 (18)	45 (100)
Whether any colour consideration was kept in mind while dressing	27 (60)	18 (40)	45 (100)
Was the deceased adorned with five symbolic 'Ks'	8 (18)	37 (82)	45 (100)
Recitation of *ardas* for the deceased before cremation	39 (87)	6 (13)	45 (100)
Donation of eyes	1 (2)	44 (98)	45 (100)

Table 5.3c: Distribution of Buddhist Respondents on the Basis of After-Death Practices for Body Preparation

Response Categories	Frequency (Percentage)		
	Yes (%)	No (%)	Total (%)
Laying the dead on the floor	22 (100)	Nil	22 (100)
Hpho-bo service: calling lama for prayers	22 (100)	Nil	22 (100)
Lighting of earthen lamps	16 (73)	6 (27)	22 (100)
Washing and cleaning of the body	22 (100)	Nil	22 (100)
Calculation of auspicious timings for the cremation of the body.	3 (14)	19 (86)	22 (100)

Table 5.3d: Distribution of Christian Respondents on the Basis of After-Death Practices for Body Preparation

Response Category	Frequency (Percentage)			
	Yes (%)	No (%)	Don't know (%)	Total (%)
Bathing/cleansing the body	30 (100)	Nil	Nil	30 (100)
Dressing the deceased in new clothes	19 (63)	11 (37)	Nil	30 (100)
Use of perfume and fragrances for preparing the deceased	26 (86)	4 (14)	Nil	30 (100)
Sprinkling of Holy Water brought from the church	30 (100)	Nil	Nil	30 (100)
Whether the colour of the coffin was chosen according to the age of the deceased	13 (43)	5 (17)	12 (40)	30 (100)
Vigil/wake and Mass at church	30 (100)	Nil	Nil	30 (100)
Prayers at the graveside	30 (100)	Nil	Nil	30 (100)

Table 5.3e: Distribution of Muslim Respondents on the Basis of Practices After Death for Body Preparation

Response Categories	Frequency (Percentage)		
	Yes (%)	No (%)	Total (%)
Closing of eyes & mouth and tying the toes of the body immediately after death, and simultaneously reciting verses from the Quran	24 (67)	12 (33)	36 (100)
***Ghusl-e-Mayyit* (bathing of the dead body)**	36 (100)	Nil	36 (100)
***Kafan-e-Mayyit* (shrouding of the body)**	36 (100)	Nil	36 (100)
***Namaz-e-Janaza* (funeral prayer)**	36 (100)	Nil	36 (100)

Method of Body Disposal

Table 5.4: Distribution of Respondents on the Basis of Method of Body Disposal

Response Categories	Frequency (Percentage)				
	Hindus	Sikhs	Buddhists	Christians	Muslims
Cremation on a wooden pyre	54 (90)	41 (91)	22 (100)	Nil	Nil
Electric crematorium	6 (10)	4 (9)	Nil	Nil	Nil
Burial	Nil	Nil	Nil	30 (100)	36 (100)
Total:	60 (100)	45 (100)	22 (100)	30 (100)	36 (100)

Before and Mid-Cremation Practices

Table 5.5a: Distribution of Hindu Respondents on the Basis of Rites Performed Before and During Cremation

Response Categories	Yes (%)	No (%)	Don't know (%)	Total
Direction kept in mind while laying the body on the pyre	44 (73)	7 (12)	9 (15)	60 (100)
***Parikrama* of the body**	45 (75)	8 (13)	7 (12)	60 (100)
***Mataka phodna* (Smashing of clay pots)**	57 (95)	Nil	3 (5)	60 (100)
***Kapalkriya* (skull breaking)**	42 (70)	8 (14)	10 (16)	60 (100)
Offering of *pindas* (rice balls) to the dead body at home, on the way, and at the cremation site	34 (57)	09 (15)	17 (28)	60 (100)
Any practices done in the light of inauspicious days	4 (7)	56 (93)	Nil	60 (100)

Table 5.5b: Distribution of Sikh Respondents on the Basis of Rites Performed Before and During Cremation

Response Categories	Yes (%)	No (%)	Don't know (%)	Total (%)
***Matka phodna* before cremation (smashing of clay pots)**	26 (58)	19 (42)	Nil	45 (100)
***Kapalkriya* (skull breaking)**	23 (51)	10 (22)	12 (27)	45 (100)

Post-Cremation/Burial Practices

Table 5.6a: Distribution of Hindu Respondents on the Basis of Performance of Post-Cremation Practices

Response Categories	Yes (%)	No (%)	Total (%)
Bathing after cremation	60 (100)	Nil	(60) 100
Bone/ashes collection ritual	60 (100)	Nil	(60) 100
Immersing of bones/ashes in the Ganges	60 (100)	Nil	(60) 100
Path of the *Garuda Purana* or any other path	55 (92)	5 (8)	(60) 100
Pinda daan at the place of bone immersion	60 (100)	Nil	(60) 100
Restrictions or abstinence from some activities during the mourning period	53 (88)	7 (12)	(60) 100
Rasam pagri/kiryakaram	60 (100)	Nil	(60) 100
Donations/alms to *pandits*	60 (100)	Nil	(60) 100
Monthly or annual memorials	60 (100)	Nil	(60) 100

Table 5.6b: Distribution of Sikh Respondents on the Basis of Post-Cremation Practices

Response Categories	Yes (%)	No (%)	Total (%)
Ardas after cremation	45 (100)	Nil	45 (100)
Phul chuggna (bone/ashes collection ritual	45 (100)	Nil	45 (100)
Immersion of bones/ashes at Kiratpur Sahib	45 (100)	Nil	45 (100)
Akhand Path/Sehaj Path followed by *bhog*	45 (100)	Nil	45 (100)
Pinda daan	8 (18)	37 (82)	45 (100)
Restrictions or abstinence from some activities during the mourning period	35 (78)	10 (22)	45 (100)
Donations in the name of the deceased	36 (80)	9 (20)	45 (100)

Table 5.6c: Distribution of Buddhist Respondents on the Basis of Post-Cremation Practices

Response Categories	Yes (%)	No (%)	Total
Ashes immersed in any flowing water	16 (72)	6 (28)	22 (100)
Ashes mixed with clay and scattered in open grounds	6 (28)	16 (72)	22 (100)
Holding memorials	22 (100)	Nil	22 (100)
Reading *The Tibetan Book of the Dead*	13 (59)	9 (41)	22 (100)
Keeping food in the name of the deceased	15 (68)	7 (32)	22 (100)
Alms to the monks or the monastery	22 (100)	Nil	22 (100)

Table 5.6d: Distribution of Christian Respondents on the Basis of Post-Burial Practices Performed by Respondents

Response Categories	Frequency (Percentage)		
	Yes (%)	No (%)	Total (%)
Memorial services on specific days after death	30 (100)	Nil	30 (100)
Practices to mourn death	11 (37)	19 (63)	30 (100)
Holding memorials on the death anniversary	26 (86)	4 (14)	30 (100)

Table 5.6e: Distribution of Muslim Respondents on the Basis of Post-Burial Practices Performed by Respondents

Response Categories	Frequency (Percentage)		
	Yes (%)	No (%)	Total (%)
Recitation of the Quran	36 (100)	Nil	36 (100)
Donations	15 (42)	21 (58)	36 (100)
Restrictions observed to mourn the death	32 (89)	4 (11)	36 (100)

Cost Incurred in Carrying Out the Practices Related to Death (Body Preparation, Cremation/Burial and Post-Cremation/Burial)

Table 5.7: Distribution of Respondents on the Basis of Cost Incurred in Dealing with the Death

Cost in Rupees	Frequency (Percentage)				
	Hindus	Sikhs	Buddhists	Christians	Muslims
Less than 50,000	Nil	Nil	Nil	8 (27)	36 (100)
50,001–100,0000	Nil	Nil	4 (19)	20 (66)	Nil
1,00,001–200,000	7 (12)	27 (60)	18 (81)	2 (7)	Nil
2,00,001–3,00,000	44 (73)	16 (36)	Nil	Nil	Nil
3,00,001–4,00,000	8 (13)	1 (2)	Nil	Nil	Nil
Above 4,00,000	1 (2)	1 (2)	Nil	Nil	Nil
Total	60 (100)	45 (100)	22 (100)	30 (100)	36 (100)

Women's Participation in Death-Related Practices

Table 5.8a: Distribution of Hindu, Sikh, and Buddhist Respondents on the Basis of Women's Participation in Terms of Lighting the Funeral Pyre

Response Categories	Hindus	Sikhs	Buddhists
Yes	2 (3)	2 (4)	Nil
No	58 (97)	43 (96)	22 (100)
Total	60 (100)	45	22 (100)

Table 5.8b: Distribution of Christian and Muslim Respondents on the Basisof Women's Participation in Funeral Rites and Accompanying to the Graveyard

Response Categories	Christians	Muslims
Yes	30 (100)	Nil
No	Nil	36 (100)
Total	30 (100)	36 (100)

Children's Participation in Funeral Rites

Distribution of Respondents on the Basis of Children's Participation in Funeral Rites

Response Categories	Hindus	Sikhs	Buddhists	Christians	Muslims
Yes	21 (35)	30 (67)	3 (14)	24 (80)	24 (67)
No	39 (65)	15 (33)	19 (86)	6 (20)	12 (33)
Total	60 (100)	45 (100)	22 (100)	30 (100)	36 (100)

The funeral Pyre

Asti Visarjan

Pinda Daan

Kusha Ghaat at Haridwar (Where rituals are done)